AFRICA'S THIRD LIBERATION

The New Search for
Prosperity and Jobs

JEFFREY HERBST and GREG MILLS

PENGUIN BOOKS

PENGUIN BOOKS

Published by the Penguin Group
Penguin Books (South Africa) (Pty) Ltd, Rosebank Office Park, Block D,
181 Jan Smuts Avenue, Parktown North, Johannesburg 2193, South
Africa
Penguin Group (USA) Inc, 375 Hudson Street, New York, New York
10014, USA
Penguin Group (Canada), 90 Eglinton Avenue East, Suite 700, Toronto,
Ontario, Canada M4P 2Y3 (a division of Pearson Penguin Canada Inc)
Penguin Books Ltd, 80 Strand, London WC2R 0RL, England
Penguin Ireland, 25 St Stephen's Green, Dublin 2, Ireland (a division of
Penguin Books Ltd)
Penguin Group (Australia), 250 Camberwell Road, Camberwell, Victoria
3124, Australia (a division of Pearson Australia Group Pty Ltd)
Penguin Books India Pvt Ltd, 11 Community Centre, Panchsheel Park,
New Delhi – 110 017, India
Penguin Group (NZ), 67 Apollo Drive, Mairangi Bay, Auckland 1310,
New Zealand (a division of Pearson New Zealand Ltd)

Penguin Books (South Africa) (Pty) Ltd, Registered Offices:
Rosebank Office Park, Block D, 181 Jan Smuts Avenue, Parktown North,
Johannesburg 2193, South Africa

www.penguinbooks.co.za

First published by Penguin Books (South Africa) (Pty) Ltd 2012

ISBN 978-0-14-352888-3

Cover by mrdesign
Printed and bound by CTP Printers, Cape Town

Good judgement comes from experience and that comes from bad judgement.

Hal Moore and Joseph Galloway,
We are Soldiers Still

CONTENTS

FOREWORD

Ghana was the first country in sub-Saharan Africa to achieve its independence from Britain. As this volume illustrates, this signal event was only the first of three liberations.

Like many developing countries in other regions, we had a difficult political and economic inheritance. Seeking the political kingdom, in the words of our first independence leader Kwame Nkrumah, was crucial, but an insufficient act in itself for development. Indeed, it gave rise instead to many excesses, and with the weakening of the opposition parties, also worsened this trait and resulted in many blind policy alleys.

In addressing this colonial legacy, we had thus to manage two other transitions. First, from the 'messianic' psyche of the liberators themselves who tainted every criticism, no matter how constructive, as a threat and, secondly, from bad policy, especially in economic management which failed, initially, to recognise the private sector as a critical partner for growth and development, and then on governance, where the individual was denied freedom of expression and association. This together stymied growth and confined us to underdevelopment. In spite of these drawbacks, Ghana has rebounded into the forefront, although it has not been easy.

It is in this light that the achievements of others give us encouragement. Southeast Asia, for example, showed us what Ghana could achieve with the right mix of visionary leadership, right policies, hard work and perseverance.

In their transition from Third World to First, they quickly instituted right partnerships between the public and private sectors which led to the attraction of skills and finance and multinational companies and placed them on the path to development.

With the right policies and politics, progress can be extraordinary. Fifty years later Singapore, for example, now has a higher per capita income than its once colonial master, Britain.

Overall, Africa has three enormous assets: A burgeoning population of high-energy young people with exposure to high education; an enviable abundant natural resource base; and a potentially powerful budding private sector.

As Africa's post-colonial history shows, without better policy aimed at developing and promoting these sources of prosperity, the African nations will continue to suffer the destabilisation that has hallmarked their immediate post-colonial histories.

Educated but unskilled young people without employment would continue to destabilise our fragile polities, entrepreneurship will be focused on subsistence activities and not wealth-creation, and the commodity dividend will continue to be prey to corruption, rent-seeking and resource nationalism.

But, as my colleagues at the Brenthurst Foundation, Drs Jeffrey Herbst and Greg Mills, vividly illustrate, a better, more prosperous alternative is available. With the application of such wisdom, the 21st century will be the African century.

John A Kufuor
President of Ghana, 2001–09

INTRODUCTION

The start of the second decade of the 21st century is a good time to consider how Africa* can accelerate its development. There has already been much progress across Africa in the past decade, and the immediate future is brighter than at any time for a generation. Growth has averaged approximately five to six per cent across the continent and prospects for many countries are improving, especially given the demand for African commodities from India and China, the policy reforms implemented by several African governments and the continent's relative insulation from the financial tumult that has buffeted Europe and the United States.

Between 2000 and 2010, six of the ten fastest-growing economies world-wide were African (namely Angola, Nigeria, Ethiopia, Mozambique, Chad and Rwanda, the others being China, Burma, Kazakhstan and Cambodia).[1] Growth is important. So, too, are the improvements in telecommunications that have enabled

---

* This book is specifically devoted to the 49 countries of sub-Saharan Africa. While many of the trends and processes we discuss also apply to Egypt, Tunisia, Algeria, Morocco and Libya, those North African countries require a separate analysis. Throughout this book, then, 'Africa' refers to the countries of sub-Saharan Africa.

new connections with the world, and among communities, citizens and states. Through this, Africa has become increasingly integrated with the global economy. In the mid-1990s African telephone connectivity was just one-tenth of the global average; by 2011 it was half, even though the global figure had increased fourfold to 70 connections per 100 people. The number of subscribers on the continent grew almost 20 per cent each year between 2006–11.[2]

While much of Africa's recent growth is thanks to better prices for the commodities it produces, previous commodity booms have not always led to development. Given this newly favourable environment and what we have learned from previous experience in Africa and elsewhere, how do Africans make sure jobs and poverty reduction follow?

Now is the right time to ask this question. Many African countries have moved beyond the old debates. They no longer depend on donors to drive development programmes, and they can, for the first time in their histories, consider how economic growth and political liberalisation should reinforce each other. Now that many African countries are looking ahead to another 50 years of independence, they are finally in a position to write their own future. This is a profound moment for countries that have struggled for so long – and acknowledging that does not deny all the challenges that remain.

The growth surge of the 2000s shows that nothing is inevitable, that the once denigrated 'hopeless continent' could transform itself. Along with higher commodity prices fuelled by Chinese demand, this surge also, as will be seen, reflects improved systems of African governance, underpinned by the spread of democracy continent-wide.

Translating growth into development – and jobs – requires other steps however. For one, African countries will have to diversify their dependency away from exporting raw materials, which is good for the fiscus but does little for local jobs. With one-quarter of the world's population under 25 projected to be from sub-Saharan Africa in 2025, ensuring the conditions to create employment is a continental imperative. Today eight in every ten Africans are self-employed.

Examples from Asia and Latin America show how such a transformation is not only possible but rapid. Only 50 years ago Asian countries were themselves seen as developmental backwaters, and Central America trapped in a vicious cycle of regional wars, economic mismanagement and faltering social cohesion.

To ensure a new future with both jobs and development, African governments will have to embark on a path down which few among their ranks have so far ventured.

They will need, at the outset, to develop a 'growth ideology' beyond the vacuous vision documents which litter the policy landscape. Rather than employing more consultants, governments and ruling parties will need to drop their animus to business, which often has its origins in racial exclusion or perceptions of rivalry. This demands government coming to an understanding with business, of remedying stultifying attitudes varying between benign neglect and ostentatious antagonism.

Indeed, governments have the key role in this transition. They also need to establish an infrastructure for economic development, especially in Africa, dealing with the binding constraints of transport and electricity. Sub-Saharan Africa's electricity production is equivalent to that of Spain, even though it has nearly 20 times as many people. And more than half of that is produced by just one country, South Africa.

If not addressed, such constraints will curtail growth or, in some cases, stop development dead in its tracks. Spending on infrastructure will pay very high dividends over a long period of time. So will better educational systems.

At its core, Africa will have to act on the realisation that to create jobs, it needs to attract the sort of investors that can go to many other countries. It is in these sectors, and not in natural resources, that the jobs exist.

For most foreign investors the decision turns on how easy it is to do business. They are interested in levels of corruption along with policy stability and predictability.

Some governments believe that they can, in this, 'pick winners' to encourage investment. The success rate from this strategy is not encouraging, not least since this is not where governments' advantage lies. Similarly, while incentives, including the establishment of Special Economic Zones, can encourage investment, not least by serving to insulate companies from government weaknesses, these are at best limited fixes. They are not a substitute for reforming the entire economy, and business inexorably outgrows such measures.

It is much more important for governments to set an overall economic environment in which the private sector can pick its own winners.

More than anything, Africa's continuing transformation demands a laser-like concentration on development for generations. There is a key political dimension to this transformation.

Instead of focusing on issues of identity and difference to be elected, including race, tribe and religion, Africa's elections will need to mature to feature hard economic choices and the record of delivery. If Africa's first liberation was from colonial and racist government, and the second from the liberators, the third is the change in focus of politics itself. Concentrating on economic development to the exclusion of much else is required. With this approach, Africa can show as did East Asia, that in development, nothing is inevitable.

And with 49 sub-Saharan African countries, there is a real premium in moving quickly. This is hardly a 'race to the bottom' as improvements in cost-competitiveness and productivity are sometimes portrayed, but rather a race to be among the first. This book shows why this should happen, and how this is possible.

The moment for Africa's 'third liberation' has arrived.

Africa's third liberation

By 2012, not only were all countries free from colonialism, but most had also overthrown the autocrats who all too often followed foreign rule. In some cases the original liberation movements have virtually disappeared. For example, Patrice Lumumba's *Mouvement National Congolais*, which led what we now call the Democratic Republic of the Congo to independence in 1960, never recovered from its leader's assassination and Mobutu Sese Seko's 32-year one-party state. In Ghana, the Convention People's Party of the first post-independence British colonial leader, Kwame Nkrumah, won just one seat in parliament in the 2008 election. The National Council of Nigeria and the Cameroons, along with the Nigeria People's Congress, which jointly led the West African giant after independence, are no longer active forces.

Outside Southern Africa, it is only in Eritrea where there has been a one-party state since independence in 1993, and in Cameroon, under Ahmadou Ahidjo from 1960 and, since 1982, Paul Biya, that the original liberation party still holds sway. Gabon's original ruling party, the *Bloc Démocratique Gabonais*, was replaced by the *Parti Démocratique Gabonais* although the Bongo thread remained unbroken, first with Omar and now his son Ali. In Kenya, the Kenya African National Union is part of the coalition government, though neither the president nor the prime minister is from the party of liberation icon, Jomo Kenyatta. In Ethiopia and Rwanda, liberation movements rule, though in both cases these removed post-independence governments. They appear, however, to have picked up bad habits, having been in power since 1991 and 1994 respectively.

It is true that the situation is more mixed in Southern Africa. Not only do Robert Mugabe and his Zimbabwe African National Union – Patriotic Front (ZANU-PF) clique cling to power at any cost in Zimbabwe, but the ruling parties in Namibia, Mozambique, Angola, Botswana, Tanzania and South Africa are the same ones that once brought democratic freedoms. Swaziland did away with political parties altogether in 1973. In Lesotho, however, the once-dominant Basotho National Party has withered to the point of virtual disappearance, as has the United National Independence Party in Zambia. Hastings Banda's Malawi Congress Party has gone from all-powerful one-party dominance to official opposition, where it has been since 1994.

The continental shift away from the one-time liberators has gone hand in hand with the extension of democracy, from just three African countries regularly holding multiparty elections at the end of the 1970s (Botswana, Gambia and Mauritius) to more than 40 today. As the next chapter reports, while many of these processes are imperfect at best and often fraudulent, and the consolidation of democratic institutions lags, democracy as an organising political orthodoxy has no ideological contenders in today's Africa. This is not to say that leaders willingly give in to these rights. Democracy is often a hard-fought process, and even today some suggest mischievously (and not without self-interest) that things would work more smoothly without the 'costs' of democratic niceties.

Africa's political evolution points to a third liberation that most of the continent has yet to experience, one that will likely prove as important as the political freedoms earned over the past half century, or perhaps even more important: the liberation from political economies characterised by graft, crony capitalism, rent-seeking, elitism and, inevitably, widening (and destabilising) social inequality. Such an emancipation is necessary to open up economic space in which business can compete, a necessary condition to expand employment.

One part of this third liberation has already happened: the evolution from seeing foreign development aid as the key source of development to more realistically portraying money brought in by outsiders as potentially useful, but only in the context of good governance. Remarkably, as recently as 2005, Tony Blair, backed by celebrity economists and a chorus of ageing pop-stars, led a campaign at the Gleneagles G8 summit to double aid to Africa as apparently the last, best hope of transforming the continent's fortunes. Within just half a decade, a combination of higher commodity prices and better governance has relegated the aid debate, which distorted economic practices and the accountability of leaders to citizens, to a secondary development consideration. The focus has refreshingly shifted to the growth imperative and the need to lessen inequality by creating jobs, especially among the youth. Accordingly, in many parts of Africa (the conversation is still somewhat different in Washington DC, and Europe), foreign aid is no longer central to debates about growth.

Instead, the debate is about how Africa can realise its enormous economic potential and thereby avoid the dashed hopes and disappointments so common in the first 50 years of independence. The stakes – which, for hundreds of millions of people in what is the world's poorest continent, include their chance of escaping poverty – could not be higher.

Can Africa join in the world's progress?

Now is a particularly appropriate time to examine Africa's prospects, because the world record on poverty reduction over the past 50 years has been excellent. All signs indicate that it will be possible for at least some African countries to participate in an international economy that continues to be robust as long as they institutionalise and enhance their reforms. Whether all, or even most, African countries can find space to grow in the international economy is a separate question. Individual nations should feel a sense of urgency to enter the international economy while the window is open.

To see how much the world has changed, it is important to remember that in 1968, when Swedish economist and Nobel Prize winner, Gunnar Myrdal, published his three-volume work *Asian Drama*, instability, corruption and poverty were widespread, and development seemed a long way off.[3] Singapore was just emerging under Lee Kuan Yew; Malaysia was a year away from the race riots that sparked Mahathir's reforms; Vietnam was in the midst of a very hot war, its neighbours Thailand, Cambodia and Laos wobbling between insurgencies and military regimes; Indonesia had just suffered a palace coup as General Suharto took over from Sukarno in March 1968; South Korea seemed caught between student unrest and the ruthlessness of a military dictator; and Taiwan was still in the iron grip of Chiang Kai-shek, not yet eased by the modernising influence of his son Chiang Ching-Kuo. Engagement by external forces scarcely helped: the United States and Soviet Union poured military resources into their allies in Vietnam, which were locked in pitched battle, while economic growth in China and India was at a standstill. In the former, development had been halted by the destructiveness of the Cultural Revolution; in India the Licence Raj and centrally planned economy drip-fed a burgeoning population.

While his pessimism seems out of place, given what we know today, Myrdal's book reflects the conventional wisdom of the day. It argued that the only way for Southeast Asia to develop was to control its population, redistribute agricultural land and invest in health care and education. While there is little wrong, even today, with these prescriptions, the region's dramatic shift from being the epitome of conflict to peace and rapid economic growth demonstrates how quickly things can change with the right ingredients of policy, political will, external opportunities and domestic ownership.

Already in 1968 there were signs of the rapid change that was to become the regional hallmark. Japan's annual economic growth averaged nearly 11 per cent between 1967 and 1970, surpassing West Germany to become the third-largest economy in the world behind the United States and the Soviet Union. And South Korea was already on the path to rapid transformation, as Figure 1 indicates, under General Park Chung-hee, who was intent on emulating Japan's rapid route to prosperity. It took the United States 164 years, from 1820 to 1984, to get its per capita income from US$1 257 to US$20 123, while South Korea managed approximately the same jump (from US$1 092 to US$19 614) in the 88 years between 1920 and 2008.[4] And Singapore, Taiwan, and Hong Kong experienced similar leaps ahead in the first roar of the 'tigers'.

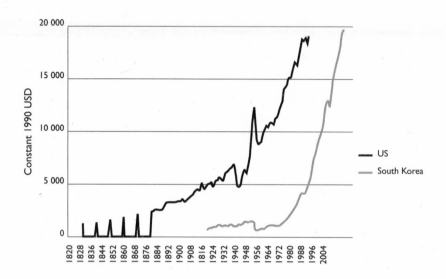

Figure 1: The US and South Korea

In 1993, a quarter-century after Myrdal's book, the World Bank published *The East Asian Miracle*, its commentary on a region that is now a byword for development. The bank concluded that the reasons for the 'miracle' lay in the massive deployment of capital and human resources coupled with market-oriented reforms. No longer did culture seem like a stumbling block to development in linking progress to societal will as, for example, the 1950 *UN Report on Development* 'Measures for the Development of Under-Developed Countries' had claimed;[5] on the contrary, Confucianism promoted development.

There is further good news at the start of the 2010s, despite the depressing economic travails of the European region and slow growth among the 34 developed Organisation for Economic Co-operation and Development (OECD) economies.[6] For one thing, there has been a dramatic change in the speed of growth and development. From the year 1000 until 1820, the advance in per capita income was very slow, the global average rising about 50 per cent as the population increased fourfold. Since 1820 there has been a dramatic change: per capita income has risen more than eight times, and the population more than five times.[7]

More recently, in the late 20th and early 21st centuries, countries have made even more rapid advances, as indicated in Figure 2. Whereas most people in the early 20th century had living standards approximating today's 'bottom billion', rapid integration with the global economy has led to significant increases in per capita incomes, led by Southeast Asia and China.

There has also been a dramatic increase in life expectancy. As Angus Maddison notes, in the year 1000, infants could expect to live about 24 years, on average. A third would die in the first year of life, while hunger and epidemic disease ravaged the survivors. Since 1820, people have lived much longer, and by 2000, the average infant can expect to live for 66 years.[8]

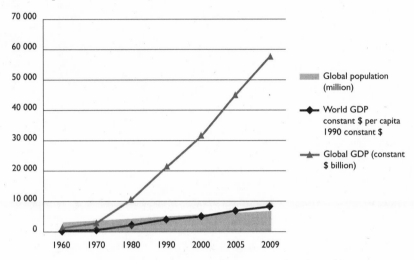

Figure 2: Global population, GDP and per capita income

Put differently, there is still plenty of space in the global economy for growth and advancement, especially for those regions with comparative advantages in agriculture and other natural resources, such as Africa.

In fact, global output is expected to double by 2030 to US$180 trillion, and to double again by 2050. The ability of countries to benefit from this environment depends on adapting technology, pursuing comparative advantages, and allowing their 'people to be free to pursue their self interest, to be constrained by competition rather than regulation'.[9] High growth is linked to high investment and a virtuous cycle of faster growth, higher savings and increasing investment. And this can be assisted, too, by increased population growth. Sub-Saharan Africa is expected to increase its numbers by around 450 million to 500 million people between 2010 and 2030, compared to China (100 million), India (260 million), Asia (excluding China, India and Japan) (300 million) and the United States (50 million).[10]

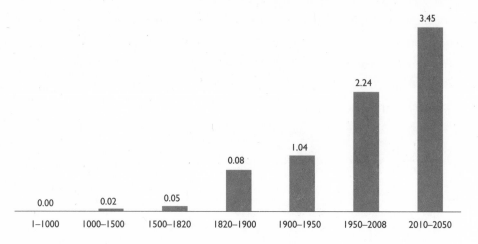

Figure 3: Global per capita growth annualised percentage increase[11]

While activists routinely decry the level of global poverty, a remarkable number of people have been lifted out of destitution over the past two decades, a fact almost universally unacknowledged. We live in the fastest period of poverty reduction ever seen, with the global poverty rate dropping more than one percentage point each year, representing some 70 million people annually. By 2005, the number of people living below the international poverty line of US$1.25 a day stood at 1.37 billion, half a billion fewer than in the early 1980s. By 2011, it is estimated that there were 820 million living below this mark.

Thus the primary target of the Millennium Development Goals – to halve the rate of global poverty from its 1990 level by 2015 – was probably achieved around 2008. As Laurence Chandy and Geoffrey Gertz note, 'Whereas it took 25 years to reduce poverty by half a billion people up to 2005, the same feat was likely achieved in the six years between then and now. Never before have so many people been lifted out of poverty over such a brief period of time.'[12]

Of course, these figures require disaggregation. China's stunning economic turnaround distorts the picture and masks the failings of others. In 1980, 16 per cent of China's population lived above the poverty line. By 2005, only 16 per cent stood below it. Without China, the 500 million decline in global poverty numbers becomes an increase of 100 million. In sub-Saharan Africa, the world's poorest region, the poverty rate remained above 50 per cent. Given the region's rapid population growth, this translates into a near doubling in the number of its poor. The international economy beckons, but Africa still must take positive steps to follow in the poverty reduction steps of others.

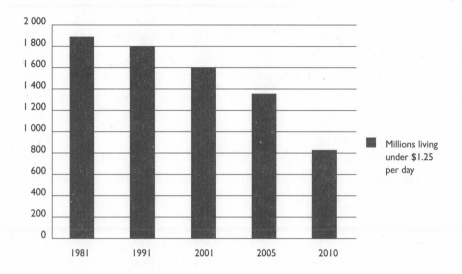

Figure 4: Decrease in global poverty

A decade of progress in Africa

Fifteen years ago, in the mid-1990s, most discussions on Africa focused on topics that are today regarded as no longer relevant, or that have, to some extent, been managed, 'dealt with' or even discredited. For example, while the continent is still coping with the consequences of HIV/Aids, and the rates of infection are the highest worldwide, the disease is no longer a defining issue. Indeed, the social fallout, including an increase in the number of parentless children, may be considerable, but the doomsday predictions about the catastrophic security and development impacts of this disease have not come true.

There is also no longer a Manichaean debate about the role of the state and that of the market. It is broadly accepted that both an efficient state and open markets are necessary for development to occur, even though some governments are uncertain about, or incapable of creating one, and lukewarm about allowing the other. As a result, debates that were focused on the pros and cons of privatisation versus continued nationalisation have moved on. However, as we note below, while the old debates are now stale, new formulations about state and market are just starting to emerge.

African countries have also largely moved towards freer political systems, albeit at different speeds. At the end of the Cold War, 70 per cent of African countries were considered to have 'Not Free' political systems as classified by Freedom House. By 2010, more than two-thirds were 'Free' or 'Partly Free'. Democracy has largely won the intellectual argument, even if the practice varies markedly from country to country. Even authoritarian countries such as Robert Mugabe's Zimbabwe hold regular elections, though of problematic quality. A good proportion of the elections worldwide in any given year are held in Africa. At the same time, democratic institutions in many African countries are still nascent, and it will take years for them to take on a permanent institutional character. For instance, few countries have legal systems that can credibly protect property rights, a prerequisite for sustained economic growth. Nor is there any guarantee that progress towards democracy will be linear, and certainly many countries, if European history is any guide, will suffer democratic reversals simply because democracy is so hard to create.

Finally, conflict is on the decline in Africa. One consequence of the degeneration of politics during the 1960s, 1970s and 1980s was the high incidence of violence in Africa. The end of the Cold War enabled some conflicts (e.g. in Angola and Mozambique) to eventually wind down, but there was also an intense period of strife after 1990, as the geopolitical cards were reshuffled. Wars in Central Africa, West Africa and Sudan, and between Ethiopia and Eritrea, signalled a continent in crisis. The failure of the United States and the United Nations in Somalia in 1993 and the Rwandan genocide in 1994 suggested that the continent could not count on external intervention to end conflict. And still, in the 1990s, Africa was shaking off the last of its colonial or liberation struggles with the advent of a multiracial democracy in South Africa.

Now much has changed. Twenty years after the end of the Cold War, the wars in West and Southern Africa have ended, although there is still conflict in the Horn and Central Africa. As Figure 5 illustrates, Africa has seen a substantial decrease in the number of conflicts, from 15 in the 1990s to five between 2000 and 2010. Accordingly, there has been a decrease in the number of global battle deaths from 160 000 a year in the 1980s to 50 000 annually in the 2000s.[13]

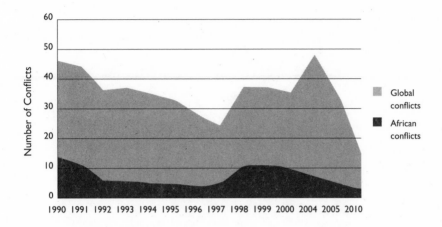

Figure 5: Sub-Saharan and global conflicts

The remaining conflicts appear to be concentrated in 'hard cases', such as the Democratic Republic of the Congo and Somalia, that have no immediate or obvious resolution. New conflicts will undoubtedly break out in surprising places, but it is hard to believe that the continental level of violence will revert to what was seen in the 1990s. The fall in the level of violence parallels the aforementioned change in democratic structures, as indicated by Figure 6.[14]

There are other dimensions to this shifting pattern of conflict. Throughout the 1960s, 1970s and 1980s, much of the African continent had become militarised. Relatively few states avoided military coups, and those that did had to find some accommodation with their armed forces. As Figure 6 shows, between 1960 and 2004 there were 105 violent overthrows of African regimes, more than half the total of regime changes in this period. Violent regime change has declined significantly as a percentage since 1990 and even further since 2000.

Aside from the implications of these military adventures for African civil-military relations, and their effect on democracy and accountability, the militarisation of society generated a culture of violence, had implications for gender structures and equality, and stimulated the growth and proliferation of armed gangs, warlord formations, death squads, guerrilla armies and proxy forces of all kinds.[15] Restoring civil governance, stability and the rule of law thus requires, as a first step, keeping the military in the barracks.

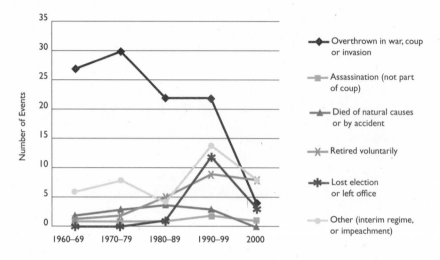

Figure 6: African leaders: Reasons for leaving office

Ending conflict can have at least as large an impact on poverty as improved growth rates. Indeed, as the World Bank's *World Development Report 2011* argues, peace is likely to lead to increased growth. The report notes that Ethiopia has, for example, increased access to potable water from 13 per cent of the population in 1990 to 66 per cent in 2009, while Mozambique, once it had ended its civil war, tripled its primary school completion rate from 14 per cent in 1999 to 46 per cent in 2007. By contrast, those countries affected by conflict are falling behind in reducing poverty. The report notes: 'For every three years that a country is affected by major violence … poverty reduction lags behind by 2.7 percentage points. For some countries affected by violence, poverty has actually increased'.[16]

Economic freedom and growth

Various indices point out the correlation between economic freedom – defined as secure rights to legally acquired property, freedom to engage in voluntary transactions inside and outside a nation's borders, freedom from governmental control of the terms on which individuals transact, and freedom from governmental expropriation of property – and economic prosperity.

As Steven Hanke and Stephen Walters clearly argue and illustrate,[17] five surveys measuring economic freedom – the Fraser Institute's Economic Freedom of the World Index, Freedom House's Economic Freedom Indicators, the Heritage Foundation's Index of Economic Freedom, the International Institute for Management Development's *World Competitiveness Yearbook* and the World Economic Forum's *Global Competitiveness Report* – have 'significant power to explain variation in per capita national income.' Similarly, the Fraser Institute's 1996 survey concluded: 'Clearly, these data indicate that during the last two decades there has been a strong relationship between economic freedom and economic growth.'[18] Countries with either a high level of or a substantial increase in economic freedom achieved positive growth. The overwhelming majority of countries with low and/or contracting levels of economic freedom experienced declines in per capita GDP.

This truth has not been lost on Africa, though the picture is becoming increasingly varied. By 2012, for example, in the Heritage Foundation and *Wall Street Journal*'s Index of Economic Freedom, the region was the 'good news/bad news story'. Africa continued to lag behind all others in seven of the ten measures that make up the Index. Four of the bottom ten (*Equatorial Guinea*, Iran, *Democratic Republic of the Congo*, Burma, Venezuela, *Eritrea, Libya*, Cuba, *Zimbabwe* and, last, North Korea) were from sub-Saharan Africa.

But the good news was that for the second straight year, sub-Saharan Africa was the most improved region, with 22 countries moving in a positive direction.[19] For the first time, an African country – Mauritius – broke into the top ten in the Index, at eighth place, behind Chile but above Ireland and the United States, and was therefore classified as 'free'. The first continental sub-Saharan African ranking country was Botswana in 33rd place, behind Jordan and above Georgia, and South Africa is next up at 70th, which makes both African countries 'mostly free'.

The new challenges

For all its progress, sub-Saharan Africa still faces extraordinary challenges, of which jobs for young people is perhaps the most important. If countries cannot leverage their better-performing economies to provide jobs (and therefore income) to young people, the tremendous opportunity afforded by the improved climate will have been wasted and the countries could face powerful poverty-fuelled unrest of the kind seen in the Arab Spring.

Sub-Saharan Africa's population is expected to increase from 800 million today to 1.5 billion within a generation, putting pressure on finite resources (notably water) and on regimes, institutions and governments. By 2025, nearly a quarter of the world's young people (under the age of 25) will be from sub-Saharan Africa – an extraordinary statistic. And many of them will be living in Africa's cities. Indeed, Africa will, by 2025, be an urban continent. One hundred years ago just five per cent of Africans lived in cities. In 1950 the figure was 15 per cent. Today it is about 40 per cent. In 2025 it will be more than 50 per cent. Accordingly, a number of African urban areas have been elevated into the megacity bracket, which includes cities with more than ten million inhabitants. Lagos, which in 1963 had just 665 000 inhabitants, is expected to become the world's 11th-biggest city by 2015 with 16 million inhabitants. Africa's other anticipated megacities include Accra (Ghana), Johannesburg–Pretoria (South Africa), Khartoum (Sudan), Kinshasa–Brazzaville (Democratic Republic of the Congo and Republic of the Congo), and Nairobi (Kenya).

With an urbanisation rate in some African countries as high as (or more than) ten per cent per annum, keeping ahead of the need for jobs for new entrants demands unprecedented continental economic growth rates. Yet, as a result of historic patterns of low growth, the majority of urban dwellers in sub-Saharan Africa live in slums 'without durable housing or legal rights to their land. At least one-quarter of African city dwellers do not have access to electricity.' Less than half have access to piped water, while waste disposal is often rudimentary at best. In Kibera, Nairobi's largest slum, which accommodates perhaps as many as half a million people, plastic bags are used as 'flying toilets'. At the same time, an estimated 60 per cent of urban employment is thought to be in the informal sector, limiting tax revenues and, for entrepreneurs, access to financing and markets.[20]

Joblessness is endemic in Africa, especially among the young, with the unemployment and underemployment of this cohort as high as 80 per cent in some countries, including relatively well-performing (at least in growth terms) states such as Mozambique and Ghana. Figure 7 displays the percentage of people in 'vulnerable employment' – the self-employed and contributing family workers – by region, and demonstrates that Africa and South Asia face the most difficult situations. While Figure 7 does not focus on levels of unemployment or underemployment (for which the statistics are notoriously unreliable), the self-employment levels shown provide a useful indicator of the availability of formal work opportunities. It also demonstrates the relatively meagre gains in employment of the past ten years, despite better growth.[21]

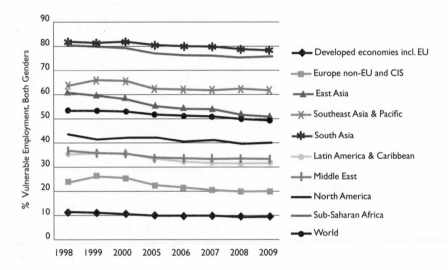

Figure 7: Vulnerable employment by region

In sub-Saharan Africa, despite the 2000s being the best growth decade on record, labour participation rates remain very low, and the proportion of informal (vulnerable) workers has declined by just 0.5 per cent per annum, half as fast as East Asia and Latin America. The growth level is still below the continent's potential and, more importantly, is not enough to meet the demands and aspirations of its burgeoning cohort of young people. No wonder politics is often fraught and people angry in spite of a recent history of consistent growth.

The problem is most acute in post-conflict countries. As Paul Collier reminds us, not only do more than half of such states slide back to conflict within ten years, but their period of recovery is at least as long as their period of collapse or decline.[22] This sad axiom is of particular relevance to some of Africa's most important and largest countries, including the Democratic Republic of the Congo, Angola and Sudan. Young people in post-conflict countries are especially vulnerable to radicalising politics and the hope and attachments that this populism offers. Governments across Africa have found it difficult to bridge the gap between growth and jobs. There are several other reasons for this poor performance, the main ones being the lack of competitiveness and productivity compared with South and East Asia and China, the relatively small number employed directly by the natural resources sector (which drives the boom times and provides a fiscal boost in the process), weak and expensive infrastructure, and a lack of suitable skills. In many cases, the economic strategy, such as it is, has been to try to leverage the comparative advantage in the natural resources sector. However, rather than creating jobs, in many cases this dependence on natural resources has instead led to a bifurcated economy and society: the small numbers who are 'in' (and pay tax) and the rest, those who remain 'out' (do not pay tax) and survive and subsist in the informal economy. Resource-led growth not only makes building a state through a widespread tax net and base difficult, but complicates the ability of the state to create a single society in which all citizens feel they are making a worthwhile contribution.

Hence the question often asked today throughout the African continent: what can we produce that China – or other countries, for that matter – cannot make cheaper than we can?

Even South Africa, the economic giant of sub-Saharan Africa, with approximately a third of continental GDP, has failed to increase formal-sector employment sufficiently. In South Africa's case, labour laws have made employment less attractive for employers. Wage rates that increase ahead of productivity, the cost of hiring and firing, and a generally inflexible labour market have strengthened existing trends towards capital intensity and outsourcing by employers. The South African Treasury has noted that just 13.1 million South Africans are employed:

> Only two out of five persons of working age (41 per cent) have a job, compared with 65 per cent in Brazil, 71 per cent in China and 55 per cent in India. To match the emerging markets average of 56 per cent, South Africa would need to employ 18 million people – five million more than are employed today. To keep pace with the number of people entering the labour market, this would require the economy to create about 9 million jobs over the next 10 years.[23]

Moreover, the unemployment rate among South Africans from 15 to 24 years old is 51 per cent, more than twice the national underemployment rate of 25 per cent, according to the South African Institute of Race Relations.[24] Such widespread joblessness is a social time bomb, as events in North Africa during 2011 show. Research by the largest temporary employment services company in South Africa provides evidence that the informal sector is much bigger than hitherto supposed – 8.3 million versus 2.1 million – and that the labour absorption rate (the percentage of the population of working age who were employed) is 55 per cent.[25] The challenge is still to generate youth employment and to move workers from the informal to the formal sector.

Figure 8: South Africa: Growth vs employment

Across the continent, the story is quite similar. To give another example, Zambia had three million people at independence in 1964, and today it has 13 million. But whereas there were 300 000 formal sector jobs at independence, today there are fewer than 500 000, excluding the public sector. And most of the three million or so young Zambians in the job market are unemployed.

Without the right environment and opportunities, Africa's youth will most likely become a powerful destabilising force, especially in the cities – but not just on the continent, as many inevitably (and with good reason) seek succour elsewhere, notably in Europe. There is also a risk of costly populist policies, with governments making promises – but, going by past practice, delivering very little – to their alienated youth. As in East Asia, where the demographic dividend was estimated to be worth as much as 40 per cent of GDP growth[26], in Africa young people could be an unprecedented and tremendous force for positive change if their undoubted energies are correctly harnessed, and the right skills cultivated.

Back to the future

This book addresses Africa's challenges now, when so much of the dysfunctional politics of the past has been cleared away. Countries across the continent have proven that they can grow. There is the promise of a significant number operating within liberalised political systems, and the regional environment for many, especially outside Central Africa and the Horn, has improved. However, these are still very fragile foundations, given the challenges that many countries face. Indeed, our central contribution will be to focus on how African countries can grow within their liberalised political systems by discussing three central questions.

1. For the foreseeable future, most African leaders will operate in political systems in which elections are routine but of uncertain quality, and in which democratic institutional development is still fragile. This is inevitably an ambiguous situation, given the difficulties of democratic consolidation after decades of authoritarian rule. What advantages can leaders leverage within this kind of political environment to promote and consolidate economic growth?

2. In many African countries, significant changes in the political and economic environment are accelerating the evolution of constituency politics. What interest groups might emerge that could help leaders promote and consolidate a growth agenda? This is a critical question as it marks the transition from an economic debate largely driven by outside actors – including the IMF, the World Bank, and bilateral donors – to a healthier situation in which domestic actors promote the growth agenda. Of course, new constituencies that oppose growth could develop.

3. What ideology, or ideologies, do the African countries that are now growing, and seek to grow faster, pursue? Even though the economic reform movement in Africa can be traced back to the early 1980s, when Ghana began its economic reforms, few African countries have articulated an ideology that explains to their own people what they are doing, what the relationship is between state and market, and what can reasonably be expected from economic growth. In other words, they have not explained their emerging political economies, a critical step

if the recent reforms are to be institutionalised. Indeed, it is striking that despite the widespread embrace of market-driven reforms, few African governments will speak of 'capitalism' or even acknowledge the private sector as a central growth driver. African countries do not need to adopt Western formulations, but it is critical that they create their own ideological constructs.

These questions, we believe, are central to the next 50 years of African post-independence development. Using examples from Central and South America, Southeast and South Asia, and the Middle East, we examine what tactics are best to match political liberalisation with growth and, in particular, why some countries have found it difficult to do so and have battled to progress. This comparative perspective is particularly appropriate now that many Africans are asking the same questions about how to ensure prosperity and democracy that have already animated other nations in what was once known as the 'developing' world. Having posed the question 'What will an African growth and development model look like?' we conclude by suggesting a way forward for higher-growth and job-absorption strategies in Africa in the context of liberalised political systems.

We will show that governments can assist in increasing levels of employment. The record from some countries outside Africa, especially in Central America and Asia, demonstrates that competitive minimum wages and clear safeguards for business are required to encourage investment, growth and employment. These lessons are especially relevant to investments in job-intensive, value-addition sectors such as services and manufacturing, but less so in oil and mining. The higher the levels of education, the greater the wages, though special qualities such as English language skills are increasingly necessary to move up the value and wage chains, as are the provision of infrastructure and favourable policy. Labour-intensive industries also require governments to do at least as much as their competitors in policy terms, including setting up special economic zones as precursors to liberalising their economies.

However, despite the emboldening of interventionist-minded government planners by the global economic crisis since 2008, the record of their ability to catalyse productive investments in the economy – to 'pick winners', in other words – remains strikingly poor. Attempts to build economies through other inter-ventionist policy measures, including populist economics, may be politically understandable in the short term, but are invariably counter-productive, not least since they risk institutionalising costly practices. Managing the short-term political fallout from longer-term policy setting is always going to be challenging, though here, too, there are good lessons from other regions in managing relationships. For example, the 'solidarity associations' of Costa Rica, essentially forums of managers and workers for the joint management of redundancy and retrenchment contributions, have created a vested interest in the maintenance of the health of companies. The associations have transformed employee–employer relations in Costa Rica for the better in the past half century.

Finally, for all of the predictions of the end of capitalism and globalisation, the economic crisis of the 2000s has highlighted, again, the importance of sound economic fundamentals and competitive practices – including prudent public expenditure, a thriving capital market, the careful management of natural resources and a productive workforce. As China and other dynamic economies vividly illustrate, the global economy today offers an unprecedented opportunity for economic growth and job creation in developing countries. Aside from the unambiguous moral desirability of freedom of choice, the empirical evidence is clear: economic growth, environmental conditions and income equality are positive functions of the degree of economic freedom.[27] All this is important for sub-Saharan Africa, where formal sector employment remains endemically low and falling, especially among the youth, and inequality correspondingly high. The extent of such inequality usually matches that of various social and political ills.[28]

Our conclusions offer a mutually reinforcing prospect of growth, stability, inclusion, development and further growth. Without it, the future appears much bleaker. The Arab Spring, the defining political event of 2011, contains its own message: empowered by technology and emboldened by their new-found power, citizens are less tolerant of leaders than they once were and more likely to take things into their own hands. The third liberation is thus less a grudging concession by ruling elites than an act of self-preservation.

Endnotes

1 'Africa Rising', *The Economist*, 3 December 2011.

2 For example, see http://www.bbc.co.uk/news/world-africa-15659983.

3 Gunner Myrdal, *Asian Drama: An Inquiry into the Poverty of Nations*. New York: Twentieth Century Fund, 1968.

4 Calculated from 'Statistics on World Population, GDP and Per Capita GDP 1-2008 AD' by Angus Maddison. Found at www.ssdc.net/Maddison/orindex/htm.

5 Cited in Devesh Kapur, John Prior Lewis and Richard Charles Webb, *The World Bank: History*. Washington: Brookings, 1997, p. 145.

6 Australia, Austria, Belgium, Canada, Chile, the Czech Republic, Denmark, Estonia, Finland, France, Germany, Greece, Hungary, Iceland, Ireland, Israel, Italy, Japan, South Korea, Luxembourg, Mexico, the Netherlands, New Zealand, Norway, Poland, Portugal, the Slovak Republic, Slovenia, Spain, Sweden, Switzerland, Turkey, the United Kingdom, the United States.

7 Angus Maddison, 'The West and the Rest in the World Economy: 1000–2030, Maddisonian and Malthusian interpretations', *World Economics*, Vol 9, No 4, October–December 2008, at http://www.relooney.info/00_New_2733.pdf.

8 http://www.fraserinstitute.org/research-news/news/display.aspx?id=18211.

9 Brian Kantor, presentation to Democratic Alliance 'Achieving 8% Growth' project, Cape Town, 23 September 2011.

10 *Ibid*, drawn from UN data and Standard Chartered Bank research.

11 The figure on global growth was kindly supplied by Brian Kantor.

12 Data on global poverty from Laurence Chandy and Geoffrey Gertz 'With Little Notice, Globalization Reduced Poverty', at http://www.yaleglobal.yale.edu/m/content/little-notice-globalization-reduced-poverty/7143.

13 World Bank, *World Development Report 2011: Conflict, Security, and Development*, p. 51. The figure is compiled from a variety of sources, including http://www.sipri.org/research/conflict/trends/sipri_publications/yearbook/yb0201a.

14 Sourced from Arthur Goldsmith, 'Donors, Dictators, and Democrats'. *Journal of Modern African Studies*, 39(3), 2001. Adapted from Roger Southall and Henning Melber, eds. *Legacies of Power: Leadership Change and Former Presidents in African Politics*. Pretoria: Human Sciences Research Council, 2006, p. 2.

15 Eboe Hutchful, 'De-militarising the Political Process in Africa', *African Security Review*, 6(2), 1997, at http://www.issafrica.org/Pubs/ASR/6No2/Hutchful.html. p. 3.

16 World Development Report 2011, p. 60.

17 Steve H Hanke and Stephen J K Walters, 'Economic Freedom, Prosperity and Equality: A Survey', *Cato Journal*, 17(2), 1997. We are grateful to Steve Hanke for bringing this to our attention.

18 J Gwartney, R Lawson, and W Block, *Economic Freedom of the World: 1975–1995*. Vancouver, BC, Canada: The Fraser Institute, 1996.

19 'Economic Freedom, Not Government Spending, Provides Path to Prosperity, 18th Index of Economic Freedom Shows', The Heritage Foundation, 12 January 2012. http://www.heritage.org/research/reports/2012/01/economic-freedom-not-government-spending-provides-path-to-prosperity.

20 Stephanie Hanson, 'Urbanisation in Sub-Saharan Africa, 1 October 2007, at http://www.cfr.org/africa/urbanization-sub-saharan-africa/p.14327.

21 This is taken from ILO, *Global Employment Trends, 2011*. Geneva: International Labour Office, International Labour Organization, 2001, p. 69. Vulnerable employment is defined by the ILO as 'the sum of own-account workers and contributing family workers. They are less likely to have formal work arrangements, and are therefore more likely to lack decent working conditions, adequate social security and "voice" through effective representation by trade unions and similar organizations. Vulnerable employment is often characterized by inadequate earnings, low productivity and difficult conditions of work that undermine workers' fundamental rights.' Interview with Lawrence Jeff Johnson, ILO chief of the Employment Trends Unit, at http://www.ilo.org/global/about-the-ilo/press-and-media-centre/insight/WCMS_120470/lang--en/index.htm.

22 Paul Collier, *The Bottom Billion: Why the Poorest Countries are Failing and What Can be Done About It*. New York: Oxford University Press, 2007, p. 26.

23 National Treasury, Republic of South Africa, Budget Review 2011, p. 40, at http://www.treasury.gov.za/documents/national%20budget/2011/review/chapter%203.pdf.

24 At http://www.iol.co.za/news/south-africa/half-of-sa-s-youth-are-unemployed-1.1019783.

25 This information was supplied by Loane Sharp of Adcorp.

26 See David E Bloom and Jeffrey G Williamson, 1998, 'Demographic Transitions and Economic Miracles in Emerging Asia', *World Bank Economic Review*, 12: pp. 419–455.

27 Bill Niskanen, at http://www.cato.org/pub_display.php?pub_id=13984.

28 Richard Wilkinson and Kate Pickett, *The Spirit Level: Why Equality is Better for Everyone*. London: Penguin, November 2010.

1

AFRICA'S GROWTH AND LIBERALISATION – A PORTRAIT

Poverty has been the defining characteristic of African countries since in-dependence. However, thanks to a combination of favourable external trends and improved domestic economic policy, the continent has experienced sustained economic growth since the early 1990s. The decade of the 2010s also seems likely to be positive: the International Monetary Fund (IMF) estimates that Africa will grow by 5.5 per cent in 2012[1], and similar rates are likely in the future as long as commodity prices remain high. Accordingly, the world has begun to take notice: many businesses report that they are investigating Africa as a potential site for investment, and China's aggressive move to Africa is seemingly being copied by other new entrants.

There has, of course, been hyperbole. The *Wall Street Journal*'s assertion that the African market is 'on par with the size of the middle classes in the billion-person emerging markets of China and India'[2] includes North African countries and people who can spend as little as US$2 per day. That level of income would not normally be considered 'middle class'. Still, the change in attitude of the business community toward Africa is palpable. The turning point appears to have been the decision by Walmart in 2011 to pay roughly US$2.4 billion to buy 51 per cent of South Africa's Massmart Holdings Ltd – ironically, despite resistance to the deal in South Africa itself, led by trade unions. This sale signalled that the African consumer market was worth taking seriously.

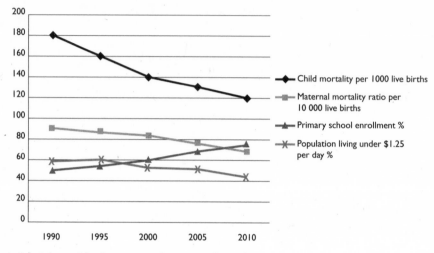

Figure 1: Sub-Saharan Africa's improving human conditions[3]

There are also important indications that the rebound in African economic development has started to have an impact on the life chances of individuals. This is no different to experiences elsewhere. Hans Rosling, a Swedish statistician and expert on the links between economic development and quality of life, has shown that positive social change, such as improvements in life expectancy and child and maternal mortality, usually happens before increases in per capita income.[4] For example, even while Vietnam was undergoing a bloody war in the 1960s (which resulted in the death of four million, or ten per cent of the population), family size was declining and life expectancy increasing. With these better conditions in place, market liberalisation in the 1980s propelled the country's rapid economic take-off.

Few dispute the imperative of growth in development. Michael Klein, for example, has observed that if Africa were to grow at over five per cent for a generation, its people would have the same wealth levels as Argentina; growth of just three to four per cent would bring it up to Brazil's level.[5] Or as Goldman

Sachs's Jim O'Neill, the author of the original BRIC (Brazil, Russia, India, China) global growth concept, notes, 'Globalization may widen inequality within certain national borders, but on a global basis it has been a huge force for good, narrowing inequality among people on an unprecedented scale. Tens of millions of people from the BRICs and beyond are being taken out of poverty by the growth of their economies.'[6] Investment in people and infrastructure is required to enable this, though radical developmental change and upliftment, Ian Morris reminds, are most difficult where the levels of social development are lowest.[7] With growth, key poverty indices in sub-Saharan Africa have, as Figure 1 illustrates, been steadily improving, although they are still pitifully low compared with many other parts of the world.

The overall African economic record

Despite the recent improvement, African performance has been exceptionally poor over the past 50 years. As Figure 2 shows, for the 50 years starting in 1960, sub-Saharan African countries as a whole managed to increase their per capita income by only US$207 (as measured in Constant 2000 US dollars), from US$429 to US$636.[8]

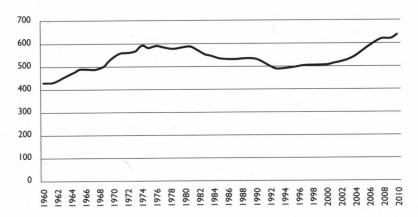

Figure 2: Africa per capita income, constant (2000) US$

The graph demonstrates that the overall growth record of the continent can be divided into three periods. The first was the time directly following independence, when per capita income increased from the base of US$429 to a high point of US$592, achieved in both 1974 and 1976. The drivers of this growth were immediate post-independence exuberance plus high raw material prices that reached a peak after the OPEC oil price hikes and the 1973 Arab–Israeli war.

There followed a long period of decline, and the regional per capita income bottomed out in 1994 at US$487, a drop of 18 per cent from the peak reached 20 years before. As Figure 3 shows, other regions were doing much better at this time, and the gap between Africa and the rest of the world widened. This period of relative and absolute economic decline was especially traumatic. While the exact causes are controversial, and different analysts offer radically divergent narratives, the combination of low raw material prices (especially after the fall of the Shah of Iran in 1979), poor governance, war and the trauma of economic reform certainly contributed to two wasted decades.

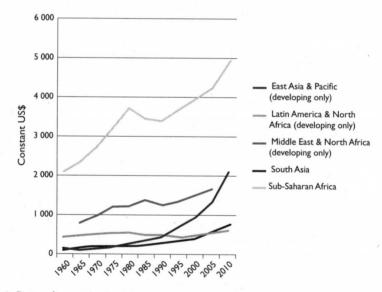

Figure 3: Regional per capita income

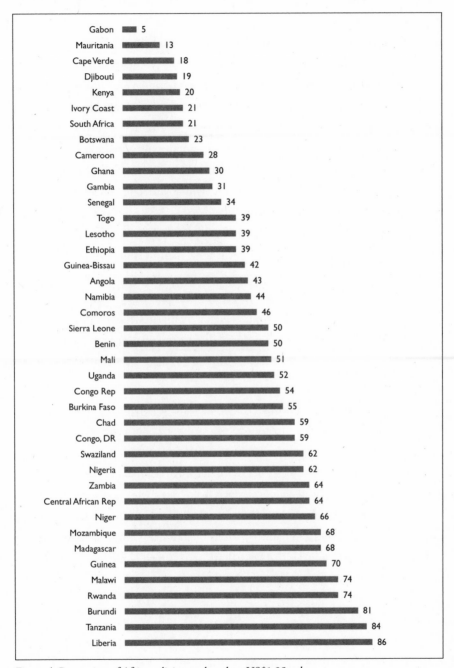

Figure 4: Proportion of Africans living on less than US$1.25 a day

Since 1994, continental per capita economic growth in Africa has been positive, propelled by governance reforms, the end of several wars, relatively high raw material prices and, for the first time in decades, external investment. Per capita income increased from US$487 in 1994 to US$636 in 2010 (an increase of 31 per cent). However, a massive amount of time and effort has been devoted to simply playing catch-up: it was not, for instance, until 2007 that Africa's previous high-water mark for per capita income of US$592 (achieved last in 1976) was surpassed. This is not a criticism of the current group of African policymakers, who have taken very difficult decisions since the late 1980s to restore their economies. Still, it is shocking that – at least at the continental level and taking just one economic aggregate into account, albeit an extremely important one – Africa, overall, accomplished nothing between 1976 and 2007. One of the most tragic and enduring effects of the preceding two-decade decline is that it took African countries so long just to get back to where they had been before. The fact that the continent now seems poised for economic growth will not lessen the trauma of a generation of essentially stagnant economic performance. And, as Figure 4 indicates, the number of Africans living below the poverty line remains high, despite the recent rise in growth.[9]

Diversity across Africa

Of course, in a region comprising 49 countries, the experience of individual sub-Saharan states varies, albeit in the context of a strikingly poor regional performance. Not only have African countries grown at different rates, but the trajectory of different countries has changed rather dramatically over time. Put simply: in 1985, if most observers of African economies had been asked which two countries were likely to perform especially well in the next ten years, they might have reasonably chosen Côte d'Ivoire and Zimbabwe, nations that at that point seemed to be doing well. By 2010, both countries had been destroyed, Côte d'Ivoire by a civil war and Zimbabwe by its own government.

Seven Poorest African Countries (poorest at the top)										
1960	1965	1970	1975	1980	1985	1990	1995	2000	2005	2010
Burundi	Burundi	Malawi	Burundi	Burundi	Ethiopia	Ethiopia	Liberia	DRC	DRC	DRC
Malawi	Malawi	Burundi	Malawi	G Bissau	Mozambique	Malawi	Ethiopia	Burundi	Burundi	Burundi
B Faso	B Faso	B Faso	B Faso	Chad	Burundi	Burundi	DRC	Ethiopia	G Bissau	Eritrea
Lesotho	Lesotho	G Bissau	G Bissau	Malawi	Malawi	B Faso	Burundi	Malawi	Liberia	G Bissau
Togo	Rwanda	Lesotho	Rwanda	B Faso	G Bissau	Chad	Malawi	S Leone	Malawi	Liberia
Rwanda	Chad	Mali	Lesotho	Mozambique	Uganda	Uganda	Niger	Niger	Ethiopia	Niger
S Leone	S Leone	Rwanda	Chad	Ghana	B Faso	G Bissau	Chad	Chad	Eritrea	Malawi

Seven Richest African Countries (richest at the bottom)										
1960	1965	1970	1975	1980	1985	1990	1995	2000	2005	2008
Senegal	Senegal	Mauritania	Liberia	Zimbabwe	C d'Ivoire	Cape Verde	Cape Verde	Swaziland	Swaziland	Cape Verde
Zambia	Zambia	Senegal	Swaziland	Cameroon	Angola	Rep Congo	Rep Congo	Namibia	Namibia	Namibia
Rep Congo	Rep Congo	Zambia	Botswana	Liberia	Cape Verde	Swaziland	Swaziland	E Guinea	Gabon	Gabon
Liberia	Liberia	Swaziland	Rep. Congo	Swaziland	Swaziland	Namibia	Namibia	Botswana	Botswana	Botswana
C d'Ivoire	C d'Ivoire	Zimbabwe	C d'Ivoire	C d'Ivoire	Cameroon	Botswana	Botswana	Mauritius	Mauritius	Mauritius
Seychelles	Seychelles	Rep Congo	Seychelles	Rep Congo	Rep Congo	Mauritius	Mauritius	Gabon	E Guinea	Seychelles
Gabon	Gabon	Liberia	Gabon	Botswana	Botswana	Gabon	Gabon	Seychelles	Seychelles	E Guinea

Table 1: Poorest and richest African countries, 1960–2010

Table 1 presents the seven richest and seven poorest sub-Saharan African countries in five-year increments, starting in 1960.[10] Over the decades there has certainly been some continuity: Malawi and Burundi, for instance, have regularly been among the poorest countries. Some nations, on the other hand, have experienced a spectacular turnabout, such as Liberia, which was one of the richest in Africa until 1980, but now, 30 years later, is among the poorest. There has also been significant evolution for many of the rich countries, with Gabon the only one to appear among them consistently over the past 50 years. In recent years, however, the relatively rich part of the list has, not surprisingly, changed relatively little. The fact that Côte d'Ivoire and the Republic of the Congo, like Liberia, were once among the richest and have now declined as a consequence of war and poor domestic decisions demonstrates the vulnerability of African countries to the disastrous decisions of their own governments.

One of the more telling trends is the increasing gap between the high- and low-performing African countries. In the early 1960s, though every country was different, they were all overwhelmingly poor. Fifty years later, some countries have broken out and are many times richer than they were at independence. Botswana, for instance, has ten times the per capita income that it had at independence in the late 1960s. Other countries are as poor as they were at independence, or poorer. Figure 5 shows how the five richest countries have evolved in comparison with the five poorest, and the widening gap that has consequently emerged.[11]

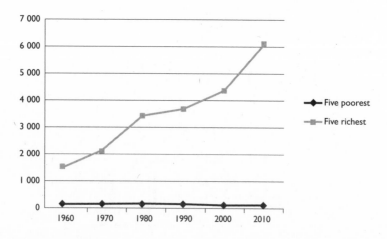

Figure 5: Five richest and five poorest African countries, 1960–2010, Constant US$ per capita

Who gets rich?

It has become increasingly difficult to make generalisations about Africa, as might be expected from a continent with 49 states south of the Sahara, some littoral, some landlocked, big and small, some resource scarce others resource rich, and with a diversity best indicated by the vast range of African languages: more than 3 000. Even so, the richest countries do have some striking characteristics in common. Notably, they have small populations and most have very small land areas. Of the seven richest (excluding South Africa), only Namibia has a population of more than two million (2.1 million), while three have populations under 700 000: Equatorial Guinea (659 000), Cape Verde (499 000) and Seychelles (86 000). The seven countries average only 1.1 million people. As for geographical extent, only Namibia and Botswana (56 673 000 and 82 329 000 hectares respectively) are bigger than the sub-Saharan Africa average of 47 690 000 hectares.

There are, of course, small countries in Africa that are poor. Liberia's relatively small population of 3.8 million has not stopped it from being one of the worst performers, at least until Ellen Johnson-Sirleaf took over the presidency in 2006. Still, the coincidence of small population, small land area and relatively good economic performance cannot be ignored. Part of the reason for smallness seeming to be a necessary (although certainly not sufficient) condition for success at this point in Africa's economic trajectory is that raw material resources inevitably have a much more dramatic effect on small populations: the same amount of, say, oil will make Equatorial Guinea much richer per capita than Sudan.

However, it is also the case that some of the small countries (notably Botswana, Mauritius and Seychelles) owe much of their economic success to good governance. Perhaps it is just easier to manage small countries because the populations are less heterogeneous, and therefore fewer political payoffs are required to keep the ethnic peace. It is easier for leaders to understand what is happening, and, if war breaks out, it is more likely that one side will win relatively quickly. In contrast, wars and their consequent economic destruction can go on for many years in relatively large countries.

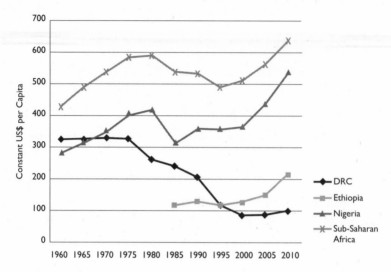

Figure 6: Per capita income in Africa's largest countries

It is also the case that the largest sub-Saharan African countries have done relatively poorly. The Democratic Republic of the Congo, with 64 million people, is among the very poorest. Ethiopia's (81 million) and Nigeria's (151 million) performances have also not been impressive, although neither is currently among the most destitute African countries. Tellingly, all three have had wars and have also had continual problems extending authority over their putative national territory. Together, the three African giants account for approximately 36 per cent of sub-Saharan Africa's population. As a result of the disproportionately poor performance by these relatively large countries, the 'average' African, has probably experienced worse economic times than is suggested by continental statistics that weight Botswana and Nigeria equally.

Figure 6 indicates that all three of Africa's giants are distinctly below the continental average for per capita income. While Nigeria has made rapid gains over the past few years because of the high price of oil and the nominal return of civilian government, both Ethiopia and, especially, the Democratic Republic of the Congo are well below the average.

The relative concentration of economic success in small countries has some immediate implications. First, some of the more optimistic pronouncements about Africa's economic growth are overstated because very small populations are being enriched quickly but disproportionately, while the large countries, where a much larger proportion of Africans actually live, have generally lagged. The 'average' African – who is probably somewhere in Nigeria – is not even as rich as the continental average suggests and has experienced more muted growth than that portrayed in the figures. In the case studies that follow, we will pay particular attention to the inter-relationship of country size and economic performance.

Growth under liberalisation

While African countries have been growing, albeit with a mix of trajectories and off different starting points, they have, to the surprise of many, at the same time liberalised their political systems. Indeed, one of the most stunning developments in Africa was the sudden outbreak of multiparty elections and, to some extent, democracy after the Berlin Wall fell in 1989. Much has been written about why the one-party, no-party or military regimes that dominated Africa in the 1970s and 1980s fell. As noted in the introduction, the most interesting development is that, after roughly 50 years of independence, elections, admittedly of radically varying quality, are the norm in most African countries.

Of course, while per capita gross domestic product is certainly not a perfect indicator of development, it is even harder to measure how much freer countries have become over time. Freedom House measures of political and civil rights provide one useful indicator, especially as the organisation has developed a long time series and has broad coverage in Africa and the rest of the world. Figure 7 presents the continental evolution of the average of the political rights and civil liberties scores over time. Freedom House uses a scale from 1 to 7, divided into three broad categories: 'Free' (1–2.5), 'Partly Free' (3–5.5) and 'Not Free' (5.5–7). The data series, which averages the political rights and civil liberties scores, began in 1972, when many African countries had already lost the veneer of democracy roughly applied in the rush to decolonisation and had largely eliminated formal multiparty electoral competition – although, as always, there were variations across the continent.[12]

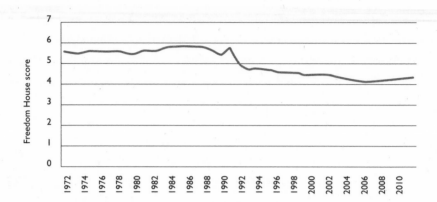

Figure 7: Evolution of freedom status 1972–2010

Figure 7 graphically depicts the stagnation in the extension of freedom in Africa between the early 1970s and the fall of the Berlin Wall in 1989. Early in Africa's post-independence history, the grip of one-party or no-party states was strong and there were many intellectual arguments against democracy in Africa. In the 1960s, it was argued sincerely (and, of course, insincerely in many cases) that democracy was not appropriate for Africa, most notably by Julius Nyerere and other theoreticians of the one-party state. In the 1970s, there were those who made the case that solving Africa's economic problems required military men or benign authoritarians. At the same time, a number of countries had adopted communism as their official ideology. Finally, the international community did not promote democracy. The strategic and ideological orientation of African countries, rather than their economic or democratic performance, often determined their international alliances and levels of aid.

As Figure 7 demonstrates, political liberties and civil rights in Africa generally began to improve in a dramatic fashion after 1989, and there were particularly important changes in the first five years of the post-Cold War era. Many of the one-party or no-party states simply collapsed because of their poor economic management.

In contrast to the 1960s, today there is no intellectual alternative to democracy, even though the urge to democratise across Africa is far from uniform, and there are many who have used current political developments for their own ends. The citizens of many African countries continue to support elections even when they are disappointed with the systems that have evolved. Now it is the norm in almost all of Africa to hold elections, and there has been a gradual evolution of other democratic institutions and consolidation of democratic practices. Of course, one can also argue, more cynically, that many African authoritarians have learned how to keep a hold on power even in a more open environment and despite elections, as is perhaps best illustrated by Robert Mugabe in Zimbabwe.

Figure 7 also reflects some deterioration in freedom since the high-water mark in 2005–6. There have been setbacks in the form of military coups and contested elections. Such reverses are to be expected, given the fragility of most liberalisation experiments and how hard it is to create a democracy. However, the movement backward is relatively slight in continental terms and does not detract from the conclusion that democracy per se is the preferred political regime for most people across the continent, no matter how difficult it is to institute in practice. Still, we need to understand clearly how complicated the environments of most African countries are for leaders and others to operate in, especially when they are trying to create pro-growth constituencies.

There are other dramatic signs of political opening across Africa, some caused by political developments and others driven by technology. For instance, in many African urban areas there are vibrant, almost riotous radio talk shows that allow listeners to call in and debate issues. This is a sharp departure from the 1970s and 1980s, when most African capitals were starved of information and debate. The international community now says it is strongly in favour of political reform, and while pressure is applied haphazardly, there is no doubt that those countries that have performed relatively well in liberalising their polities have managed to garner some international advantages.

As impressive as African political progress has been, there is, again, considerable variation from country to country. This diversity is especially important to understand given that the average African country has moved from 'Not Free' to 'Partly Free' according to the Freedom House Index. 'Partly Free', while obviously hard to define precisely as a category, does accurately describe the position of many African countries. They have elections, but they have not managed to consolidate democracy by developing a robust set of those institutions that normally support a free society. Thus, while electoral competition seems a given, the population cannot be certain that the next electoral cycle will be fair and, critically, that those elected will leave power peacefully at some future date. Of course, the willingness of those in power to leave office when voted out is the absolute bedrock of democracy, failing which people would be tempted to contest every election violently and illegally, fearing it is the last. Likewise, there is considerable uncertainty over the ability of other democratic institutions – including the parliament, the press, the armed forces, and the courts – to play a constructive and enduring role.

1972	1975	1980	1985	1990
Gambia	Botswana	Botswana	Botswana	Botswana
Mauritius	Gambia	Gambia	Mauritius	Gambia
	Mauritius	Ghana		Mauritius
		Nigeria		Namibia
1995	2000	2005	2010	
Benin	Benin	Benin	Benin	
Botswana	Botswana	Botswana	Botswana	
Cape Verde	Cape Verde	Cape Verde	Cape Verde	
Malawi	Ghana	Ghana	Ghana	
Mali	Mali	Lesotho	Mali	
Mauritius	Mauritius	Mali	Mauritius	
Namibia	Namibia	Mauritius	Namibia	
São Tomé & Príncipe	São Tomé & Príncipe	Namibia	São Tomé & Príncipe	
South Africa	South Africa	São Tomé & Príncipe	South Africa	
		Senegal		
		South Africa		

Table 2: African countries ranked 'Free' by Freedom House

Table 2 lists those African countries that Freedom House has rated as 'Free' at set intervals since the rankings were started.[13] Clearly, few countries earned that status before 1990: only Botswana, Gambia, and Mauritius featured consistently. After 1990, the category explodes, with ten countries, more or less, so indexed. There is less volatility in these freedom rankings than in the economic indicators. Certainly, since 1995, a country that has attained the 'Free' category seems likely to retain it. It is also interesting to note that, after the burst of progress immediately following the end of the Cold War, there was a levelling off in the number of countries considered 'Free', with no apparent growth in this category in 15 years.

Again, in this category of high performers, there appears to be a bias toward small countries. Certainly, not all the countries that appear on this list are small:

Ghana and South Africa have some demographic heft, and Mali, Namibia, and South Africa are not small in extent. However, overall the countries in this group are small. Five of the nine rated 'Free' in 2010 – Botswana (2 million), Cape Verde (498 000), Mauritius (1.3 million), São Tomé & Príncipe (161 000) and Namibia (2.1 million) – have populations of 2 million or fewer. They are also, in the main, geographically small.

Arguably the same factors that we have noted as favouring good economic performance apply to high scores for political liberalisation. In particular, the fact that small countries have less ethnic heterogeneity could be important, as could the fact that some, though certainly not all, 'Free' countries are small. (Not all small countries are 'Free', by any means!) Indeed, the correlation between political performance and size is a little less obvious than that between economic performance and size. The fact that South Africa, a large country with a diverse population, can achieve a 'Free' rating demonstrates that size, in and of itself, does not solely determine the pace of political liberalisation.

African economic performance: the link with outside

There are, of course, other criteria shaping Africa's growth performance, including the nature of its integration with the global economy. Here there have been both improvements and changes in countries' trading relationships, brought in part by the commodity boom and in part by increased openness to trade, technology and capital flows. Historically, African economic performance has been driven by improvements in its terms of trade: in other words, when it exports more (usually commodities), and/or commodity prices go up, economic growth increases. Contemporary African export performance continues to track commodity prices closely, as indicated by Figure 8. Little wonder, given that more than two-thirds of Africa's exports are, as of early 2012, oil or other minerals.[14]

Although new markets, especially in Asia, are becoming increasingly important, as demonstrated in Figure 9, much growth is, as before, driven by the needs of and access to traditional developed markets in the United States and Europe. Hence it is hardly surprising that African economic growth continues to track global growth closely, particularly given its resource endowment and the continued demand for such commodities, including the expansion in demand from Asia.

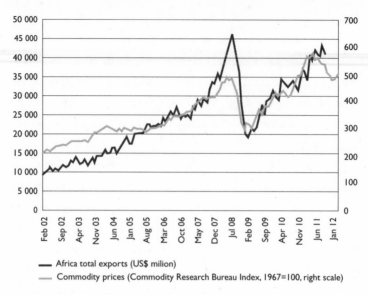

- Africa total exports (US$ milion)
- Commodity prices (Commodity Research Bureau Index, 1967=100, right scale)

Figure 8: African exports and commodity prices

The potential for further resource-driven growth is significant. Africa possesses an estimated 95 per cent of the world's platinum-group metals reserves, 90 per cent of chrome reserves, half of all cobalt reserves and more than 20 per cent of global reserves of manganese, vanadium and titanium.[15] These minerals are in high demand by the fast-growing countries of Asia, and Africa's trade patterns are changing accordingly. By 2012, for example, two-thirds of African iron ore exports were to China, a percentage set to increase with the projected expansion of China's steel production by nearly a third between 2010 and 2015.

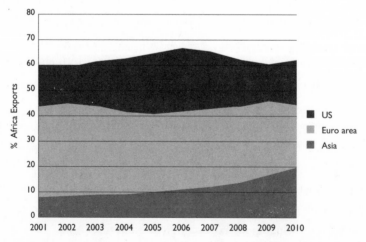

Figure 9: Africa's dependence on mature markets

It is not only in the area of mining, however, that Africa is the world's 'last frontier'. It is estimated that more than 60 per cent of the world's available and unexploited cropland is in sub-Saharan Africa. Land availability is of increasing importance, especially in view of projected global population increases (demanding a concomitant increase in food production of 70 per cent by 2050) and the simultaneous decline of this resource in China, home to 20 per cent of the world's population and less than eight per cent of its arable land, where total cropland is expected to shrink from 135 million hectares in 2011 to 129 million in 2020.[16]

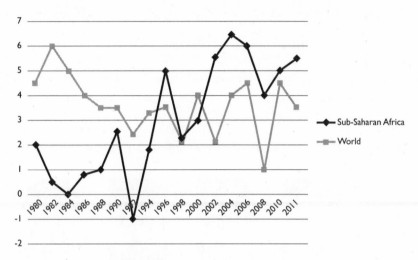

Figure 10: Comparing African and global growth

African economies therefore remain integrated with global fortunes, especially since the 1990s, as Figure 10 above illustrates. And it seems improbable, for all the doomsday prophesies about globalisation and growth, that the global pie will not continue to expand fast enough, at least, to accommodate the aspirations of many in the developing world. More than 200 years ago the Reverend Thomas Malthus forecast in his 'Essay on the Principle of Population' that the human race faced worldwide famine. There have been repeated similar apocalyptic warnings about the environment and energy, yet humans continue to demonstrate remarkable powers of adaptation. Supposedly unbreakable development ceilings have not stopped growth and progress, with, as has been noted, hundreds of millions of people lifted out of poverty since the Cold War, notably in countries once considered development backwaters, such as China and India.

Indeed, the moment of 'peak oil' (defined as the point where the rate of new oil discoveries and production is lower than the rate of consumption) had not, for all the gloomy punditry, been reached by 2012. Some, such as Richard Heinberg,[17] still argue that there are 'fundamental barriers to ongoing economic expansion' due to the depletion of natural resources and the inability of current regimes to regulate today's financial system and environmental problems, though efficiency and other improvements offer a distinct upside, especially in poor economies such as in Africa.

Thus for every stark warning – of unsustainable population numbers, for example – there are opposite trends and opportunities. Half the world today lives in countries where the rate of population growth, 2.1 per cent, is just enough to keep the figures constant, while populations in Europe, China, Russia, Japan and Brazil are all ageing. Moreover, the demographic dividend – the moment at which today's children become tomorrow's workers – offers exciting development opportunities, especially in sub-Saharan Africa.

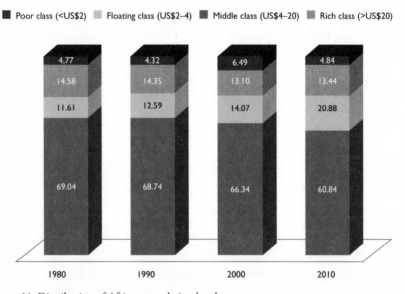

Figure 11: Distribution of African population by class

Of course resource-driven growth in many countries across the continent has not been enough by itself to reduce poverty and increase jobs. The African Development Bank has noted that Africa's poor make up about 60 per cent of the population. (Those living in absolute poverty are around one-third.) Also, the very slow pace of development of Africa's middle class, shown in Figure 11, indicates the failure of countries to translate growth into permanent employment.[18] It also demonstrates the limits and inefficiencies of the state as a distributor of such external incomes and as an employer.

Estimates project that Africa's middle class will account for more than half of the continent's population in 2050, when two out of three Africans will be living in cities. Yet diversifying economies away from natural resources and creating widespread employment remain difficult to achieve, given skills levels, the cost of doing business and policy choices to date. Despite improvements in growth and governance, Africa's ability to attract private investment, especially outside the natural resource sector, lags, as demonstrated in Figure 12, behind other developing regions.[19] Accordingly, efforts to promote efficiencies in African economies, and notably the communications boom, the expansion of finance, improvements in political and economic governance, and the larger number of people congregating in the cities, creating economies of development scale, are likely to have a positive impact.[20]

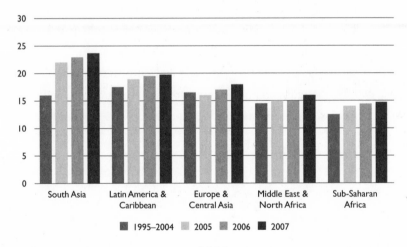

Figure 12: Private investment as a percentage of GDP

Political and economic freedoms in Africa have improved, albeit off a low base. But African countries still rank consistently at the bottom, according to most international indicators. The improvements are not uniform across the continent, and can be said to be institutionalised in only a few countries. Little development is possible without a functioning state. Consequently, through much of sub-Sarahan Africa, although there are outwardly respectable institutions and democracy has spread, human development has been slower than in other regions. While Africa was declining in the grip of political economies characterised by graft, crony capitalism, rent-seeking, elitism and, inevitably, widening (and destabilising) social inequality, other developing regions were rapidly increasing their incomes. African governments, urged by a variety of international governmental and non-governmental institutions, both bilateral and multilateral, today place a lot of store in improving governance scores and rankings. This attention is welcome as a indicator of government efficiency, though these improvements will remain insufficient by themselves in bringing prosperity where rulers prefer development to be driven at the centre where a complex regime of party, ideological and personal interests are best served, rather than through a multitude of independent, entrepreneurial sources. Such suffocating political systems will have to be changed to open up the space in which business can compete. Without these changes sustainable employment will not expand at the rate required to meet the aspirations of citizens, especially of those whose horizons are informed by international media. Allowing all-powerful elites to dominate simply encourages the patronage-ridden systems of government at the heart of Africa's underperformance.

The next chapter explores these histories and outcomes in a number of case studies, demonstrating the complexities of reform beyond statistics, and the role of political dynamics, personalities and circumstances.

Endnotes

1 International Monetary Fund, *World Economic Outlook*, April 2012, p. 73.

2 'A New Class of Consumers Grows in Africa,' *Wall Street Journal*, 2 May 2011.

3 This figure is drawn from the material presented by the World Bank Chief Economist for Africa Shantayanan Devarajan at the 'Africa's New Era' conference, SAIS, Washington DC, 1–2 March 2011.

4 http://www.ted.com/talks/hans_rosling_shows_the_best_stats_you_ve_ever_seen. html, and http://www.ted.com/talks/hans_rosling_reveals_new_insights_on_poverty. html.

5 Cited at 'Africa's New Era' conference, SAIS, Washington DC, 1–2 March 2011.

6 Jim O'Neill, *The Growth Map: Economic Opportunity in the BRICs and Beyond.* London: Portfolio Penguin, 2011.

7 Ian Morris, *Why the West Rules – For Now.* London: Profile Books, 2010.

8 All per capita income, demographic and land mass data is from the World Bank's World Databank, at http://databank.worldbank.org/ddp/home.do?Step=12& id=4&CNO=2.

9 'The Middle of the Pyramid: Dynamics of the Middle Class in Africa.' *African Development Bank Market Brief*, 20 April 2011, at http://www.afdb.org/fileadmin/ uploads/afdb/Documents/Publications/The%20Middle%20of%20the%20Pyramid_ The%20Middle%20of%20the%20Pyramid.pdf.

10 This table excludes South Africa in order to focus on recently decolonised countries, and because South Africa has been richer than the African average for many years.

11 These are the five richest and five poorest at a given moment, so the same countries are not necessarily included at every stage covered by the figure, although there are continuities.

12 Freedom House data found at www.freedomhouse.org.

13 South Africa is only included since the first democratic election in 1994. (In 1972, South Africa was rated as 'Free' for whites but 'Not Free' for blacks.)

14 Figures 8, 9 and 10 are based on International Monetary Fund data presented by Razia Khan of Standard Chartered Bank in Zambia in February 2012. Also relevant is Simon Freemantle's presentation to the 6th African Economic Forum at the IMAX Theatre in Cape Town on 6 March 2012.

15 Standard Bank, 'Time to Act on Opportunities in Africa', February 2012, at http:// www.standardbank.com/Article.aspx?id=-162&src=.

16 http://www.ghanabusinessnews.com/2011/12/03/attention-on-africa%E2%80%99s-agriculture-as-food-becomes-world%E2%80%99s-%E2%80%98new-oil%E2%80%99-%E2%80%93-standard-bank/.

17 Richard Heinberg, *The End of Growth: Adapting to our New Economic Reality*. Canada: New Society, 2011, p. 2.

18 As sourced from the African Development Bank at http://www.afdb.org/fileadmin/uploads/afdb/Documents/Publications/The%20Middle%20of%20the%20Pyramid_The%20Middle%20of%20the%20Pyramid.pdf.

19 Figure 12 is sourced from the material cited at the 'Africa's New Era' conference, SAIS, Washington DC, 1–2 March 2011.

20 For an explanation of this impact, see the McKinsey Report, 'Lions on the move: The progress and potential of African economies', June 2010 at http://www.mckinsey.com/Insights/MGI/Research/Productivity_Competitiveness_and_Growth/Lions_on_the_move, and the Standard Bank's 'The Five Trends Powering Africa's Enduring Allure' at https://m.research.standardbank.com/DocumentSearch?keyword=The+five+trends+powering+Africa%E2%80%99s+enduring+allure&allRegions=true.

2

THE COMPLEXITIES OF
AFRICAN REFORM

Africa's record of job creation specifically, and human development more generally, is poor. This history, as noted in the introduction, hardly improved even during the continent's recent period of economic growth. Part of the blame for poor job creation lies in the failure of African countries to follow commodity-led growth with institutionalised, permanent reforms. Nominally almost all African countries have embraced such reforms, but their implementation is patchy, and particularly deficient where politics and vested personal and other interests, as well as the sheer weight of inheritance and circumstance, trump the execution of plans.

This chapter examines a variety of African case studies – big states and small, performers and laggards, fragile and relatively developed economies – in identifying patterns of reform across the continent. Why have some countries failed to carry out the reforms necessary for job creation, as Chapter 1 has shown? What is the relationship between economic choices and politics in these countries – their political economy – and does this militate against or encourage far-reaching policy advances?

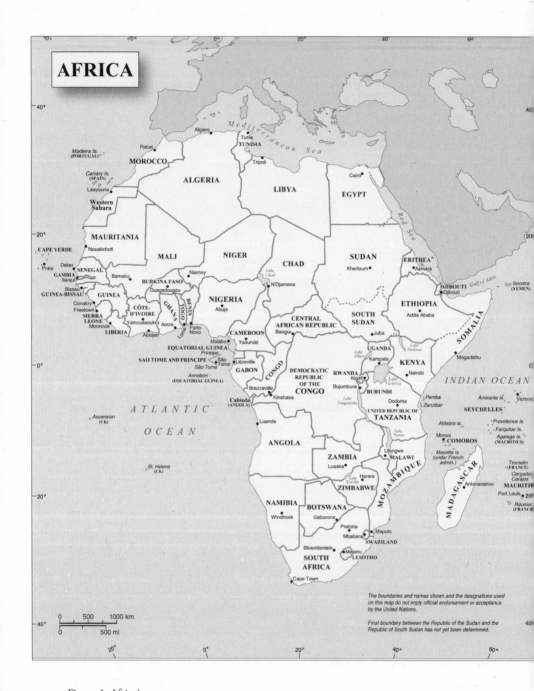

Figure 1: Africa[1]

South Africa: a model reformer?

South Africa's levels of human development are unimpressive, despite the fact that it is widely regarded as a model reformer. Its transition from apartheid to democracy in 1994 was a source of great continental pride and hope, and of anticipation that the end of white rule would be the catalyst for a new African growth phase. As then President Nelson Mandela put it to the 15th anniversary summit of the Southern African Development Community (SADC) in Johannesburg on 13 September 1995, 'We owe it to all the peoples of the sub-continent to ensure that they see in us, not merely good leaders waxing lyrical about development, but as the front commanders in the blast furnaces of labour, productive investments and visible change.'[2]

The town of Dimbaza, on the road to Alice from South Africa's east coast port of East London, 20 km west of King William's Town, was created under the apartheid 'border industry scheme' with ridiculous subsidies (peaking at more than 50 per cent of wages per worker), ensuring that they would remain uncompetitive without such protectionism. But rather than wean at least some of them off the subsidies into sustainability after 1994, the government cut them off completely. The industrial park wilted and quickly died.

In August 2011, the oldest factory there, Dimbaza Foundries, gave notice to its 314 staff of its imminent closure, reducing the number of factories to just one functioning entity. The foundry, part of giant Anglo American's Scaw Metals Group, had made crushing equipment for mines, with more than half its output destined for export. A combination of distance from the markets and from the necessary raw materials, plus Chinese and Malaysian competitiveness (around 20 per cent cheaper for the same products landed in South Africa), made the business a target for closure. 'The quality of our castings is the best in the world,' said its local CEO at the time of the announcement of the closure, 'but there is no way we can compete on price.'

The contribution of South Africa's manufacturing sector to GDP shrank more than six per cent during the 2000s. While manufacturing comprises over 30 per cent of GDP in Malaysia and the Philippines and more than 20 per cent in Indonesia, in South Africa it has fallen to 15 per cent.[3] In Dimbaza, where once 120 factories operated in the 1980s, many of the buildings have been picked clean of their steelwork and fittings, like rotting animals in the bush. Even the railway no longer runs, not least because it would need four different power source changes (between electric, coal and diesel) to get to the desolate station.

A similar sight is sadly repeated elsewhere across South Africa, from once-thriving industrial areas such as Botshabelo outside Bloemfontein to the Eastern Cape's Berlin and Butterworth. The domestic textile sector, as seen below in Figure 2, once a key employer in these areas, lost about 75 000 jobs during the 2000s to mainly cheaper Chinese and South and Southeast Asian competition.[4]

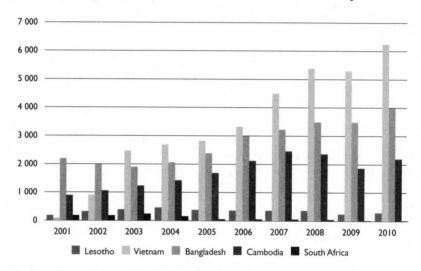

Figure 2: Garment exports 2000–2010 (US$)

Compare this deindustrialisation to South Africa's port city of East London, where Mercedes Benz has specialised in state-of-the-art technology to manufacture its C-class sedan. Here the industrial picture seems comparatively rosy, at least from the outside. But that business has returned to virtually what it started out as 60 years ago: an assembly plant called 'Car Distributors Assembly (CDA) Pty Ltd'. Today robots weld and spray the steel panels imported from Germany, while workers screw together a kit consisting almost entirely of foreign-supplied parts. Little wonder that the number of workers declined to 3 000 in 2011 from 7 000 a decade earlier.

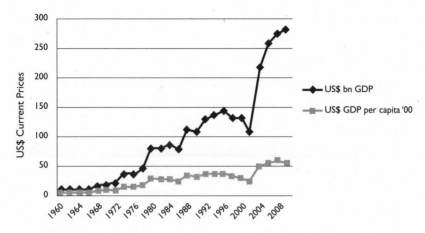

Figure 3: South Africa's GDP performance

While the government lauds the R70 billion contribution (a shade under US$10 billion in 2012) South Africa's seven car manufacturers have made to the balance of payments, the costs to the economy have to be considered too. In 2010 the South African National Treasury calculated that the annual subsidy to the motor industry was R17.8 billion, comprising tax allowances, cash grants, preferential financing from the Industrial Development Corporation and the costs to consumers from higher prices due to import tariffs. For the 36 000 workers directly employed, this worked out to R585 000 per worker for a sector where workers earned, on average, R143 000 annually, or, if the downstream 80 000 workers were included, R205 000. Little wonder the car companies think it's worth it; but why should the government – or taxpayers?

South Africa's GDP, touching US$300 billion in 2010, as demonstrated in Figure 3, is equivalent to one-third of the combined GDP of all of the 49 states of sub-Saharan Africa. It follows that the future of the subregion is entwined with the country's fortunes. However, despite improvements, South Africa's economy has underperformed, relatively speaking, for a variety of politically inspired and structural reasons. During the 1960s, South Africa's annual real GDP growth averaged five per cent, significantly increasing average living standards over a decade. This put it on a par with the aspirant Southeast Asian 'tigers', admittedly with extreme differences between the races – black, white, so-called 'coloured' and Indian. South Africa's average growth rate then fell to four per cent between 1970 and 1975, 2.8 per cent from 1975 to 1980 and 0.6 per cent from 1980 to 1995.

Income per head decreased by 17 per cent between 1981 and 1993. While growth has recovered since the end of apartheid in 1994, with an annual average of 3.2 per cent, only in 2006 did the average living standard return to its 1981 level.[5]

Many of the problems that lay behind this earlier downturn still exist. First, there has been a constant balance of payments crisis, with South Africa's shrinking share of global merchandise exports unable to fund the economy's import requirements. At the same time, the economy has remained reliant on imported technologies, and over-dependent on mining. In 2011, mineral products were equivalent to over half of South Africa's merchandise exports.[6] Attempts at diversification and value addition have been complicated by the valuation of South Africa's currency, the rand, itself a reflection of global trends, including vast portfolio capital flows towards the country and a volatile gold price.

Second, South African productivity remains low, despite the government spending 20 per cent of its budget on education (more than five per cent of GDP). This expenditure ensures free education in two-thirds of schools, yet fewer than half the pupils who enter the educational system reach the final year, grade 12, and the quality of education is among the lowest in Africa.[7] As a result, between 1990 and 2009, multi-factor productivity increased only two per cent per year, but unit labour costs rose 5.7 per cent. This unimpressive performance was due in part to inefficiencies in protected industries as well as high salaries in what is still a highly regulated labour market. For example, while in developed countries (that is, members of the OECD) starting wages were on average 30 per cent of the average occupational wage, in South Africa this figure was 60 per cent. Additionally, public sector wages rose by 23 per cent in real terms from 2006 to 2010, compared to 19 per cent in the private sector.[8]

Third, government spending has crowded out private sector investment. By 2012, government spending, including the projected deficit, amounted to 30 per cent of GDP, much higher than comparable developing countries – including Costa Rica, Vietnam, Singapore, the Philippines, Malaysia and India. High levels of public debt and expenditure are usually negatively associated with per capita GDP growth, as the incentives for individuals to work, save and invest diminish, and private borrowing for businesses is more difficult and costly.[9]

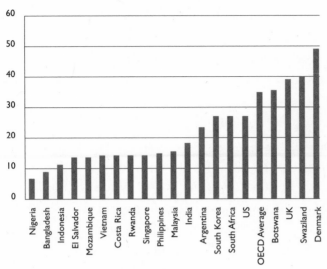

Figure 4: Tax-GDP ratio: Selected countries[10]

Indeed, investment and savings rates have remained low, at 20 per cent and 16 per cent of GDP respectively, the latter being at the level of the 1980s and early 1990s. South Africa has been starved of domestic growth capital.

Finally, actions to promote investment have been constrained by vested political and economic interests. In particular, the labour unions – a critical part of the governing alliance – have consistently resisted calls for deregulating the labour market, which, while lowering wages, might increase the number of jobs. At the moment, heavy regulations on employment, including real constraints on restructuring workforces or firing workers, incentivise businesses to employ capital rather than labour. According to the World Bank, real rates of return on capital in South Africa have risen sharply since 1994, averaging 15 per cent from 1994 to 2008 and 22 per cent from 2005 to 2008.[11] The result is a frustrating lack of jobs in a still-poor economy, pointing to concerns about labour market rigidities and other political factors as impediments to investors. Calls for nationalisation and the rise of the ruling African National Congress's (ANC) radical Youth League as a political force are therefore both a cause and a consequence of this malaise.

Once considered a model of democratisation and liberalisation, the post-apartheid economic reform process has slowed to the point that David Williams, then deputy editor of the *Financial Mail*, has described South Africa as a 'stalled state'. Such rhetoric has led to a crisis of confidence on the part of business in

South Africa, in sharp contrast at times to the reported statistics. Indeed, during the global commodities boom of the 2000s, South Africa's real mining output fell by one per cent annually, and investment shrank by just under one-third between 2003 and 2005. In 2009, South African mining production fell to its lowest level since 2000.[12]

Put differently, investor confidence remains a major inhibitor, reflecting concern about crime, corruption, labour market issues and political populism. Nearly 30 million worker days were lost to strikes in 2011 and wage demands have consistently been four times the level of inflation of five per cent.[13] The government's focus on job retention, by making it hard to fire workers, has had a negative impact on employment, and for both the problems have been related to policy drift fuelled by the ruling ANC's internal dynamics and leadership hesitancy. Whatever the government's attempts to assuage these concerns and to span the gulf between investor perception and reality, the absence of a pro-business faction and lobby in government has been telling.

South Africa's economy and society have remained schizophrenic, often characterised as both Third and First World. By 2011, 15.1 million South Africans were receiving a state welfare grant, around one per household, having increased from 3.5 million over a decade. The number of registered individual taxpayers in South Africa numbered 5.9 million in 2009/10, and the number of businesses 1.9 million.[14] In this, the political dilemma facing the South African government has been very real. The ANC was elected by the racially marginalised. Since those elected were largely of a socialist persuasion – no matter the penchant of some members for decadent Western trappings – it figured that they would be sympathetic to having the state at the centre of all matters, including the economy, while they did not fully appreciate, or want to know, how the private sector operated. The ruling party has tried to find a development route different from Asia's low-wage manufacturing, a political imperative given the nature of the ruling coalition. As Tony Ehrenreich of the Congress of South African Trade Unions (COSATU), and Cape Town mayoral candidate in 2011, has highlighted, 'In South Africa, we've made a choice: we don't want to build a low-wage economy that's premised on exploitation of workers. We want to ensure that people have decent wages; that they participate in the economy; that they drive up demand for domestic products; and that that in itself contributes to creating jobs. And that's what our focus must be. The ANC does not want its people working in "sweatshops".'[15]

This statement highlights the policy limitations of having the unions, with their constituency interests, as a member of the ruling tripartite alliance (with the ANC and the SA Communist Party) – and hence the costs of the structure that brought democracy and liberation to South Africa. Admittedly, however, the ANC did take over at a difficult time. Not only had the Cold War ended, and South Africa begun democratisation, but high-speed globalisation was coming on stream, forcing governments to expose previously protected industries to fierce competition, against which many simply folded.

Thus the government's strategy has been to leverage South Africa's comparative advantages (the natural resource sector) in conjunction with the establishment of a tougher tax regime to generate resources to ensure the redistribution of wealth to the less privileged. This strategy has been executed through the ending of white preference in the civil service and the expansion of that service, along with the extension of a welfare system through pension and child-support payouts. Unsurprisingly, the greatest current job gains in South Africa are in the public sector. This redistributive model is unsustainable for several reasons, beyond the programmes' large slice (around 40 per cent) of the South African public wage bill.

First, there is the tax burden. While revenue from corporate tax almost tripled in the five years to March 2009, the bulk of such tax collected has come from less than ten per cent of registered companies. The bulk of individual tax has come, as noted, from little over ten per cent of nearly 50 million people.

Welfare, second, is not only expensive, it is also distortive. Like aid generally, it removes the incentives to seek work or even subsist through informal jobs or agriculture. There is a high social cost to this too. As the South African National Treasury's 2011 budget review states, 'Employment is not only about earning an income – it is the condition for a decent life.' It is about establishing a framework for social engagement and stability, and giving people meaning to their lives.

Third, the extent of concern about South African political direction and its policies means that the country has been ill-positioned to gain fully even from its comparative advantages, especially given the polemic around the nationalisation of mining assets. A 2011 Citibank survey found South Africa to be the world's richest mining country in terms of its reserves, worth an estimated US$2.5 trillion.[16] Yet South Africa's mining sector declined at an average of one per cent per annum during the 2000s, while the top 20 mining producers grew annually at five per cent. In 2011, South Africa's global share of greenfield mining projects was just five per cent; Australia's was 38 per cent. As a result, the global resource boom of the 2000s became a missed opportunity for South Africa.

As a result of the regulatory uncertainty generated by extant policy (such as that over the convertibility of mining rights) and especially concerning debates around 'resource taxes' and nationalisation, many new projects have gone begging. According to a 2011 survey conducted by the Fraser Institute, South Africa's rank as a mining investment destination slipped as a result of 'obscuring government involvement in the sector'. The report ranked South Africa just 67th out of 79 in attractiveness for exploration investment among countries such as Zimbabwe, Venezuela, and the Democratic Republic of the Congo. According to the institute, the survey was launched, 'to examine which jurisdictions provide the most favorable business climates for the industry'.[17] Resource nationalism is not unique to South Africa, of course, and has been a historical feature of oil politics in the Middle East and increasingly in Latin America, with the rise of Hugo Chávez's brand of 'revolutionary' nationalism. But it does add a premium of uncertainty for investors seeking long-term policy predictability and the rule of law.

The South African government, however, like others in Africa, has got hung up on the need for investors to beneficiate mineral products, rather than focusing, first, on the importance of starting production in order to realise the benefits of resource endowments. For example, Chile, today the world's largest copper producer, with one-third of global output, has not opened a major new smelter in 25 years. It has focused instead on attracting investment, expanding production and establishing a tax regime that enables maximum benefit in partnership with private investors. It has used this income to unleash other opportunities.

At the time of the Citibank report, experts[18] maintained that with the right regulatory environment, South Africa could at least double coal, platinum, iron and manganese outputs within five years. It is estimated that this expansion could add a further 100 000 direct and the same number of indirect jobs to the 500 000 already directly employed and the 150 000 indirectly employed in this industry; an industry that accounted for more than half of South Africa's merchandise and more than 40 per cent of all exports.

The basis of any sustained growth will lie in a political structure capable of earning widespread popular support for pro-growth and pro-jobs policies, even in the face of vested constituencies demanding high-wage, anti-job policies. This scenario requires governments, too, to use their mandate to create an environment in which entrepreneurs will invest and can create jobs. After all, as noted in the Introduction, the best method of ensuring a good wage for workers and protecting their rights is to increase employment opportunities and numbers not just to protect a few formal sector jobs. Essentially, South Africa is not rich enough for even a radical redistributive regime to provide a viable standard of living to a large percentage of the population. Ironically, however, the relatively hostile stance to investment and, in particular, to mining, has resulted in declining investment in the sector that still provides most of the wealth in the economy. South Africa's democracy has not allowed it to develop a constituency system that would reward politicians who seek to follow a high-employment, (relatively) low-wage strategy. Until the emphasis shifts from redistribution to the politics of growth, frustration over the slow development of the now-enfranchised, but still poor, African majority will remain.

Long fingers, warm heart

Malawi has a very poor resource endowment and throughout the past half century it has been among the seven poorest African countries. Given the desperation, it is surprising that its leaders have not felt compelled – or been compelled – to take drastic measures to improve popular welfare. Instead, they have taken decisions to safeguard their rule and enrich a coterie. Malawi therefore epitomises the difficulty that African countries have had in institutionalising reforms that promote jobs and development.

A little under a decade ago, we ran a diplomatic summer school at an exclusive resort on the banks of Lake Malawi. Two things struck us about this central African country. The first was that it seemed to have very little going for it, especially given its small land mass, distance from markets and poor infrastructure. President Hastings Banda, Malawi's leader from July 1964, when the country gained its independence from Britain, until 1994, apparently realised his country's restraints and forged a controversial relationship with apartheid South Africa. Whatever the criticism of his democratic intolerance and repressive instincts, the country more or less functioned, aided by the annual 200 000 or so white South African visitors to the 'Warm Heart of Africa', desperate to visit a slice of 'black' Africa. Soft loans from the apartheid regime helped too, including R300 million in the 1970s to build a new capital in Lilongwe, located in Banda's own Central Region.

The second was the desperation of the population. One did not have to take a boat out onto the lake to see the poverty on either side of the carefully raked sand of the resort. The desperation of the curio sellers in the local market verged on physical aggression, vented against other vendors and the few tourists. Very little has changed since, apart from the government. Malawi remains one of the world's poorest countries, with three-quarters of the population living on less than US$1 a day.

Banda, who declared a one-party state in 1966 and himself president-for-life four years later, ruled until his ousting by Bakili Muluzi with the advent of multiparty democracy in 1994. By then the former president, a US- and Scottish-trained doctor and Church of Scotland elder, was 96 years old. He died three years later, laid to rest in a humble grave in Lilongwe. Politically rehabilitated, partly by time and partly by the inadequacies of his successors, the autocrat who preferred relations with Taiwan now lies in a mausoleum squeezed between the country's parliament and a five-star Chinese-built hotel. Someone in Malawi has a sense of humour.

Whatever his political tendencies and the violence meted out by the Malawi Young Pioneers in his name, Banda's economic policies were at the time seen as a model for what to do with a poor, landlocked country: making peace with the devil (South Africa) for aid, running the economy centrally like a giant (by Malawian standards) conglomerate and pumping up tourism. But while Banda believed in private enterprise, he did not believe in free enterprise. That things have got considerably worse economically since those autocratic days – not by the judgement of foreign visitors, but according to Malawians themselves – is a sad if not shocking indictment.

Muluzi started with great promise. But having broadened political freedoms, he did little to improve the efficiency of the economic system he had inherited, to transform it from an unsustainable import-substitution economy to one based on exports. The biggest difference, however, was in the nature and extent of corruption. 'During Banda's time,' notes Jabbar Alide of the Malawi Law Society, 'corruption was very centralised. During Muluzi, it became widespread and open. Now it has become more sophisticated, underground and in a carefully developed chain.'

In 2002, we were invited to Malawi by Muluzi's government to prepare a strategy for growth and development. Our suggestions then included privatising the airline and removing onerous layers of taxes that were suffocating the tourist industry. Nothing happened. Indeed, the country is still grappling with the same problems as it tries to resuscitate tourism. Banda's successor preferred to keep in place the economic structures he inherited, including the all-powerful Press Corporation, which controlled around half the economy. Analyst Mabvuto Banda contends, 'Muluzi failed badly. Politically he did well for the first five years, but totally messed up his second term, mainly because of his personal greed, wanting to get involved in every business himself.' Indeed, a pattern has been established in Malawi of a good first presidential term and a hopeless, damaging second one. In particular, Muluzi's interest in a third term upended politics and made any focus on growing the economy extremely difficult. Justin Malewezi, who served as Muluzi's vice president for ten years, admits, 'We lost focus in the second term, mainly due to the third-term issue. Our performance was not that rosy.'

No one could accuse Bingu wa Mutharika, elected in 2004, of similar inaction. Born Brightson Webster Ryson Thom, the son of a local teacher, he changed his name during the wave of African 'authenticity' sweeping the continent in the 1960s. Graduating with economics degrees from India, he later 'earned' his PhD from the Pacific Western University, a do-it-yourself life-experience college usually advertised in magazine classifieds. In 1991, after a career as a Malawi civil servant and UN official, he was appointed secretary-general of the Preferential Trade Area for Eastern and Southern Africa, better known today as COMESA, the Common Market for Eastern and Southern Africa.

Any thoughts Muluzi might have had that he could control Mutharika should have been removed by the 2004 inauguration speech, in which the new president set himself apart from his predecessor. Mutharika then broke with the United Democratic Front and formed his own Democratic Progressive Party in 2005. As a result, in Bingu's first five presidential years he led a minority government, which did not allow him the freedom of action his second term provided after he secured a two-thirds majority.

In order to build support, as Malewezi recounts, 'Bingu believed that the best way to ensure popularity was to appeal to people, not parliament, hence the agriculture subsidy programme and spending on roads infrastructure.' Given that more than five million of his people were subject to incessant food shortages, and with over 80 per cent of the population of 14 million living in rural communities, the new president lost little time in instituting a radical programme to build food self-sufficiency. Going against the advice of donors, on whom the government depends for about 40 per cent of its budget, Mutharika implemented a sweeping fertiliser input subsidy programme.

By 2011, about 1.6 million farmers had benefited from the programme, which provided them with 100 kg of subsidised fertiliser, 5 kg of open-pollinated and 7.5 kg of hybrid maize seed, and 2 kg of legume seed (bean, groundnut, soya, or pea). Initially this programme boosted production, improving the quality of life in Malawi and lifting economic growth rates to over six per cent annually from 2004 to 2009. But this was at a cost.

While donors, always desperate for any success, praised the results, the programme's sustainability, governance and impact were questionable. For one, it has been criticised for using up scarce foreign exchange for a sector that did not generate export revenues. Much of the maize also went to waste because of limited storage facilities, and because the overvalued currency made it difficult to export to a needy region already lacking the efficient systems and routes to do so.

Malawians say the subsidy scheme not only institutionalised a culture of dependency among farmers, but offered plenty of scope for corruption among both farmers (by on-selling fertiliser) and the elite (who organised the process). One Chikoti farmer's experience is typical. 'I went to buy the fertiliser. Instead of the subsidised price [of 500 kwacha for a bag usually costing 7 500 kwacha], they charged me 3 000 kwacha [about US$18],' pocketing the difference. Moreover, the resultant high GDP growth had little impact on formal sector employment, which has remained at about ten per cent of the population, with manufacturing and tourism particularly hard hit. The situation was worsened by fuel shortages leading to Zimbabwe-style queues and regular blackouts in a country where little more than five per cent of the country had access to electricity anyway. As a result, Mathews Chikaonda, a former minister of finance under Muluzi, who has been CEO of the listed Press Corporation for several years, was not alone in saying, 'We need an exit strategy urgently from this [fertiliser] programme.'

Politics and personality explain why such rational arguments fail. After his second term began in 2009, Bingu, who turned 77 in 2011, seemed to lose the plot altogether – or, as Malewezi put it late that year, 'He has lost his mind.' In a parallel to Robert Mugabe's transition in neighbouring Zimbabwe from his first wife, the popular Sally, to his second, the much younger socialite, Grace, Bingu's Zimbabwe-born wife, Ethel, said to be a stabilising factor, died in 2007. In 2010 he married former tourism minister Callista Chapola-Chimombo in a lavish event costing over US$1 million of taxpayers' money at which the couple were surrounded by a 'small' group of close friends and family in Lilongwe's main stadium.

His wedding was not the only excess. In 2009, Mutharika purchased a Dassault Falcon 900EX presidential jet costing US$20 million. He said it was to save money on his trips overseas. While it may have improved his legroom, it provided scant comfort to his people, worsening a scarcity of foreign currency and, consequently, of fuel. And it did little for tourism, a key potential foreign exchange earner and domestic employer, severely constrained by the collapse of Air Malawi, the local airline, and a failure to open the skies.

The president blamed currency shortages on externalisation and money laundering by 'Asian traders' and others, and fuel scarcity on hoarders. But the jet purchase led the UK government, a major donor, to cut its budget support by the cost of the aircraft over the following two years. The president later expelled the British high commissioner, Fergus Cochrane-Dyet, over a leaked cable in which he described the Malawian president as 'becoming ever more autocratic and intolerant of criticism'. The truth apparently hurt.

With the country falling off the IMF wagon too, other donors followed the UK's lead, reducing direct donor budget support to zero, though indirect aid remained at just under US$1 billion annually. In addition, the United States put on hold the Millennium Challenge Corporation energy sector compact worth US$350 million, pending improvements in governance and economic policy. The result was worsening blackouts, exacerbating the problems of factories, schools and health facilities, and discouraging investors. Malawians at every level of society realised the importance of such investment and reportedly begged the US government to 'do it for the people' in spite of the 'one man' they acknowledged to be at the root of the problem.

Donor problems and the jet purchase did not help, but the root of the foreign exchange shortage and price instability lay in issues that were within the power of the government to remedy, if it chose to do so. The self-induced problems included an increase in expenditure on non-export-earning inputs and rampant consumerism led by the government (each of Bingu's ministers had three official vehicles, says Mabvuto Banda: 'a Land Cruiser VX, a Mercedes and a shopping basket'), plus the rapid increase in money supply, especially during the Muluzi years. Government is the major employer, with 160 000 civil servants on the books, consuming nearly one-third of the annual $2 billion budget in salaries alone. The budget itself is already one-third of GDP; with an unsustainable high tax burden. And then there was the US$95 million Chinese-built 'President's Hotel' and conference centre in Lilongwe, which would have to be paid off at around $7–8 million annually for 15 years from 2014, a vanity project if ever there was one. All of this is not someone else's fault.

Self-interest extended into the political domain. Joyce Banda, a former NGO activist who became vice president, and the second vice president, Khumbo Kachali, were fired in December 2010 for 'anti-party' activities. This move, however, was blocked by the courts, given the constitutional provision that a vice president can only be removed by impeachment. The president's action was widely interpreted as trying to position his brother, Peter, a former US law professor and, in 2012, minister of foreign affairs, as his successor 'so that he would be safe'.

Mutharika also went back to basics to firm up support. By November 2011 the minister of finance, secretary-general of the treasury, army commander, inspector general of police, head of the anti-corruption unit, director-general of the Malawi Revenue Authority, director-general of the Malawi Broadcasting Corporation, director-general of posts and telecommunications, governor of the reserve bank, chief executive officers of the cities of Blantyre and Lilongwe, director of public prosecutions, attorney-general and many of the most powerful businesspeople were all from the president's ethnic group, the Lomwe, which constitutes less than five per cent of the population. 'With that kind of setting,' says Jabbar Alide, 'one can only expect things to get worse, where all good governance norms and practices are being respected only in their breach.' Or, as Malewezi notes, 'This type of thing is unprecedented in Malawi. One result is that the mood has become particularly unpleasant, and the president the subject of open ridicule.'

The president stubbornly refused to liberalise the currency, thereby causing the black market rate to move from the 2011 level of 167 kwacha to the US dollar to around 300 kwacha per dollar by 2012. This stance was partly, it is assumed, due to the need to continue to fund elite consumer purchases and maintain the political illusion that all was well.

Joseph Mwanamvekha, Bingu's secretary of the treasury, defended this stance irascibly if unconvincingly in October 2011: 'If we do devaluation at the wrong time, it will do a lot of damage. We were once 1:1 with the pound. Now it's 265 kwacha to the pound. And what has that changed for us? Why has it happened?' Apparently not understanding the laws of economics and over-estimating the influence of government – a common regional failure – he suggested that Malawi should have left it at parity.

Similarly the government undermined attempts to fix the tourism sector. No longer able to milk a captive apartheid South African market, it has had to compete with other destinations worldwide. Yet its tourist facilities currently offer African charm by 1970s standards – with added chaos, and at 21st-century prices. The government still owns six of the top hotels in the country, though these were suffering from a lack of investment – and clientele.

Then, suddenly, in April 2012, it was 'ye-bye Bingu, *jambo* Joyce!' President Mutharika died of a heart attack, thus undoing plans to install his brother as president. Dead before an air ambulance arrived from South Africa, after much wrangling at the airport given the crew's refusal to load a dead person, he was regardless sent 'down south' to allow his brother's cohort time to get their own succession plans in place. It was to no avail. The army in particular stood firm in protecting the constitution against such blatant rigging. Joyce Banda was steadfast, too, in ensuring that these plans quickly foundered, and she assumed the presidency as constitutionally ordained, 60 hours after her predecessor's death. The Malawian succession demonstrated, among other things, that the presence of democratic structures, even if only partly adhered to by a given incumbent, can suddenly have powerful effects when there is a sudden shock to the political system. That is why even the partial liberalisation of most African countries, still falling well short of institutionalised democracy, is such an important development.

As President, Joyce Banda will have to be just as resolute in restoring Malawi's economy to health and in building unity, thus ridding the nation's politics of its fractious, malicious tendency. A Malawian recovery plan would have to allow the kwacha to adjust to a market value in order to get petrol flowing – which 'JB', as she is widely known in Malawi, carried out in the first month of office; change the tobacco sales system from auctions (involving costly intermediaries, as is the character of the Malawian economy per se) to direct contracting between seller and purchaser; improve competition in international airlinks through opening the skies and boost tourism by concessioning the broken airline; and set a long-term economic vision for the country, especially its stressed cities. For example, Lilongwe, once a sleepy administrative hollow, is expected to double its population to over two million in the next decade. To achieve stability in the immediate term, she would have to convince the donors that governance had changed positively enough to get funds flowing once more, that the government was committed to its own austerity.

Yet donors do not offer the long-term solution to Malawi's plight. The country's fundamental overall challenge is that it imports more than it exports, that government spends at least 25 per cent more than it gets from taxes though the tax burden is already very high, and that it lives on the charity of others. Even if it were to grow at five per cent per annum and thus double its economy in 15 years, Malawi would still be a very poor country. It needs to find the means to put itself on a different diversification and growth trajectory. Unless all this changes, Malawi's descent into state failure seems assured.

King Cobra or Monty Python?

At independence in 1964, Zambia's future looked rosy – much more so than that of Malawi, its one-time partner in the Central African Federation. Zambia was generously endowed with copper and other minerals, and had a sophisticated transport and energy infrastructure. It fell victim to a series of bad choices around nationalisation, the effects of which were worsened by the liberation wars in neighbouring countries and the long reign of one man, Kenneth Kaunda.

It has also partly squandered a second opportunity. When Frederick Chiluba defeated Kaunda in the 1991 election, Zambia was among the very first African countries to vote out of power a dysfunctional liberation figure and elect a seemingly dedicated reformer. Since then, there has been some progress as the Copperbelt has been revitalised by private investment and higher commodity prices, but there have also been missed opportunities, greater corruption and a squandering of the resource dividend by the failure to diversify the economy during relatively good times. Policies have been guided less by a desire to attract investment than, again, by the short-term impulse to distribute largesse. It should thus be no surprise that the population elected someone who promised them more radical delivery – Michael Sata.

Michael Sata arrived punctually for the meeting at the restaurant in Lusaka in January 2011, the expatriate staff greeting him warmly if somewhat fawningly. His mobile phone chirped continuously during the friendly meeting, the 74-year-old finding himself at the centre of a controversy over Barotseland's mooted secession. The callers all, without fail, received a tongue-lashing from the veteran politician known as 'King Cobra' because of his venomous tongue and forthright manner.

His style and the prospect for change he offers appeal to Zambian voters. Sata was elected as the fifth president of Zambia on 22 September 2011, roundly defeating the incumbent Rupiah Banda of the Movement for Multiparty Democracy (MMD) by 43 per cent to 36 per cent. In so doing, the former policeman and British Rail station sweeper not only tapped into the ethnic vote among his northern Copperbelt brethren, but also rode the groundswell of discontent among urban Zambians who have not seen the country's recent growth translate into improved living standards.

At independence in 1964, there were 300 000 formal sector jobs for Zambia's three million people. By 2011, there were fewer than 500 000 such jobs, 44 per cent of them in the public sector, for nearly 13 million people, with widespread unemployment, especially among the youth, who make up about two-thirds of the population. The failure to create jobs can be tied directly to the country's poor economic record. In 2010, Zambia finally managed to return to its 1972 production record of 720 000 tonnes of copper. It had taken the industry that long to recover from the ruinous nationalisation policies of Kaunda's one-party government. During the late 1980s, keeping Zambia Consolidated Copper Mines alive cost the government US$1 million a day. Unsurprisingly, it was starved of fresh investment. Privatisation followed five years after the advent of multiparty democracy in 1991, and a long, slow process of getting an industry back on its feet ensued. As the copper price picked up in the 2000s on the back of Chinese demand, the industry not only righted itself, but drove Zambia's growth beyond five per cent during the 2000s to 7.6 per cent in 2010.[19]

Even so, Sata's Patriotic Front supporters voted for accelerated, radical change.

On the record, there also was much to fear about Sata, known to be a supporter of Mugabe's land and business seizure policies. 'What Robert Mugabe has done is sensible,' Sata was reported as saying after he cast his vote in Lusaka during the 2006 election. 'He hasn't roasted any white persons. He has just taken back what belongs to them [Zimbabweans].' He also earlier pilloried Zimbabwe's opposition leader Morgan Tsvangirai, describing him as a Western puppet 'financed to cause trouble in Zimbabwe'.[20]

Ironically, in addition to the Copperbelt turnaround, another reason for Zambia's recovery has been the influx of farming and entrepreneurial skills from Zimbabwe. Not for nothing has Mugabe been known as Zambia's 'honorary minister of agriculture and tourism'.

Sata has also been very tough on the widespread and burgeoning presence of the Chinese in Zambia, who were seen to have a special relationship with the Rupiah Banda regime. During the 2006 election contest with Levy Mwanawasa and two years later, following that president's death, Sata ran on a populist anti-Chinese platform against Rupiah Banda, even threatening to establish formal ties with Taiwan.

That rhetoric was not a feature of his 2011 campaign. Indeed, for all the blustering about Mugabe, Sata's official pronouncements, at least regarding mining, were generally quite sensible in the run-up to the poll. He called on Banda's government to reinstate the 'development agreements' governing investments by mining companies that had been abrogated in Banda's ill-fated attempts to impose a windfall tax on mining profits in 2008.

To some extent, his rhetoric has vacillated depending on his audience. He has not only praised Mugabe, but promised new state enterprises, tax cuts and a cap on foreign mine ownership, tapping into popular, if misguided, resentment based on the belief that Zambia had sold too cheaply the assets that have, in recent years, provided up to 90 per cent of the country's export earnings. He also promised to develop Zambia within 90 days: less King Cobra than Monty Python! Yet after the election, 'develop' was quickly changed to 'initiate development' and 'restore dignity' within this period.

The polemic should not, however, disguise the enormous positive change Sata could make if he chose to use his mandate for good. In 2010 we worked with President Banda's government, at its request, on establishing the terms for a fast-track development strategy known as 'Enterprise Zambia'. This programme focused on the changes that the government could make to encourage investment and bring growth. These include: in government services, the creation of all-hours customs posts at key crossing areas; in agriculture, the establishment of a private-sector linked extension service; in encouraging diversification, the targeting of tourism and agriculture value-addition; and in mining, establishing a practical regime for retaining existing investment, beneficiation and expansion.

However, little was implemented. Despite Banda being an affable and likeable person, his government lacked energy. Sata has the energy – and if he could recognise the difference between being a candidate and a president, and that the rules of economics and geography remain the same whatever the government, he could accelerate development. Rather than forcing mining companies, against prevailing competitive conditions, to give up ownership and merely beneficiate ore, Sata could instead lead a further stage in the country's recent mining boom if he set achievable production targets such as doubling copper output to 1.5 million tonnes by the time of the next poll in 2015.

But to achieve this aim, he will have to avoid the sort of increased taxation and domestic ownership stipulations that more than a few of the electorate (and his government) would like to see. The government continued, even by 2012, to hold between 10 and 20 per cent ownership in nine mining operations. More importantly, with an investment stake totalling over US$5 billion, mining companies paid more than US$2.5 billion in tax in Zambia following privatisation between 2000 and 2010, by which time they employed 45 000 (producing around 15 tonnes of copper per employee per annum, compared to 100 tonnes in Chile). Research by Deutsche Bank surveying the four largest mining companies worldwide between 2004 and 2010 shows that the cumulative return to shareholders was 184 per cent, compared to the 447 per cent going to governments, a figure that excludes the increase in income tax realised from higher miners' wages.[21] Zambia's Kansanshi mine in the North-Western Province alone paid US$1.6 billion in taxes between 2010 and 2012, or some 62 per cent of total gross distributable income, amounting to US$1.5 million per day, making it one of the highest-taxed copper operations in the world.

The frustration felt by many Zambians is no doubt compounded, however, by the absence of job opportunities in other sectors. In the early 1970s, Zambia manufactured Mitsubishi trucks and cars, assembled Fiats, Peugeots and Land Rovers, produced batteries at Mansa in Luapula, bicycles at Luangwa Industries in Chipata, glass and clothing at Kapiri Mposhi and Kabwe, and canned pineapples at Mwinilunga in the North-Western Province, and processed cashews at Mongu in the Western Province. Dunlop made tyres in Ndola for export in the region, Serioes International stitched designer suits for export to the UK and Germany, Lever Brothers, Johnson & Johnson and Colgate-Palmolive manufactured household goods and toiletries, and ITT Supersonic produced televisions and radios in Livingstone.

Where Zambian industries used to rank only behind Zimbabwe and South Africa in the region, by 2012 very few existed: the Chipata bicycle factory had become a beer warehouse, Livingstone Motor Assemblers (one of only seven Fiat factories worldwide) a small timber factory, Kabwe's Mulungushi Textiles a piggery, and Kafue Textiles a maize storage site. With the disappearance of the tax incentives once administered by the government's former Industrial Development Corporation, the centrepiece agency for the import substitution industrialisation strategy, these industries left too. This was hastened by the lowering of protectionist tariffs. The consumers voted with their money for cheaper and often better-quality imported goods. And the producers themselves had other problems with difficulty in accessing financial resources, worsened by policy change and uncertainty, along with 'legal, regulatory and judiciary constraints'.[22]

Most Zambian goods were destined, however, for a small domestic market. Although the Sata government stated at the outset its intention to reclaim these glory days of manufacturing, with the aim of doubling the contribution of this sector to GDP to 20 per cent by 2015, they will have to deal with these enabling constraints by improving the business climate and making it easier for investors, instead of trying to make imports more difficult and expensive.

Zambia has experienced a great deal of difficulty in building a domestically-owned economy. In part this can be explained by the overvalued exchange rate (a symptom of the dependency on copper exports) and the high cost of domestic capital (around 25 per cent in real terms) which in turn reflects heavy government borrowing in the local market. Zambia's earlier collapse and ongoing contemporary challenge of jobless growth illustrates the importance that investors and government take a long-term view. To do so, investors seek clear rules, policy predictability and the rule of law. Governments naturally want tax revenue, but only as onerous as the market will permit. All of this has to be underpinned by a sense of trust. The mining of Botswana's diamonds is one illustration of how such a partnership might work, where both parties had a vested interest in taking a long view: the government, because it wanted price stability of the product offered by De Beers' engagement along with the necessary capital and mining technology; De Beers, because Botswana had the diamonds in its soil. Without such long-term investment horizons, businesses inevitably seek short-term payback periods and politicians attempt to extract maximum rents, sometimes for their personal pocket rather than the national purse.

Sata's election and the parliamentary outcome are proof of the extraordinary democratic progress made by Zambia and sub-Saharan Africa in two decades. Although Zambia was an early African democratiser, political reform did not force a departure from the distributional model of government, because copper was the only game in town. Indeed, the way the resources generated have been used has undermined attempts to diversify into other industries. The result is a politician who has, with his forceful personality, the potential to break the mould, but who can, if he lacks pragmatic focus, prove an obstacle to investment and destabilise the country.

Out of the genocide into the ...?

Like Malawi, Burundi has consistently been one of the poorest seven countries in sub-Saharan Africa. To be fair, it is in a difficult neighbourhood. But its decision-making around ethnic preferences has shaped its history and is an example, in extremis, of what happens when ethnic politics subvert the logic of economic reform.

One hundred kilometres south of Bujumbura, near Rotovu, on the road to Tanzania, is 'the southernmost source of the Nile'. Several East African countries lay claim to the great river's origins, but at least the Burundians are specific about it.

The second-most densely populated African country after neighbouring Rwanda, Burundi can be split into two parts. The first is the great Imbo plain stretching north to south, enveloping Lake Tanganyika, which covers nearly one-tenth of the territory, and borders on Tanzania, the Congo, and Zambia. The second comprises the mountainous highlands, quickly rising from the lake, where the capital Bujumubura sits at its northernmost tip, to over 2 000 m. This is the site of the agricultural export backbone of coffee and tea. It is here, too, that large mineral reserves are to be found, notably of nickel, but including cobalt, copper, platinum, tantalum, tungsten and a range of rare earths.

Yet for all its natural resources, Burundi's people are among the ten poorest populations worldwide in terms of per capita income, with 70 per cent of ten million people living below the poverty line. Part of the reason for this is a population growth rate touching 3.5 per cent, which means that the country doubles its population approximately every 20 years.

Despite abundant water resources, Burundi faces chronic energy shortages. It is one of the most energy-scarce economies in Africa, with just 36 MW of production for the whole country. As one government official put it, 'There is not a single product that Burundi can make which is competitive, even in the region, because of energy [shortages].'

Such problems are indicative, however, of a wider social and political malaise: endless inter-communal violence and conflict between the Tutsi minority (15 per cent) and Hutu majority (85 per cent) have plagued the country since independence in 1962. An estimated 550 000 people have died in inter-ethnic pogroms. Unlike neighbouring Rwanda's 1994 genocide, though, much of the violence has been perpetrated by the Tutsi-dominated army on the Hutu majority.

Indeed, the Tutsi dominated politics until the advent of multi-party democracy in 2005, staging no fewer than five coups between 1965 and 1993. Pierre Nkurunziza, a former Hutu rebel leader, was elected president in 2005 and re-elected in 2010. With armed attacks continuing in isolated areas, he would have a difficult enough job if he were supremely capable. But strip away the usual pro forma government documents of 'Vision 2025' and the like, and the country's lack of direction is exposed. It appears to move only when the donors apply pressure.

The reason for government inertia is partly bureaucratic, partly geographic, partly educational, partly cultural and partly political. For instance, one of the few local industries is the Heineken-owned brewery Brarudi. The brewer cites two persistent problems with their manufacturing and logistical business: the electricity shortage and stifling bureaucracy. Landlocked and over 1 000 km from the nearest seaport, Dar es Salaam, Burundi is expensive to operate in and to get to. The journey takes a petrol tanker no less than four days; for a 20-foot container, it costs about

US$3 000 and takes as long as three months. Paperwork requirements are stifling and, of course, provide an opportunity for incessant corruption.

Indeed, difficult economic conditions are compounded by widespread corruption. Not for nothing has the government number plate suffix 'AGB' become known as 'Association des Grands Bandits'. One of the reasons for this, says a senior defence force officer, 'is that the government came into power with nothing, nothing in their pockets. This was a big mistake. They are trying to make up for lost time.' Apparently this phenomenon applies from the top of government to the bottom.

Despite the government spending over eight per cent of GDP on education, only 60 per cent of Burundians are functionally literate, the result of years of exclusion and lack of effective investment. In a vicious cycle, agriculture continues to support 90 per cent of the labour force, and comprises nearly half of economic output. Children are a labour asset, their work in the fields keeping many from already inadequate schooling institutions.

Many of these problems stem from problems of political identity aggravated by Belgian colonial practices and exacerbated by independence leadership.

Upon Burundi's independence in July 1962, under its constitutional monarchy, King Mwambutsa appointed a Tutsi prime minister. The Hutus, making up the parliamentary majority, felt hard done by. An attempted coup by the Hutu-dominated police was brutally put down by the army, led by a Tutsi officer, Captain Michel Micombero. Mwambutsa was eventually deposed in 1966 by his son, Prince Ntare, but Micombero soon returned to the political fold to topple Ntare and abolish the monarchy. By 1972, violence escalated with the launch of systematic attacks by the extremist Hutu organisation, Umugambwe w'Abakozi b'Uburundi (Burundi Workers' Party), which intended to exterminate all Tutsis. Amidst ongoing violence in 1976, another Tutsi, Colonel Jean-Baptiste Bagaza, led a bloodless coup and promoted various reforms. In August 1984, Bagaza was elected head of state of a single-party regime.

Bagaza said in October 2011, 'There was confusion everywhere. There was civil war. We had to find a solution to this and we also needed to transform our country, end chaos, and put us back on our feet.' He added, 'There was no electricity, no water and no roads, so we had to create industry and improve the transport system.' Out of this came a number of flagship enterprises, including the coffee and tea parastatals, SOGESTAL and OTB respectively, as well as the SOSUMO sugar plantation and mill in the south. 'We were trying then to drive development,' reflects Bagaza. Then in 1987, at the instigation, Bagaza claims, of France and Belgium in alliance with the Catholic Church, Major Pierre Buyoya, yet another Tutsi, staged a coup, suspended the constitution and reinstated military rule. 'He was just an instrument of others,' says Bagaza today, 'at a time when things were different, where we had Mobutu on one side [Rwandan Hutu president], Juvénal Habyarimana on the other, and the US and Russians were providing the Cold War context.'

Following the appointment by Buyoya of an ethnically mixed government, in June 1993 Melchior Ndadaye of the Hutu-dominated Front for Democracy in Burundi won the first democratic election. However, in October 1993, Tutsi soldiers assassinated Ndadaye, sparking widespread violence in which an estimated 300 000 people were killed. The next president, Cyprien Ntaryamira, also a Hutu, had the misfortune to hitch a ride with President Habyarimana in April 1994, and was killed together with his Rwandan counterpart when their Falcon aircraft was shot down on its approach to Kigali airport. Amidst further waves of ethnic violence and refugee flows, Buyoya seized power again in a second coup d'état in 1996. A power-sharing arrangement, the result of long peace talks, was agreed on from 2000, followed by the 2005 election.

By 2011, there appeared to have been a shift in the nature of the political conflict. Instead of the obvious Tutsi-versus-Hutu, minority-versus-majority-rule struggle, the conflict has transformed into low-level violence between Hutu parties: the ruling National Council for the Defence of Democracy (CNDD) and the National Forces of Liberation (FNL), which preferred to stay out of the 2010 polls and return to the bush. And as it plans to consolidate its power, the CNDD has not only become more deeply engaged in business, but is building elaborate party headquarters countrywide. This gambit has resonance with liberation movements across Africa, though the party's introspection and fascination with power has many critics, not least Bagaza. 'I believe the only solution for the current government is for the president to quit,' he snorts. Yet out of such negatives there is progress. The Hutu-Tutsi struggle no longer defines the country. 'We spent 40 years fearing genocide,' says one Tutsi officer. 'That is now over. The army is integrated fifty-fifty, to insure against this threat reoccurring.' But Bagaza warns, 'Congo is a very fragile country. Violence will be in the region, not only here [in Burundi], but everywhere.'

A substantial number of parastatals established in the 1970s and 1980s were also slated for privatisation in 2012, along with Air Burundi, ONATEL (telephones), OTRACO (transport), *stations de lavage* (coffee washing stations), ECOSAT (government land) and ALM (government roads and bridges). These will be difficult to unwind, but the move indicates at least some effort to move beyond the distributional politics of the past.

Finally, there is the upside of regional integration through the East African Community, offering the prospect of lowering logistical costs and moderating political behaviour. How this matches with local ownership of the development process is important – whether it is seen as further interference by outsiders or assistance from like-minded Africans. However, the external environment will not answer Burundi's development challenges. Ethnic politics has starkly shaped both policy choices and the nature of the distribution of economic assets. Without breaking this model, Burundi is destined for violent failure.

Two Kenyan tribes – one rich, one poor

The combination of ethnic politics and entrenched systems of patronage has defined Kenya's history, where decisions are made on a fundamental basis of 'What's in it for me and my supporters?'. Kenya is richer than Burundi or Malawi and, unlike them, has a much more favourable geography that includes a potentially world-class transportation infrastructure, significant agriculture assets both for local consumption and export, a diversified economy including a significant tourism component, and a sophisticated business class with international links. When given the choice between long-term growth investment and the benefits of short-term consumption, however, the balance has invariably tilted towards the latter.

In 1982, 80 per cent of Kenyans were employed in the formal sector and 20 per cent in the informal. Twenty-five years later, these proportions had been reversed. By 2011, a million young Kenyans were coming onto the job market annually, though an annual average of only 50 000 jobs had been created during the first decade of the 21st century. With nearly four out of every five Kenyans under 32 years old, inflation at 20 per cent and unemployment at 40 per cent, Kenyan corruption fighter John Githongo noted that economic crisis threatened political stability.[23] The population has grown from just 8.1 million in 1960 to 40 million in 2011.[24]

Indeed, for all of the focus on which tribe – Kikuyu, Luo or Kalenjin – will lead and thus whose, as the Kenyans would say, 'turn it is to eat', in reality the two dominant 'tribes' in Kenya are the rich and the poor, and between them is a middle-class continuously squeezed by a volatile currency and high inflation. Ingrained corruption combined with bouts of ethnic domination of the political status quo has slowed the economy. Widespread violence following the contested election outcome of December 2007 saw an almost total collapse of the economy, with all-important tourism numbers and horticulture exports falling dramatically.

Yet this waxing and waning has been constant since independence in 1963. Although initial post-independence economic growth was around six per cent, it had fallen to 1.5 per cent by the 1990s and to 0.2 per cent by 2000.

By 2011, however, growth had recovered to five per cent on the back of improvements in key elements of its economy. Agriculture, on which 75 per cent of the population depends, is dominated by export crops of coffee, tea and, notably, flowers. By 2011, the latter employed 100 000 people directly and a further 1.5 million indirectly, with production volumes increasing rapidly from just 14 000 tons in 1990 to 81 217 tons in 2005. By 2011, 21 international weekly 'flower flights' were reputedly bringing in over US$1 billion in export earnings.[25] About 30 per cent of Kenyan flowers are exported to the UK, a US$2 billion market, while Kenya also supplies 25 per cent of cut flowers sold in the European Union (EU), a €3.5 billion import market.[26] There are 5 000 flower farms in Kenya, but 75 per cent of exports are supplied by 25 companies.[27]

Tourism dominates the services sector, though it has been extremely vulnerable to terrorist events and perceptions of insecurity, including the 1998 Nairobi US embassy bombings, the violence after the 2007 election and the abduction of tourists from the coastal resort of Lamu in 2011. Regardless, tourist numbers topped one million in 2010, generating US$1 billion in income.[28]

But, attaining Kenya's tourist growth target of two million visitors by 2012 will depend on getting the politics right, which, in turn, will allow more rapid progress to be made on key infrastructure projects, including upgrading the wholly outdated Jomo Kenyatta Airport in Nairobi and the roads through and around the capital.

A 2011 report, *Termites at Work: Transnational Organised Crime and State Erosion in Kenya*, from the International Peace Institute, highlighted the scale of corruption in Kenya and its impact on state and society. The corruption dynamic includes the presence of networks smuggling heroin from Pakistan and Iran and cocaine from Latin America through Kenya to markets elsewhere, with the proceeds being used to attain positions of influence, especially in politics. The same dynamic applies to counterfeit goods and small arms, as well as the smuggling of people. It is estimated that US$2.1 billion found its way into the Kenyan economy in 2010 without the government being able to explain its origins.[29]

While smugglers move many goods with relative ease, it is hard for Kenya to handle legitimate commerce. For instance, it is extraordinary that an airport acting as a hub for Kenya Airways, one of Africa's most dynamic and successful airlines, is little more than, in Prime Minister Raila Odinga's words, 'a bazaar',[30] barely improved since 1977. Its volumes of passenger traffic by 2025 will, according to projections, be ten times the installed capacity of 2.5 million annually, and are already at ten million in 2012. Put differently, it is a Boeing 707 airport for an Airbus A380 age.

Kenya Airways traces its history back to 1946, with the formation of the East African Airways Corporation (EAA). Initially, EAA had a good reputation for service and reliability. With the formation of the East African Community, EAA passed into the joint ownership of the governments of Kenya, Tanzania and Uganda. Shortly after the collapse of the original variant of the East African Community in 1976, EAA was placed in liquidation. Kenya Airways was incorporated in January 1977 as a company wholly owned by the Kenyan government until April 1996.

In 1992, Kenya Airways was given priority among national companies in Kenya to be privatised. In 1995, with assistance from the World Bank's International Finance Corporation, Kenya Airways restructured its debts, while KLM purchased 26 per cent of its shares, thereby becoming the largest shareholder. In the same year the airline started trading on the Nairobi Stock Exchange. The Dar es Salaam bourse followed in October 2004. In April 2004, the company reintroduced Kenya Airways Cargo as a brand and in July 2004, the company's domestic subsidiary Flamingo Airlines was reabsorbed. As of 2011, the airline was owned by individual Kenyan shareholders (32.5 per cent), KLM (now Air France-KLM) (26 per cent), the Kenyan government (22 per cent), Kenyan institutional investors (15.7 per cent), foreign institutional investors (4.36 per cent) and individual foreign investors

(0.07 per cent). It has a shade under 3 000 employees and also owns 49 per cent of Precision Air in Tanzania.

Kenya Airways has now captured a large slice of the African market, opening up routes across East, Central and West Africa. It has done so largely because no one else did or could, and because it is respected as having a good business model. Its networks have been built on the SkyTeam alliance (around KLM and Air France), thereby ensuring the international connectivity, frequent flyer programmes and booking systems that give it a passenger advantage that none of its (private) domestic competitors currently enjoy.

Since 2004, much of Kenya Airways' success can also be attributed to the KTAP (Kenya Airways Turn-Around Project), which has overhauled the airline's revenue management, cost structures, and route and fleet planning. In the 2005/6 financial year, after-tax profits nearly tripled over 2003/4 to US$50 million, with more than two million passengers carried. Passenger numbers in 2006/7 were 2.6 million. In 2010/11, the airline's net profits were US$44 million on revenues up nearly a fifth over the previous year at US$1.07 billion.[31] Kenya Airways carried 3.16 million passengers in 2010/11, up from 2.89 million, with the load improved to 69.2 per cent from 66.5 per cent.[32]

Kenya Airways' inter-African routes reputedly generate up to 40 per cent of its profits. At home, its success has spurred greater domestic competitiveness, with the emergence of private airlines. By 2011, Kenya was flying into 55 cities worldwide, including 45 in Africa. It planned to increase the number of destinations by 60 per cent between 2011 and 2015, and to triple its fleet of aircraft to 107 by 2020, so that it could fly to every country on the continent, an average of five new aircraft each year.

Kenya Airways has become a poster child for the liberalising of African skies, an illustration of what is possible with the right incentives and policy context, in Kenya and across the continent.

How might this experience be translated into other sectors? Kenya, like many African countries, has an obligatory development vision, in its case 'Vision 2030'. But, while long-term and long-winded framework documents stating a multitude of priorities might be politically understandable, in that they offer a sense of direction along with considerable wiggle-room, given their vagueness and inclusiveness, they are in effect meaningless in the absence of clear goals and a strategy and instruments to achieve them. Israel's president Shimon Peres asked, in response to entrepreneur Shai Agassi's idea of building an electric-car network across the Jewish state, 'Nice speech, but what are you going to do?'.[33]

Changing Kenya's trajectory depends, however, not only on doing things, but also on stopping the 'business as usual' approach to politics and the economy in Kenya, thus helping put an end to the elite's culture of impunity. Ultimately Kenya cannot afford any other choice.

The politics of the pocket

If an outsider had looked at Africa in the 1960s and then been asked 'What are the most likely successes?' the answer would conceivably have been Kenya and Côte d'Ivoire. Both were led by liberation icons. Both had export-oriented economies, based on crops that brought benefits to a large number of small farmers. Yet these apparent advantages served to deceive. And while Kenya's record has been disappointing, and highlights the cost of managing ethnic politics, Côte d'Ivoire's has been calamitous.

Nanette works at the Hotel Ivoire, a somewhat bizarre Israeli-designed, French-run grand statement surrounded by a giant swimming pool. The elegant 40-something travels 15 km from her home every night, a journey that soaks up six dollars daily of her US$240 monthly salary. But she is grateful to have a job, especially now that her husband is paralysed from the neck down, the result of an accident at work. And the hotel is being renovated, occupancy is climbing and the pool, empty and decaying during the past decade, is freshly painted and once more sparkling and full.

But Nanette's prosperity is linked to things she cannot see and, in a fragile democracy, has little power over: the effectiveness of the process of political reconciliation, economic growth with the governance necessary to ensure it is spread beyond a tiny elite and, above all, the maintenance of peace. Indeed, Côte d'Ivoire's challenge is best summed up by the 2012 Africa Cup of Nations final. 'Half the country was supporting the team,' reflected an Ivorian business leader. 'The other half refused to as they felt it could benefit [President Alassane] Ouattara. And there were those in the stadium in Libreville,' he observed, 'shouting not for the team, but "Let Gbagbo go!" at Ouattara,' referring to former president Laurent Gbagbo, who was removed in 2011 to stand trial in The Hague.

At first glance Côte d'Ivoire seems to have everything that much of Africa lacks. Skyscrapers and outwardly classy hotels perch on the 'Plateau', Abidjan's business centre, above a beautiful lagoon. There is even a bespoke capital at Yamoussoukro, manufactured in the style of Canberra or Brasilia that includes its near-replica of Rome's St Peter's Basilica, built at a cost of US$400 million in the 1980s. This church mouse, it appears, is quite prosperous.

A French colony from 1893, Côte d'Ivoire was a constituent unit of the Federation of French West Africa until December 1958, when it became an autonomous republic while remaining within the French community. Independence followed on 7 August 1960, when Félix Houphouët-Boigny, the son of a wealthy chief, assumed the presidency.

He inherited an economy geared towards the export of cocoa, coffee and palm oil, contributing 40 per cent of the entire region's exports, and dominated by a sizeable population of French 'settlers', numbering at their peak in the 1970s some 50 000 (out of a population then of seven million). The new president promoted agriculture, stimulating production with high prices. For 20 years from independence in 1960, the country maintained an economic growth rate of over ten per cent per annum. By the 1970s, Côte d'Ivoire had become the world's third-largest coffee producer (behind Brazil and Colombia) and the leading producer of cocoa. By 2012, despite industry struggles, it still supplied more than 40 per cent of world cocoa demand. It was also Africa's largest producer of pineapples and palm oil, and second only to Nigeria in the West African region in terms of its economic size. 'With nearly 7 000 km of paved roads,' reminded Minister of Commerce Dagobert Banzio in 2012, 'even today Côte d'Ivoire possesses one-third of the region's highways.'

French domination and Houphouët-Boigny's firm hand were tolerated in an environment in which, for 20 years, the country maintained a high economic growth rate. GDP per capita nearly doubled in the 1960s. The focus on farming meant that these benefits were comparatively widespread, much of it in the hands of smallholders. Literacy also doubled to 60 per cent during this period, while virtually every town was reached by roads and electricity. Not for nothing was Abidjan labelled the 'Paris of West Africa', a cosmopolitan hub of commerce, people and nightlife.

But the collapse was sudden. A decline in the price of cocoa coupled with the burden of excessive state spending caused GDP per capita to fall from US$1 300 in 1970 to US$700 by 1992. The decline was compounded by expectations that Houphouët-Boigny would step down on the 25th anniversary of his accession. When he stayed, businesspeople adopted a wait-and-see attitude rather than investing in the economy. 'There is not a single major building in Abidjan or bit of infrastructure built after 1985,' says business leader Jean-Louis Billion, 'aside from a half-completed mosque.'

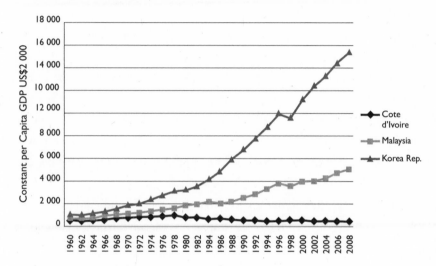

Figure 5: Côte d'Ivoire: What Might have Been

And a culture of corruption had begun to bite. The private stabilisation fund for cocoa established with liberalisation in the 1990s was empty, raided with impunity by the administrative elite.

It was a double whammy, with political change paralleling economic stress. GDP tumbled as the country's external debt trebled. The government's response – to call in the IMF, slash government spending and bureaucracy, and send home a third of the expensive French advisers – did little to help, especially as it included cutting cocoa prices to farmers by half in 1989. It is little wonder that Houphouët-Boigny received 'only' 85 per cent of the vote in the 1990 election, the first open to parties other than the ruling Democratic Party of Côte d'Ivoire (PDCI), compared to the usual 99.9 per cent.

In January 1994, there was a 50 per cent devaluation of the CFA franc (the regional currency used in 12 former French colonies plus Equatorial Guinea and

Guinea-Bissau, whose value is underwritten by the French government), making exports less expensive but significantly raising the cost of imports. Accordingly there was a a jump in inflation and further instability, even though export prospects improved.

Although the economy partly righted itself, the situation worsened overall with the political chaos that followed Houphouët-Boigny's death in 1993. His personality had helped mask weaknesses of administration already developing before that time, says Amadou Gon Coulibaly, minister of state in the Ouattara presidency. 'In a single-party state, transparency was not the best one can have,' he says. 'The press did not play a positive role either, and while the private sector was important, actually it was the government on which the economy depended. It was very difficult for the state to maintain an acceptable level of management and efficiency.' In part this was down to the culture inculcated by Houphouët. As a Wharton-educated Ivorian business consultant adds, 'The country had a well-educated elite, but not an entrepreneurial elite. As a result, they were dependent on handouts, not on making money for themselves.'

Lacking the old man's national appeal, those who followed found it all too easy to play the identity card – xenophobia – spurred on by a combination of economic difficulties and the widespread regional immigration encouraged by Houphouët during the best of times. Today, perhaps as many as four out of ten Ivorians can trace their origins to elsewhere in the region, particularly neighbouring Burkina Faso, Guinea, Ghana, Liberia and Mali.

Houphouët-Boigny's hand-picked successor and speaker of the parliament, Henri Konan-Bédié, was forced out in late 1999 by a military coup led by General Robert Guéï. Following a presidential election in October 2000 marked by violence, Gbagbo came to power. However, Ouattara was disqualified from running due to his alleged Burkinabé nationality. Violent protests culminated in a September 2002 armed uprising, when troops mutinied, launching attacks in several cities, and France deployed soldiers to stop the rebel advance.

When Guéï was killed (some say assassinated), Ouattara took refuge in the French embassy, and Gbagbo returned home to negotiate an accord resulting in that African speciality resorted to when no one can admit defeat – a government of national unity. Amidst ongoing violence, Gbagbo's original mandate as president, which expired on 30 October 2005, was extended when elections were finally held in November 2010.

With both Gbagbo and Ouattara claiming fraud and victory, and both staging inaugurations, the UN certified Ouattara as the victor. This move led to a further crisis and violence as pro-Ouattara forces seized control of most of the country. Gbagbo was eventually evicted from his hideout in Abidjan in April 2011 by UN forces, with external support, notably a French battalion, active in the final stages of the operation. With civilian casualties estimated at around 3 000, and looting of factories, ministries and homes widespread in the last two weeks of the struggle, many businesspeople fled into the region. The trauma of the violence was palpable and lingered 12 months on. In the absence of economic growth, and without any great ideological differences, the rivals naturally reverted to the politics of identity. A little less than half have seen the Christian southern Gbagbo as their man; the others preferred the Muslim northerner Ouattara. These crude stereotypes are perpetuated by the choice of international partners – Ouattara being portrayed by opponents as Paris's choice.

The French connection cuts deep. Nanga Emile is one of the managers of an association which 15 years ago sold the produce of the 2 000 banana and 3 000 pineapple farmers. It all fell apart in 2003, when the EU imposed strict import quotas on bananas from African producers. The export volume from Ivorian farmers dropped from 230 000 tonnes to 20 000 tonnes. Although the EU restriction was rescinded in 2006, the damage had been done, worsened by the costs and difficulties experienced by farmers in accessing affordable finance. By 2012, only one local producer was active in an export market dominated by three multinational companies. Similarly, the number of local pineapple exporters had fallen to just 150, their position complicated by issues of quality. Whereas Côte d'Ivoire once exported 300 000 tonnes of pineapples, providing 85 per cent of European requirements, today the gap has been filled by Costa Rica, which has rapidly grown its exports from 40 000 to 1.5 million tonnes. Recovery has been difficult, says Nanga. 'We did not have enough exports to charter our own ships, but the main French competitor made it too expensive for us to share space on their ships, which was more expensive than space in a commercial container.' And aid from the EU was tied to using European companies, rather than cheaper and more appropriate African, including South African, services, Nanga added.

The economy thus not only has to recover, but needs to be restructured. There is little compelling reason to simply getting back to the point where the precipitous decline began.

President Ouattara and those who follow will have to pursue a diversification strategy away from 'an old scheme based on planting and exporting cocoa,' says Billion, one of the country's most successful businesspeople, who runs extensive palm oil, cocoa and sugar plantations, 'to one that we can support our expanding population on'. The population has increased fivefold in 50 years to over 20 million people by 2012.

'While Ouattara's rule represents a deal between [former president Henri Konan-Bédié's] PDCI and his RDR [Rally of the Republicans], he thus has to recognise that the rebels put him there,' says a UN official. This is no small task, given the presence of various armed groupings within the government. They include the rebel New Forces, the former government Defence and Security Forces (Gbagbo's *mélange* of the police, gendarmerie and military following the civil war), grouped in roughly equal proportions by Ouattara's government into a 40 000-strong army known as the Republican Forces of Côte d'Ivoire, and more than 20 other militias, along with UN and French foreign forces.[34]

Restoring growth would require a focus, first, on reinvigorating cocoa production, which still accounts for 12 per cent of GDP and as much as US$5 billion in export income (now second to oil exports by value), and on providing for more than four million Ivorians in farming households. A second economic imperative is the need to diversify into mining and energy, the latter into hydrocarbons and expanding hydropower.

However, growth will require spending on new infrastructure, including roads and housing, along with health and education. Public–private partnerships are the lexicon of Ouattara's government, and are quickly being given shape, for example in the creation of Air Cote d'Ivoire, a joint venture between the government, Air France and private investors. At the start of 2012, all these ideas were being formulated into a national plan, picking up on Houphouët-Boigny's planning preferences that started in five-year cycles in 1965.

This is not all about hard infrastructure, though. The ten years of civil war have seen the country virtually cut in half. The rebel forces controlling the north still, in 2012, 'taxed' trucks passing into Mali and elsewhere at a reported €1 000 a load. Aside from the problem this poses to national governance and political authority, along with the security challenge, it places a premium on the costs of doing business.

Any reform process worthy of the name also has to recognise the existence of various 'economies'. The formal sector (today not even a 'few hundred companies' says one foreign businessman who has been there for 35 years) is heavily taxed, paying a combination of 18 per cent value-added tax (VAT), punitive customs duties, 35 per cent company tax and electricity rates 'two to three times the European average'. A second sector is the 'Lebanese' economy, 'comprising officially 100 000 people ... many of whom do not pay tax and operate on a cash-only basis, though they are important employers'. Lebanese entrepreneurs scooped up many former French businesses at bargain prices when the violence erupted in the early 2000s. The goal of the government is to broaden the base of the economy beyond the French and Lebanese interests. To do so, however, they will need to open up to other investors and incorporate the informal economy in which the bulk of Ivorians subsist. Government plans scarcely acknowledge such realities, though there is a general awareness that employment has to be driven by the private sector and that growth in the cocoa sector, because it reaches so many families, will rapidly alter the fortunes of a large number of people.

Things quickly improved in Côte d'Ivoire after Ouattara's inauguration in May 2011. Where there were once 11 roadblocks between the airport and the Plateau, each a private tollbooth, within six months of Ouattara taking over there were none. Much thus depends on changing the inner stuffings, moving from a political economy characterised by corruption and a lack of accountability and justice – from the 'politics of the pocket', where to be in politics is to be in business – to a system instead characterised by a separation not only of powers, but also of commercial interests. Such a malady, as Houphouët-Boigny wisely realised, afflicts all. 'There is no easy remedy for two diseases,' he reportedly said, 'for when you become rich and when you are poor.' Political leadership also has to shake the recent habit of highlighting and playing to differences within the population and play the national game instead.

A land of irony

What can be done with a torrent of cash from a single export pouring into an environment of impoverishment, long-term conflict and poor governance? Such a question can be asked of a number of African countries, especially the oil-rich nations on its western coast. Angola is the epitome of this challenge. It is a land of ironies, some delicious, others less palatable.

A key African site of Cold War struggle, Angola is where the Soviet- and Cuban-backed People's Movement for the Liberation of Angola (MPLA) and the US-armed National Union for the Total Independence of Angola (UNITA) slugged it out for 27 years. Today American executives tout business in Luanda. Indeed, even during the conflict, business interests reigned supreme. In all likelihood US intelligence tipped off the Angolans about the raid by South African special forces commandos led by Captain Wynand du Toit on the Cabinda oil facility in May 1985. It was one thing to support UNITA; another altogether to endanger oil supplies.

The South African phase of the war came to an end with the Angola–Namibia peace accords in 1989. Out of a population of seven million in the 1980s, by the end of the war an estimated 1.5 million had been killed and four million refugees created. Hard and soft infrastructure, from roads, ports and railways to education and health systems, had to be rebuilt, in many cases from scratch. Under the terms of the Angola deal, South Africa would stop supporting UNITA (which it did not really do until later), Namibia would get its independence (which happened in March 1990) and Angola would stop hosting the ANC. In spite of the latter, relations between the ANC and MPLA remain close – in fact they have never been closer than they are between presidents Jacob Zuma of South Africa and José Eduardo dos Santos of Angola, where business and politics reputedly intersect.

It is perhaps the greatest irony – and contradiction – of all that the MPLA, an avowedly Marxist–Leninist party, has presided over a period of highly unequal economic growth. During the 2000s, following the fatal shooting of UNITA leader Dr Jonas Savimbi in February 2002, the economy grew at over 11 per cent annually, with a peak of 22.7 per cent in 2007. Despite an average per capita income of nearly US$9 000 and enormous mineral riches, more than two-thirds of the approximately 8 million Angolans live under the US$2-per-day poverty line, with one-third reliant on subsistence agriculture for their income. There is little formal sector employment outside the public service.

Yet Luanda is officially the most expensive city in the world in which to live. A mid-quality hotel room costs US$400, a bottle of water US$5 and an omelette a gagging US$37. Nowhere better illustrates the unfortunate axiom: Africa is poor because it is expensive, and expensive because it is poor.

One reason for this is the dominance of oil in the economy, accounting for half of the GDP and 90 per cent of export revenue, inflating prices and the value of the local currency, the kwanza. Little more than a token effort has been made to develop other sectors, notably agriculture. There is huge potential in this sector, which drove economic growth at 25 per cent per annum between 1963 and 1974.

Another reason is the state's lack of capacity to plan and to deliver to anyone apart from themselves.

José Severino, who was in the military frontline in Benguela for the MPLA against the South African military incursion in 1976, heads Angola's industrial chamber. He describes the state and the party as akin to a giant, sprawling baobab, accumulating powers along with business interests, but never giving fruit, except to a chosen few. Despite President dos Santos's 21 November 2009 call for a zero tolerance policy against corruption, the presidency itself is seen as the 'epicentre of corruption', engaged in a variety of self-enrichment enterprises encompassing petroleum, telecommunications, banking, media and diamonds. When describing their state, Angolans routinely use the phrases 'rent-seeking', 'clientalism', 'patronage', 'elite interests' and 'party control'. The result of the systemic corruption is a land of stark contrasts, of swish BMW X6s moving in a sea of street sellers hawking everything from South African fruit to toilet seats, car deodorants and second-hand mobile phones.

A combination of oil and war also explains why traditional sectors such as coffee, once a major employer, have been neglected since independence in 1975. Angola was once the world's fourth-largest coffee and sisal producer, most of it farmed on large colonial-style plantations. From a peak of US$180 million in coffee exports in 1974, the figure fell to just US$250 000 in 2010. Angola remains stubbornly near the bottom of the United Nations Human Development Index: life expectancy was just 50 in 2010, for example, and one-third of adults are illiterate.[35]

Still, the money benefits some. By 2012, the traffic chaos in the capital, Luanda, was world class, clogging the streets and commerce alike. These failures are due in part to poor planning and a lack of discipline, highlighted by the pathologically selfish taxis and drivers who routinely double-park in busy streets, bringing traffic to a standstill. Yet the swarms of cars and the endless roadworks, along with the cranes and skyscrapers dotting the capital's skyline, all illustrate that progress is being made. However, the lack of government planning is keenly felt in its vain attempts to keep up with the demands of the population, especially in terms of basic services. As bad as it is, the situation is a far cry from 2002. One indicator is the national budget, which was, in 2011/12, at an effective US$60 billion – ten times the figure a decade earlier.

The new riches should not excuse the general antipathy towards private business. The MPLA wants to dominate – to control the political and economic environments, partly for the power and wealth such control brings, and partly because the sentiment of Marxist–Leninist centralisation and triumphalism over UNITA remains. Tellingly, there are still avenues named after iconic left-wing figures, from Frederick Engels to Vladimir Lenin. 'Comrade is in the MPLA's blood,' says one observer. 'It sees the world in terms of competitors and threats, not as potential partners.'

But to grow and to create employment it will have to let go, allow space for the private sector to operate, and permit UNITA the space to act as a proper political opposition, providing a check and balance on untrammelled power, a means of ensuring greater competitiveness. As Dr Onofre Santos, one of Angola's seven constitutional court judges, notes, 'If there is no diversification in the economy, poverty will continue. The government cannot be the only source of wealth or the agent of development.'

UNITA has virtually disappeared as a political force, winning just ten per cent of the popular vote and 16 parliamentary seats against the MPLA's 82 per cent and 191 seats (of 220) in the 2008 parliamentary elections. Abel Chivukuvuku, a leadership contender who, in 2012, jumped ship to the smaller Party for Social Renewal and the civil society-based Democratic Bloc, says that UNITA's old guard have been bought off by the MPLA to ensure that stability prevails over greater political competitiveness. This strategy, while understandable, is very short-sighted, he argues, a point that a surprisingly large number of MPLA cadres agree with.

The MPLA has adopted a similar strategy in attempting to dominate the media, says journalist Mario Paiva. The withholding of state advertising has forced the sale of several titles, suffocating public debate in favour of the MPLA's view.

The absence of a parliamentary or public popular voice and debate has led to the youth taking things into their own hands à la the Arab Spring. Starting in September 2011, youth-led demonstrations against the MPLA calling for President dos Santos's resignation have been a regular occurrence, drawing as many as 15 000. With Libyan leader Muammar Gaddafi's departure from power in 2012, it was not lost on activists that dos Santos was by just one month short of being Africa's longest-serving head of state, after Equatorial Guinea's Teodoro Obiang. Both had taken power in 1979. And dos Santos has only once tested his popularity at the ballot box, in the aborted 1992 run-off with Savimbi, which he narrowly won. Activists routinely ask: what will the day after dos Santos look like?

Angola's investment environment is ultra-challenging and ultra-expensive. It is also potentially ultra-rewarding, which is why there are so many businesses jostling for entry, many of the foreigners at best under-informed about the status of intermediaries, legal and other challenges, barriers and loopholes. But few of them come to do much apart from sell stuff, being what are pejoratively termed 'container businesses', disgorging their contents on the locals. Importing rather than making goods is encouraged where duty-free allowances correspond to political contacts.

Only the Chinese have arrived in large numbers to settle: about 300 000 by 2012. As one veteran Portuguese settler put it, 'It is their turn.' But they, too, are here to pick up construction and other government contracts, at one end of the scale, and open up small businesses – 'Konicas', as they are known locally – at the other. And their number is inevitably causing some tension. Diplomat turned businessman, José Patrício, reflects the sentiment of many when he says Chinese immigration is 'out of control'.

Greater democratisation is only a part of the story, if an essential one. Another is to accelerate projects by reducing red tape and improving the efficiency of government institutions. However, it is also not enough to use oil parastatal Sonangol as a piggy bank for projects, including the gargantuan 80 000-apartment Kilamba Kiaxi 'new city' housing project 30 km north of Luanda, near the Viana special economic zone. 'Nothing happens,' said one observer in late 2011, 'unless the government and the party hierarchy takes a slice of the action, and Sonangol is usually the provider of the funds to skim.' President dos Santos's promise to deliver one million new homes by the end of 2012 has, in the case of Kilamba, in fact been delivered by a Chinese contractor with a US$3.5 billion Chinese credit line. The shareholders of Delta Imobiliária, which has the job of selling the apartments, include many of the same shareholders involved in other deals. Onofre Santos says, 'Angola is like Russia. The people who are millionaires got the money via the state, where the party is like a monarchy, and remains both hegemonic and a distributor of wealth. Yet,' he says, 'we don't discuss this. There is a conspiracy of silence.'

This method will not provide even a roof for all. For one, it's costly. Most cannot afford apartments like Kilamba's, which cost US$125 000 to US$200 000. Chivukuvuku argues eloquently that reforms must prioritise 'remoralising society' by ensuring transparency along with basic services and getting government out of business. These reforms include cleaning up the city, freeing up visa and airline access, and transforming Luanda's famed waterfront boulevard, the Marginal, once more into a tourist destination. But that requires the elite to give up some of its privileges, something African leaders with few exceptions – South Africa's F W de Klerk, Zambia's Kenneth Kaunda and Ghana's Jerry Rawlings among them – have historically been reluctant to do. Yet, Severino reminds us, 'Government will only do what the pressure will oblige it to do, since it firmly believes that its philosophy of a centralised system, where the main resources are under the control of a small group of people, is the right one.' The fact that Angola has oil revenues does not render it immune to the fundamental development fact that other countries have to accept: that job creation requires leaders to create systems incentivising investment, rather than distributing patronage.

Peeling the onion

Few states have recovered as quickly as Mozambique. By the time its ruinous civil war ended in 1992, per capita income was less than US$50. Twenty years later it was just under US$1 000. In part this process has been driven by the peace dividend, in part by improved governance, and in part, too, by the advent of so-called 'mega' projects, including the Mozal aluminium smelter, the gas pipeline to South Africa and, more recently, the development of huge coal deposits in Tete Province.

However, such schemes bring only limited benefits to Mozambique's 23 million people, among whom, especially the young, unemployment remains endemic.

The youth-led unrest in the capital Maputo in September 2010 had its roots in the sense of alienation and anger resulting from joblessness. There are investments that have delivered widespread poverty alleviation, notably through Mozambique Leaf Tobacco's involvement in Tete and Niassa provinces, providing the extension services for some 100 000 small-scale 'outgrowers' and income for over a million people.

But this success has been a notable exception to the otherwise general rule of failure in large-scale agriculture initiatives. Similarly, the record of private sector investments in tourism, another potential large-scale job creator, has been patchy, especially outside Maputo, and hamstrung by the cost of getting to the country. The failure to attract private funds is linked to overall tensions in Mozambique's business sector, cited by both investors and donors, that arise from widespread protectionist sentiment against investors and a state-centric and interventionist response to development demands, where the private sector is over-regulated, subject to over-bureaucratic practices, crowded out by state-linked actors, and a target for elite rent-seeking and resource nationalism. Put differently, there are those in government who favour state-run capitalism and distribution à la Angola rather than the free-market alternative.

The slow pace of development of the Ilha de Moçambique as an iconic tourist destination is indicative of many of these challenges. The Ilha sits sweltering in the Indian Ocean just 15 degrees south of the equator. Its remoteness and uncomfortable heat made it even more unusual to find a Swedish couple running a hotel there.

But they had not only come here to thaw out the Scandinavian permafrost. Instead, following a tourist trip, they bought three old interlinked warehouses once used for storing Mozambique's signal colonial crop, cashew. Over five years they restored them into an 11-room boutique hotel, notable for its setting, understated taste and serenity.

It was not all plain sailing. Building materials had to be brought 175 km down from Nampula to where they had originally been imported. Very little was made in Mozambique. Licensing took time in a country where computerisation was, especially more than five years ago, a novelty.

And some things have remained problematic in establishing a commercially sustainable business. There are no scheduled flights to the nearby strip at Lumbo, which houses a neo-classical architectural gem of a terminal. The cost of flights within Mozambique and the region to nearby Nampula is shockingly high. 'The cost of my ticket from Amsterdam to Nairobi was less,' one observer reflected, 'than the leg from Nairobi to Nampula.' Uncertainty over visas adds to the perception of risk, even though these can now be purchased on arrival at airports by many nationalities. Although Mozambique received 2.2 million tourists in 2010, the vast majority were businesspeople or drive-in visitors. The number of fly-in tourists, a high-yield source of income, remains at 50 000 annually, compared to ten times that for neighbouring Tanzania and 20 times for Kenya. Mozambique's international tourism receipts were US$230 million in 2010, but over US$1 billion in both Kenya and Tanzania.

Then there are the ongoing challenges of running even a small facility on a water-scarce island, including the absence of fresh produce, which has to be brought in from afar. The average length of stay is just three days, and most (foreign) visitors are low-yield backpackers, with little to entice them to remain longer. While hoteliers can put on boat trips to entertain, there is concern about dwindling fish stocks, given the pressures of overpopulation on the 32 000-strong mainland, connected to the Ilha by a three-kilometre causeway. And the shopping, another 'essential' tourist pastime, is very limited.

Despite these perceived deficiencies, the island, a UNESCO World Heritage Site, is an extraordinary tourist asset, even in a country where there is much to choose from along 2 800 km of virgin coastline.

An Arab port before Vasco da Gama's arrival in 1498, the island became the capital of Portuguese East Africa and a centre for the trade of spices, slaves and gold until the end of the 19th century, when it moved to today's Maputo. The Chapel of Nossa Senhora de Baluarte, built in 1522 in the fort at the end of the peninsula, is said to be the oldest European building in the southern hemisphere.

Tourism has been slowly growing on the Ilha over the past decade, up to 7 000 visitors in 2010. By 2012 there were big choices to be made, which could transform the island from an adventure to a jet-set destination.

The most iconic building is the 19th-century hospital, once the largest health facility in sub-Saharan Africa, but today badly dilapidated. There are tensions over this pending restoration process: who would pay for a new hospital, and where should it be, island or mainland or both? And could an investor move the primary school, accommodating over 1 400 children, which obscures the view from the hospital over the sea?

Yet the government lacks a clear vision and plan for what it wants to achieve on the Ilha, despite the development of various 'master plans' which have amounted to little more, in the opinion of experts, than 'project catalogues'. As a result, several wide-ranging proposals have been submitted for the hospital development.

There has also been a lack of clarity about who makes necessary decisions. As the hospital, for example, is likely to fall under the government's 2011 PPP (public–private partnership) law, it would, as such, require approval by the ministries of culture (as a UNESCO site), finance (to transfer land off the public registry), education (since a primary school might have to be moved), health (because the developers are expected to build a new clinic on the island and a 40-bed hospital on the mainland), fisheries (given local livelihoods) and agriculture (given both the livelihood dimension and the likely transfer of land).

Any PPP would thus require a 20 per cent local ownership stake, though the law is unclear on the modalities. It would also require approval by the Investment Promotion Centre, based in Maputo, if incentives are sought, and of course by UNESCO if the status is to be maintained. There are also other approvals required, from the regional authorities (based in Nampula, 175 km away) and from the local authorities based on the island. The latter are especially critical with regard to building regulations, though there have been allegations of corrupt practices in this regard.

It is a complex, multilayered process, in which stifling Portuguese colonial bureaucracy has been overlaid with new governance practices and demands, and it's not clear who is in charge, even though the tourism ministry should be the lead agency.

Moving this project from concept to implementation will also entail confronting the usual chicken-and-egg dilemma. On the one hand there is a need to catalyse the tourism development process to the next level, up from guest-houses and home-stays to a five-star hotel. A hospital-to-hotel rehabilitation could be this spark.

It's a balancing act. Any development will have to manage the crush of the local population (17 000 people on an island built to accommodate 7 000), especially in the barrios or Makuti Town area (so named after the reed dwellings), resulting in sanitary deficiencies and water shortages. The only way to depopulate is by offering attractive employment prospects on the mainland. Yet the island currently has much better livelihood alternatives than the continental side, and that gap would likely widen with the establishment of a new hotel. Integrating the local economy into foreign-led tourism is also a challenge, as is maintaining the delicate balance between tourism, fishing and the environment. The Ilha's attraction of being part hotel, part home, part business and part tourism would have to be maintained.

Moreover, since local ownership and leadership are crucial, some of the very people expected to carry out this process are those who have overseen the island's decay. Yes, they have undoubtedly learned from their mistakes, but it is still a big ask, not least because they have their own constituencies to accommodate, aside from investors. Consensus is required between the government, local and central, the community and tourism operators. Without investors it is impossible to conceive of a situation where there is no poverty; with poverty, it's difficult to imagine a sustainable and profitable business model.

Finding the balance and breaking the cycle of underdevelopment demands leadership to establish both vision and policy. Progress will require people to think beyond the advantages of keeping things just as they are today, and instead to focus on tomorrow's opportunities.

Kiliba and Kabila

Of all African countries, few are as blessed with resources as the Democratic Republic of the Congo. In addition to its vastness, it has a wealth of mining, hydrocarbon, water, energy, forestry, land and agricultural assets. Yet the Congo demonstrates perfectly the phenomenon we noted in Chapter 1 – that large countries, precisely because of their size, are blighted by particular governance problems that reflect in their record of economic performance and political stability.

The contrast between the Burundian and Congolese sides of the border at Kavimvira was stark. At the former, a sullen official, the one with the badly stitched gash on his forehead, spent ages trying to find fault with the multiple-entry visa in between calls to and from the four mobile phones on his desk, before he finally wrote the details into a giant, lined ledger, stamped the by now well-thumbed travel document, grimaced and handed it over with a grunt.

The Congolese side said, 'Welcome to the 21st century.' The passport was scanned along with thumb and index finger, stamped and handed back with a gap-toothed smile. This was not the Congo we remembered. Yet the border is a facade, quite literally. While the Congo's boundaries are better – or rather, not as badly – policed, it's the inside which remains badly governed, or even ungoverned. Passing over a single-lane rickety steel bridge, we left behind Burundi's tarred road and turned onto a dusty dirt one to Uvira at the northern end of Lake Tanganyika. Twenty minutes later we headed north to the turnoff for Kiliba, down one of the last tarred roads Mobutu Sese Seko's regime built, the disused sugar factory down a five-kilometre track dotted with electricity poles shorn of their cabling, standing like giant crucifixes commemorating some tragic event.

For the inhabitants of this eastern part of the Democratic Republic of the Congo, disaster occurred when the SUCKI sugar plantation and mill was closed down in 1995 due to a combination of political instability, a falling Zairean franc, which made it difficult to afford spares and to budget, and a drought in the late 1980s. By the time of its closure, production had fallen from a peak of 21 000 tonnes of sugar in 1989 to just under 5 000 tonnes. Started by a Belgian baron in 1958, the business was forced into partial government ownership in 1969, this event being followed inevitably by slow decay and eventual collapse.

We were greeted by a six-man management team, who had patiently remained *in situ* hoping against hope that the plant would restart – a latter day *Mary Celeste*, if you will, but with a crew. There is little doubt that the demand exists. The Congo's 60 million people each, on average, consume three kilos of sugar a year. Currently the single operational mill in Bas-Congo province, near Kinshasha, meets less than half of this need.

Ushered into the dank boardroom down an unlit parquet-floored corridor, the institutional enamel cream paint dotted with photographs of the founder of the business, a smiling Baron Kronacker, and successive white, and then black, general managers, we were treated to an update on the plant. No fewer than 683 personnel remained on the books, though they were owed more than US$4 million in unpaid wages. The management team, with more than 170 years of experience among them, ran us through the plans to reinstate production, telling us how they had kept the plant under a form of rudimentary care and maintenance (including sending the local electricity transformer to Burundi for safekeeping to ensure it did not go the way of the looted 20 km of electricity cabling linking the plant with Uvira), and how they had kept income trickling in through doing machining and woodwork.

Around the unlit room were relics of a past era – a blackboard denoting annual sugar production from 1958, a chalk drawing of the production process from cane through juice extraction and separation to heating and drying, a world map of sugar producers and a hand-painted diagram of the concession. On the table were heavy brass Primus beer ashtrays. No one smoked. But at least one shed a tear when I asked how they had coped over the past 15 years, the threadbare collars and stained shirt-pockets telling their own story of struggle and poverty. They were drawn from virtually all corners of the Congo – including Equateur, Bandundu, Katanga, Uvira and Bukavu – illustrating how the country might work together with the right leadership and direction.

Then it was off for a tour of the run-down plant, skipping the goats resting where the management's cars once rolled. A wrap-up at the ramshackle successor to the Baron Kronacker staff club followed. There is something lump-in-the-throat humbling about folk who have precious little offering you a cold Coke or Fanta Citron.

Kiliba is located on the fertile Ruzizi plain. It's also where the Banyamulenge Tutsi began their insurrection against the rule of Mobutu, which led to the despot's toppling in 1997. Today it remains wild and woolly, a sometime refuge for the radical Burundi FNL Hutu movement and the renegade Rwandan Interahamwe *genocidaires**.

While local politics have become institutionalised, they have not brought prosperity and, in some cases, not even stability. In nearby Uvira, flags of a huge variety of political parties were flying in preparation for the Congo's second democratic election scheduled for 28 November 2011. Every acronym was on view: MSR, PPRD, UNC, PNR, PRM, PK, UNADF, AFDC, PANADER, UDPS, and so on. There was even a cyclist sporting a red T-shirt proclaiming 'Popov for President', hopefully referring to the one-time Chechen prime minister, rather than any possibility that the Russian might be coming to the Congo. That's all they needed!

President Joseph Kabila has shown little instinct for governing the country and every instinct for enriching himself and his coterie. Instead of attracting the sort of investor interested in sitting things out for the long term, Kabila has closed

---

*   The term *genocidaires* is used to refer to those responsible for the mass murder of close to one million people over 100 days in 1994 in Rwanda.

down those who did not toe his line. For example, the mining licence 'revisitation' process, so-called, which aimed at forcing companies to cut government-connected individuals into deals, saw the Canadian firm First Quantum evicted from its projects in Kolwezi (later sold to a Kazakh-led concern) and at Frontier near the Zambian border. If First Quantum had gone ahead as planned, it would be paying US$400 million in annual tax revenue to the government, increasing Kinshasa's income by not less than ten per cent.

According to the British MP Eric Joyce, who chairs the House of Commons all-party parliamentary group on the Great Lakes region, such deals are part of what he describes as a 'startling pattern of corruption' in the Congo.[36] Understanding corruption helps to explain why, although Congo's mineral wealth is estimated at over US$20 trillion, the country ranks last on the UN's Human Development Index of 187 countries and territories.

The first election, in July 2006, followed a decade of conflict, the eviction of Mobutu from power in 1997, and the ongoing UN peacekeeping mission, one of the largest and most expensive in the organisation's history, with over 23 000 personnel and a US$1.4 billion annual budget. This election, which cost the Congo's international sponsors a further US$500 million, was won by the incumbent, Joseph Kabila. His main rival, Jean-Pierre Bemba, who disputed the results, was later arrested and sent to The Hague on war crimes charges.

On 28 November 2011, the second democratic election in the giant central African country went predictably badly, being characterised by allegations of extreme fraud. But this time, Kabila faced his toughest challenge yet in the form of the veteran politician Étienne Tshisekedi, 79, a man whose personal poverty illustrates perfectly his political principles, breaking the mould of the Congo big man. He was one of the few who stood up to Mobutu. He also refused to participate in the 2006 election, citing concerns about fraud.

Tshisekedi and his party, the Union for Democracy and Social Progress (UDPS), alleged widespread electoral swindling, including ballot-stuffing, vote-tallying 'adjustments' and flights from South Africa of three million pre-endorsed ballot papers.[37]

The Carter Center said that the results 'lack credibility',[38] while the EU election observer team joined others in citing 'serious irregularities' at the polls.[39] After some delay in announcing the results, Kabila officially won 49 per cent of the vote and Tshisekedi 32 per cent. The UDPS claimed their man had won 52 per cent of the vote, compared to Kabila's 24 per cent. The Archbishop of Kinshasa, Cardinal Laurent Monsengwo, observed that 'after analysing the results … it is indeed normal to conclude that they do not conform to the truth or justice. How, for example, is it possible that on 6 December, Mr Tshisekedi had 5 927 728 votes out of 17 329 137 votes cast, but on 9 December he was credited with 5 863 745 votes out 18 144 154 votes cast? He lost 64 000 votes, even though the results from 34 000 more polling stations had been added.'[40] Private tallies put Vital Kamerhe, who officially finished in third with just seven per cent, ahead of Kabila. Kamerhe, who enjoyed support, especially in the restive east, subsequently joined forces with Tshisekedi.

The problem in the Congo is that, for all the fluttering flags and computerised border posts, its leaders don't think like nationalists and instead act as individuals or as representatives of narrow groups. Their people are powerless but to follow this example. But the Congo is not a failure for everyone. Some people become rich because of failure and the absence of governance, and have a vested interest in perpetuating the bottlenecks, inefficiencies, absence of rule of law and transparency, and bureaucratic obstructionism. In this environment, predatory politics and access to resources are the goals of victory, where government's aim is not to reap the reward of investments in terms of development, but to prosper from the transaction costs. A failure to recognise and address this root problem will simply prevent the type of investment that leads to growth and jobs.

Ethiopia

With the Congo and Nigeria, Ethiopia is one of the three biggest sub-Saharan African countries in terms of population, with more than 80 million people. After a bloody civil war, in May 2012 it celebrated 21 years of peace. And it economy took off during the 2000s, registering consistently high growth figures. This surge was not, contrary to many African examples, based on natural resource prices. And nor was it reliant on foreign investment, but rather public sector-led expenditure, where the need for political and economic control has trumped development needs. This has a cost, however, both in terms of sustainability and relative under-performance.

The sign proclaimed: 'Ethiopian Airlines welcomes you'. But Ethiopia did not.

The visa queue was so long that it started halfway up the descending escalator, creating a scene of chaos as the dominoes of arriving passengers descended.

Then it snaked around the corner, following several switchbacks, before disappearing into a doorway behind which five officials nonchalantly peeled visas off paper, stuck them in passports, took your US$20, and laboriously wrote out receipts.

It was exactly 1 hour and 55 minutes long. It was slower than Heathrow, and that says it all. Remarkable too, for a country considered Africa's conference centre. The Commission of the African Union alone holds more than 200 events annually in Addis Ababa.

The purpose of visa regimes is unclear, especially for those countries wanting to encourage tourism. Why slow down and charge people wanting to spend money in your country?

The defence of such regimes is similarly shaky. The arguments included the usual 'Well, the West imposes visas against us'. However irritating it might be, if African countries want richer Western visitors more than the West wants Africans, some pride will have to be swallowed. Another perennial excuse is the need for security, though again a proper airport immigration system would just as easily flag bad guys than a perfunctory peel-stick-and-stamp visa method with no computerisation.

Among all the arguments in favour of retaining visas, seldom is the need for foreign-based African embassies to fund themselves through such charges.

Before Ethiopia we took a group to Victoria Falls among whom was a Latin American colleague. On previous visits he had acquired a Zimbabwean visa at the border. Not this time, the problem only being resolved by the uttering of the Open Sesame phrase: 'How much for an emergency visa?'.

How many Costa Ricans have overstayed their welcome in Zimbabwe? And is it not a good idea to allow a Costa Rican (average per capita income US$12 000) into Zimbabwe (average per capita income US$300)?

Georgia, the Black Sea country, not the peanut state, has had the right idea on visas. They did away with the need for them for citizens of all countries with higher incomes – Georgia ranks just outside the top 100 worldwide in this regard. And it also removed the need for work permits for citizens of these countries. The logic is they are likely to contribute more to Georgia's economy than they could possibly take away.

Georgia did this unilaterally, not insisting on reciprocity from these countries.

As a result of this policy, Georgia got three million visitors a year, up from 300 000 in 2004. Tourism receipts are now US$1 billion, up from virtually nothing before. To put the number of visitors in perspective: Georgia's population is 4.5 million. South Africa's population is 48 million, to take a comparative example, give or take, and the African country receives 10 million visitors annually. On a per capita basis, Georgia now receives nearly three times as many.[41]

What apparently motivates such visa regimes is a deep-rooted sense of pride and a need for extra funding combined with a statist instinct. In the case of Ethiopia, despite its economy growing, at least according to the government, for eight years from 2003–11 at double digits, its development path has been state- rather than private sector-led. While in certain sectors, such as chemicals and horticulture, where foreign investors have been given red-carpet treatment, by some estimates the share of private sector activity in the economy has declined during this period. The extremely rickety telecom sector remains, for example, closed to the sole government operator, ranking in 142nd and last place in the World Economic Forum's 2012 mobile telephony sector competitiveness listing.[42] A 2012 law in Ethiopia, which criminalises the use of Voice Over Internet Protocol services such as Skype or Google Talk and carries a prison term of up to 15 years, further illustrates the tension between the embracing of new technology and policies driving openness and growth and the old, autocratic, militarised, closed economy and society. Not only does this measure ensure use of the more easily monitored state monopoly services, but it curbs Internet and media freedoms. Already Ethiopia has the second-lowest Internet penetration rate in Africa.[43]

The government has identified four priority export sectors: textiles and garments, leather and footwear, agro-processing, and pharmaceuticals, with ambitious targets for each. For example, the textile sector has a target of over US$1 billion by 2015 and leatherwear US$500 million. This is to be achieved in part through discouraging unprocessed exports (such as the export levy on raw leather) and incentives for those operating in various special economic zones, including duty-free status for manufacturing and capital machinery inputs.[44]

Ethiopia's ambitious vision of wanting to become a middle income country by 2023 coupled with a fear of the consequences of openness, the failure to open some sectors including transport to foreign activity, low interest rates, an infrastructure budget of more than US$40 billion over five years (the same as the national budget), and high public expenditure has led to high inflation (by some estimates over 35 per cent, second highest in 2012 world-wide only to Belarus) and very low foreign investment (less than US$200m annually during the 2000s).

With low FDI inflows and very low rates of tax collection (just ten per cent of GDP, compared to the sub-Saharan average of 17 per cent), the government has driven growth up through public spending on construction projects. In April 2011, the government obliged private commercial banks to buy National Bank of Ethiopia (NBE) government bonds to the value of 27 per cent of their gross loan disbursement in order to finance onward government infrastructure spending, much of it carried by out Chinese firms through 'direct awards' rather than public tenders.[45]

Of course the government does not like any criticism of its approach. It is one of only four countries (the others being North Korea, China and Brazil) which have refused publication of the 2011 IMF report on the country which reportedly chided government policies. Part of the problem is, too, that there is little informed domestic debate between the government's view – 'everything is fine' – and the other extreme of the especially US-based disapora. The government's response to economic fragility is instructive and predictable given command economy instincts – it's because of market and trading inefficiencies, where private sector hoarding and lack of innovation has stunted growth. Its centrist instincts also can be seen in the bureaucratic nature of regulation. As one foreign economist based in Addis Ababa observes, 'Every law is extremely complicated. They would like to follow China, and micro-manage the economy, but they don't have the quality of the administration. It's a thoroughly Marxist approach to the nature of economic management and thinking.'

Ethiopia is trying to find a different African development path through exports rather than the common natural resources route. It also has a bonus of more than US$2 billion in annual aid from the EU and United States alone along with more than US$1.5 billion in remittances each year. And it's not that the government of Meles Zenawi is not smart. To the contrary.

Its development could really accelerate with more openness. But the government prefers lower growth than the emergence of competing centres of power that greater private sector activity would inevitably involve. 'So while the government talks about the private sector a lot,' says one EU observer, 'in reality they are cutting it out.' There are 'three types of enterprises', he says, 'the public sector with the biggest chunk; the private sector which is shrinking; and then Sheikh Al-Amoudi [the Saudi–Ethiopian businessman and philanthropist] who controls one-third of the private sector.'

The reason for the continuation of antediluvian visa regimes is related to the same reason why governments are fearful of opening their economies to outsiders: control and its benefits.

True reform means not returning to the past

Zimbabwe was once one of Africa's most diversified economies, rich in natural and human resources. It then went down a path of calamitous political choices: first, the Unilateral Declaration of Indepedence by white Rhodesians in 1965, which was followed by international isolation and the enhancement of import substitution policies that had already become a major feature of the regime. After Robert Mugabe won the first non-racial elections in 1980 and became prime minister, there was a recovery. Eventually, Mugabe's strategy floundered because he, like the whites, preferred redistribution to growth. However, unlike the whites – who had to support, in their eyes, only roughly 250 000 people – Mugabe, after formally deracialising politics, has tried to win much bigger constituencies with patronage, a play that was doomed to fail because there is simply not enough wealth to go round – a fact that made it even more tempting for populists to try to seize the land and the mines.

In the early 1960s Supersonic exported radios from its factory in Bulawayo to the United States. By the 1980s, Zimbabwe was reputed to be one of the most industrialised economies *per capita* in the world, the sector accounting for one-quarter of national production.

Thirty years later, Zimbabwe is a commodity exporter, reliant on sending unrefined gold, agricultural products, diamonds, platinum and people abroad to keep itself going.

Most, apparently, know the 'story' of Zimbabwe's decline. A bitter liberation war, which ended in 1980, was followed by a period of political reconciliation and economic progress, marred by the Gukurahundi ('the early rain which washes away the chaff before the spring rains', in Shona): the violent suppression of political opponents in the eastern Matabeleland region. In the mid-1990s, however, faced with the option of continuing painful structural economic reforms or taking another route, the government chose the latter, easier way out. This was hastened by a decision taken in November 1997 to offer a gratuity and pension to 50 000 war veterans, amounting to an *ex fiscus* payment of US$1.5 billion, as a result of which the Zimbabwe dollar plunged from Z$14 to Z$26 to the US dollar in a single day and the stock exchange lost 46 per cent of its value as investors dumped local shares.

And so began the seizure of land from 4 000 white commercial farmers and their redistribution, in part, to political lackeys of President Robert Mugabe's ruling ZANU-PF, along with an attempt to force through a new constitution cementing ZANU rule.

The rejection of the new constitution in a national referendum in February 2000 saw ZANU accelerate the land seizures and the economy tumble as agricultural outputs and exports fell, investor confidence eroded and the politics hardened with the emergence, around the referendum, of a union-based opposition in the Movement for Democratic Change (MDC).

Fast forward a turbulent decade, and the MDC had become ZANU's government partner after a disputed election in 2008 prompted the creation, through South African mediation, of a unity government in February 2009. Under MDC stewardship, the Zimbabwe dollar was scrapped amidst record hyperinflation, and the economy stabilised.

By 2012, tobacco production, once the export mainstay, had recovered to about one-third of its previous levels, mainly through the efforts of smallholder farmers and the remaining 200 or so white commercial farmers. Half of the required two million tonnes annually of maize, the staple, is imported. Gold production, which fell from 27 tonnes in 1999 to 3.5 tonnes in 2003, has recovered on the back of higher prices, operating now at about 50 per cent of capacity. The MDC finance team had managed to increase monthly revenue income from US$4 million in 2009 to US$300 million in 2011, and diversify the sources from solely customs and excise to one-third each from VAT, direct tax and customs.

But huge problems remain, especially staggering rural poverty and countrywide joblessness. There is the same number of formal sector jobs in 2012 (850 000) as in 1980, though the population has more than doubled to 13 million.[46]

The analysis that suggests Mugabe and ZANU are responsible for all of

Zimbabwe's problems is incorrect, even though the country's leaders since independence have undoubtedly made those problems far worse. The problem is that no Zimbabwean, white or black, at least until the advent of the MDC, ever believed in market forces. White racial socialism in an isolated, import-substitution economy gave way in 1980 to black socialism. Neither could work. As Ronald Reagan once remarked, the problem with socialism is that you eventually run out of someone else's money.

There is little surprise that Mugabe's government ran into trouble in the mid-1990s. Not only did the Cold War end – and with it the ability to play one side off against the other and appear, at least, the moderately good regional guy in Southern Africa, the model non-racial state – but this coincided with the emergence of a democratic South Africa. No longer could Zimbabwe present itself as the best regional non-racial example, and the global race card, played for aid and sympathy, suddenly lost its currency.

So Mugabe went back to creating a feudal system, where the elite were kept onside through patronage and the remainder left poverty-stricken and dependent on handouts in the rural area. In doing so he has adroitly used a combination of land distribution, diamonds and indigenisation of foreign property. He has kept Zimbabweans pitifully poor, poorer than they were, on average, at independence in 1980. Male life expectancy has declined since 1990 from 60 to 42 years. Infant mortality rate has climbed sharply from 53 to 81 deaths per 1 000 live births over the same period. Not surprisingly, Prime Minister Morgan Tsvangirai has noted that the country's troubles boil down to two socio-economic challenges: 'a young population which is ill-educated and unemployed, and an economy that has shrunk by 50 per cent over a decade.'

Yet a different future requires, the prime minister realises, changing the economic make-up and not simply reinstating the traditional drivers of minerals, tourism and agriculture which, along with remittances and transportation fees to the Congo and Zambia, is what most businesspeople are focused on for future improvements. Among the steps that will be required are, first, moving from short-term stabilisation and subsistence to enabling longer-term policies to attract all-important foreign investment, acquire debt relief from the US$9.1 billion borrowings and arrears, and deal with the infrastructure backlog. Second, Zimbabwe must discard its protectionist mindset, one linked to the liberation struggle, a 'them and us' mentality. And third, as finance minister Tendai Biti has reminded us, Zimbabwe has to break out of the cyclical crises that have characterised its economy and politics for the past 100 years.

And the requirement for all of these reforms, the finance minister says, is to be 'liberated from politics'. However, it is not only the politics – white colonial and racial, and Mugabe's perpetuation of this thread – that have to be reformed. Zimbabwe's economic model has to change overall, from one focused on redistribution and patronage to one embracing growth, and also from its intent on bucking the market through protectionism to a focus on harnessing market forces and interests.

Why do countries get stuck?

Lesotho, completely surrounded by South Africa, has had a number of development advantages, yet remains one of the poorest countries in the world. It has abundant natural resources in diamonds and, especially, water. It has a regular source of income from the shared revenue of the Southern African Customs Union (SACU) and the migrant workers who ply their trades in South Africa. Yet its attempts at diversification have met with only limited success, being dependent on external tariff preferences (notably the US African Growth and Opportunity Act, AGOA). Moreover, it has failed to transform these industries, not only from apparel assembly to textile manufacturing, but also into other areas of industrial activity. Lesotho's development through diversification has got stuck.[47]

The Taiwan-based Nien Hsing Group has been operating in Lesotho for two decades. In 2001 its three factories employed 7 500 people and produced 70 000 pairs of jeans a day, with Levi Strauss its biggest customer. The reason they were in Lesotho, said local CEO Lin Chin Yi, was the duty- and quota-free access to the US market under AGOA. 'Where the US market goes, we go,' he admitted.

In 2004 there were 45 garment-exporting factories in the mountain kingdom employing 52 000 and exporting 111 million square metres of clothing. Seven years later there were 23 factories with 35 000 employees manufacturing 72 million square metres for export. By 2012, 45 per cent of the 840 000-strong workforce was unemployed. There are several reasons for the downturn.

The first is the end of quota limits with the termination of the global Multifibre Agreement in 2005, a change which 'favours those with cost efficiencies, essentially

Asia over Africa,' says Mr Lin. 'Asian salary costs are lower, and their governments offer greater incentives, including tax-free imports and local sales.'

The minimum wage in Lesotho, circa 2011, was US$127, including benefits and overtime. Even though Bangladesh's was less than a third of this, and Vietnam's, India's and Cambodia's little more (US$43, US$52, US$49 and US$50 respectively), it is difficult to see how it can be brought down in Lesotho, given the South Africa-linked cost of living. This situation is exacerbated by payment on a piece-by-piece basis in Asia, which promotes higher productivity, but is not permitted in Lesotho, and worker absenteeism of 8–10 per cent. The latter is partly related to the high level of HIV/Aids among workers of around 25 per cent (though this has come down from over 30 per cent as a result of factory-led awareness and antiretroviral programmes).

How Maseru might respond with improved incentives is more complex and political, however, given its membership of the century-old SACU, along with South Africa, Namibia, Botswana and Swaziland. Nien Hsing has more factories in Mexico, Nicaragua, Vietnam and Cambodia. 'While our other factories can sell overruns locally without incurring duty,' laments Lin, 'we cannot do that in SACU without incurring duties, which leaves us vulnerable to overseas demand and lots of expensive stock.' The duty on jeans made in Maseru but sold into the SACU market was, in 2011, 32 per cent plus VAT.

Lesotho has had only limited scope to develop the types of incentives preferred by investors. This has been limited to corporate tax (at zero for export industries), personal income tax (which is paid at local rates) and work permits. The latter, however, have gone in the opposite direction, with increases of up to 500 per cent in the cost of various permits. 'Without incentives ... we will see more factories closing,' says Johnny Lin, secretary of the Lesotho Textile Exporters Association.

Another constraint has been the appreciating value of the local currency, the loti, against the US dollar, coupled as it is to the South African rand. The average exchange rate went, for example, from ZAR8.25 to the US dollar in 2008 to ZAR7.33 in 2010. Yet lower dollar export incomes were matched by higher costs for services: water and electricity tariffs went up by 16 per cent and 17 per cent respectively over the same period.

Not only have downstream industries struggled to emerge in this environment, but their absence has impeded the competitiveness of the garment sector. While

Formosa Textiles established a local upstream denim mill in 2006 to take advantage of the then imminent end of the AGOA preference for least-developed economies such as Lesotho's to use third-country-supplied material for garments, this provision was extended until 2012. The result is that locally spun, dyed and woven denim costs around five per cent more than landed imported textiles, due to limited economies of scale. The absence of zipper, label and yarn manufacturers adds costs.

Local shipping times have been longer and costs much higher than in Asia – US$4 620 for the export sea-freight of a 40-foot container, compared to the competitors: US$2 600 for Vietnam, Cambodia's US$2 800 and US$3 100 for Bangladesh. Land-freight costs have been higher still: US$2 250 compared to US$400, US$800 and US$1 350 respectively. Part of the reason has reportedly been cargo handling dues at the South African port of Durban of US$632 for imports and US$341 for exports. Vietnam, Cambodia and Bangladesh have no such charges. The long immigration and customs queues at the Maseru crossing point add costs and hassle.

Locally based producers have found it difficult to replace declining American demands by moving into European markets, not least because the EU 'already has its suppliers from the Middle East and North Africa, and because they have a more high-end, high-quality style', say Lesotho producers. The US demand for jeans, a Lesotho speciality, was in 2010 no less than 460 million pairs annually. Johnny Lin sets out the prospects: 'If the duty-free, tariff-free access of AGOA is opened to others, Lesotho's textile factories will close. What we need is an operational SADC duty-free, tariff-free arrangement to replace AGOA.'

It's not only Asia and Central America that are competitors. Kenya, Lin notes, is also 'stealing' jobs from Lesotho and other Southern African garment producers, with cheaper labour and more aggressive incentives.

The results of the downturn have been more than just figures, though. In Mafeteng, 60 km south of Maseru, the closure of the P&T Garments factory in 2011, with a loss of 2 300 jobs, hit the town hard. Nothing is likely to replace it. P&T was the district's sole remaining factory after the closure of ceramic and pharmaceutical firms. 'One can say with certainty that Mafeteng is now a district that cannot promise any jobs,' says Seabata Likoti, the secretary-general of the Factory Workers Union.

Efforts to encourage local ownership have been stymied by limited motivation combined with a lack of financial wherewithal, even though the start-up costs for a 300-employee factory are relatively small for an entrepreneur, at around US$4 million. Diversification away from textiles has also proven, so far, a non-starter, apart from the establishment of a small lighting factory outside Maseru. As Johnny Lin puts it, 'The level of investment required in garments is small, even if the margins are small. If you are not going to make it in this industry, you will not survive in any other.'

Countries get stuck in their development path by not pushing through reforms. This reflects the absence of political will along with the presence of vested interests. Such interests – combined with macroeconomic structural links with South Africa through SACU membership and the currency pegging – have proven to be hurdles too great for Lesotho's manufacturing sector, not only to remain viable, but also to transform into areas of production other than textiles. It is difficult enough to manage the competitiveness challenge that China and others present to growing a manufacturing industry without domestic suffocation of the 'space' for this industry to operate – land, wages, electricity costs and transport hurdles.

The search for a reform model

African governments, like others, face a tremendous challenge, having to juggle long-term developmental aspirations with the need to maintain short-term political support, especially from vested constituencies. This challenge is made more difficult in the larger states with the greater diversity of their populations and larger extent of the territory they have to govern.

The long-term answer to Africa's development challenge is for leaders to make a profound commitment to economic growth as their highest priority by reforming institutions and by making and then adhering to a set of policy choices that encourages private sector expansion. However, rather than sticking to their reformist guns, governments, when faced with a set of economic problems, revert to populism, patronage and economic nationalism, rather than venturing reforms that will expand the economy. They search for vehicles for less reliance on market factors, so that they can favour specific communities through redistribution, insulating them from the consequences of poor performance by co-opting potentially competing elites. One reason for this failure relates to scepticism about the market and an inability to see that economic growth can, of itself, address development problems. Pessimism about the market is also related to the slow pace of elite and middle-class wealth creation in Africa.

Despite their obvious differences, the examples in this chapter show a number of common trends. While many of these countries have experienced economic growth in the past few years, this has largely been in spite of, rather than because of, their politics. Moreover, their record of job creation and diversification remains pathetic. Given the dependence on commodity prices and external demand, their trajectory remains uncertain at best.

An African model has yet to emerge that can demonstrate how to use the economic dividend provided by the commodity boom to promote job growth more generally and dissolve the patronage politics that has characterised countries since independence. We therefore look elsewhere for guidance.

Many of the same conditions – colonial history, inequality, vulnerability to external prices, conflict, weak borders, ethnic make-up, the role of outside agencies and powers – apply at least as much to Asian and Latin American countries as they do to Africa. The explanation for the growth in these other regions, compared to Africa, resides largely in policy changes. Equally, the failure of Africa to develop at comparative rates is owing to such decisions not being made. The reasons behind the African failure often relate to the existence of a patronage-ridden system of government, where investment and economic decisions are, for example, not made solely on economic principles, but rather to serve the imperatives of redistribution and maintaining allegiances for the sake of political control and holding on to power. In such situations, the need for stability on a narrow political power base is all-important to leaders, overriding the imperative to extend growth and development beyond a tiny elite, as has been shown in many of those African countries that have formed part of this study.

Can Africa replicate the successes of other regions, notably Southeast Asia and Central America, in building a diversified, high-growth, initially low-wage, job-intensive economic model? Or must African countries be required to develop their own growth model? We will attempt to answer these questions in the following chapters, which examine the development experience of countries on several different continents.

Endnotes

1   Map No 4045, Rev 7, UNITED NATIONS, November 2011.

2   http://africanhistory.about.com/od/mandelanelson/p/qts_mandela2.htm.

3   See http://www.businessweek.com/news/2012-05-29/south-africa-gdp-growth-slows-as-mining-production-slumps.

4   These figures were supplied by various sources, including from the Lesotho Textile Exporter's Association.

5   The figure is drawn from World Bank *World Development Report* data. The following section is in part derived from South African Treasury and World Bank reports as assembled in an unpublished report by a South African consultant. This section is based on first-hand research during trips in 2011 and 2012 to the countries analysed.

6   According to the Chamber of Mines, the South African mining industry contributes: 8.8 per cent directly, and another 10 per cent indirectly, to the country's GDP; about one million jobs (500 000 directly); about 18 per cent of gross investment (10 per cent directly); approximately 30 per cent of capital inflows into the economy via the financial account of the balance of payments; 93 per cent of the country's electricity-generating capacity; about 30 per cent of the country's liquid fuel supply; and between 10 per cent and 20 per cent of direct corporate tax receipts (together worth R10.5 billion). http://www.southafrica.info/business/economy/sectors/mining.htm.

7   See Oxford Analytica, 'South Africa: Leadership gap prolongs economic drift', 28 July 2011 at http://relooney.fatcow.com/SI_FAO-Africa-2012/Oxford-South-Africa_6.pdf.

8   See http://www.iol.co.za/business/business-news/public-sector-wage-bill-slammed-1.1290147 and Laurence Schlemmer's analysis on 'South Africa: Will there be an Arab Spring?' at http://www.africa.fnst-freiheit.org/news/south-africa-will-there-be-an-arab-spring.

9   See, for example, 'The Impact of High and Growing Debt on Economic Growth,' Working Paper 1237, 2010, European Central Bank, at http://www.ecb.int/pub/pdf/scpwps/ecbwp1237.pdf.

10 Tax-GDP data can be found in the 'fiscal freedom' data at http://www.heritage.org/index/fiscal-freedom.

11 See Oxford Analytica, 'South Africa: Structural constraints check growth rate', 11 August 2011, at http://relooney.fatcow.com/SI_FAO-Africa-2012/Oxford-South-Africa_5.pdf.

12 Interview, SA Chamber of Mines, September 2011; and see http://www.chinamining.org/News/2009-02-13/1234507005d21487.html and http://www.businessweek.com/

news/2012-06-10/south-africa-pressed-to-cut-rates-as-rand-worries-gain.

13 See http://www.iol.co.za/business/business-news/fewer-strikes-expected-as-wage-deals-are-reached-1.1222557.

14 The figures in 2002/03 were 3.4 million individuals and 815 000 businesses. http://www.southafrica.info/news/business/27466.htm.

15 Interview, Carte Blanche, 14 August 2011.

16 http://www.polity.org.za/article/minister-in-major-overhaul-of-ambiguous-mine-laws-licence-tracking-to-go-public-2010-08-18.

17 http://www.stillmanexchange.com/international-business/south-africa-finds-itself-hole-foll.

18 This section is partly drawn from a telephonic discussion on 23 September 2011 with Roger Baxter, then outgoing chief economist of the SA Chamber of Mines.

19 See http://web.worldbank.org/WBSITE/EXTERNAL/COUNTRIES/AFRICAEXT/0,,contentMDK:20224588~pagePK:146736~piPK:226340~theSitePK:258644,00.html.

20 http://www.newzimbabwe.com/pages/sadc8.16163.html.

21 http://www.telegraph.co.uk/finance/newsbysector/industry/mining/8979101/Boom-time-for-workers-at-the-mining-giants.html.

22 This is taken from a Zambian Association of Manufacturers audit cited in 'Bringing Back the 'Glory Days' of Zambian Manufacturing', *The Bulletin and Record*, March 2012, pp. 14–15.

23 Discussion with John Githongo, Nairobi, 13 October 2011.

24 http://www.us-passport-service-guide.com/kenya-population.html.

25 Discussion with a flower producer, Nairobi, 13 October 2011. See also http://www.kenyarep-jp.com/business/industry/f_index_e.html.

26 http://www.proverde.net/2009/10/eu-cut-flower-imports-2008-eurostat-figures/.

27 http://www.fairtrade.org.uk/producers/flowers/finlay_flowers_oserian_ravine_roses_kenya.aspx.

28 http://www.tourism.go.ke/ministry.nsf/pages/facts_figures.

29 'Powerful Criminal Networks Intent on Holding Kenyan State Hostage', *Daily Nation* (Nairobi), 10 October 2011.

30 Discussion, Tswalu Kalahari Game Reserve, October 2011.

31 http://www.flightglobal.com/news/articles/why-kenya-airways-is-a-poster-child-for-liberalising-african-skies-359896/.

32 http://www.kenya-airways.com/home/uploadedfiles/Global_Website/About_Kenya_
Airways/Investor_Information/Financial_Reports/2010-2011%20annual%20report.
pdf.

33 Cited in Dan Senor and Saul Singer, *Start-Up Nation: The Story of Israel's Economic
Miracle*. New York: Twelve Books, 2009.

34 For a breakdown of these, see http://www.humansecuritygateway.com/documents/
SAFERACCESS_armedgroupspolpartiesCoteDIvoire.pdf.

35 See http://hdrstats.undp.org/images/explanations/AGO.pdf.

36 http://www.voanews.com/english/news/africa/Congo-President-Rejects-British-MP-
Accusations-of-Mining-Fraud-135509493.html.

37 These observations were made during several telephonic interviews in December 2011.

38 http://www.cartercenter.org/news/pr/drc-121011.html.

39 http://www.france24.com/en/20111201-elections-democratic-republic-congo-
irregularities-fraud-voting-africa-kabila.

40 http://congoplanet.com/news/1926/dr-congo-presidential-election-results-not-
truthful-cardinal-monsengwo.jsp.

41 This information was supplied by Lado Gurgenidze, the former Georgian Prime
Minister, May 2012.

42 At http://www3.weforum.org/docs/WEF_GCR_Report_2011-12.pdf.

43 At http://www.theatlantic.com/international/archive/2012/06/why-does-ethiopia-
want-to-give-people-15-years-in-jail-for-using-skype/258558/#.T98YO_mnl2E.email.

44 This data was acquired from various foreign embassies and the Ethiopian government
during a visit to Ethiopia in May 2012.

45 See for example http://www.ezega.com/news/NewsDetails.aspx?Page=news&
NewsID=3181.

46 http://www.google.co.uk/publicdata/explore?ds=d5bncppjof8f9_&met_y=sp_pop_totl
&idim=country:ZWE&dl=en&hl=en&q=zimbabwe+population.

47 The information here was gathered during a research trip to Lesotho in August 2010.

3

CENTRAL AMERICAN PERSPECTIVES

Central America is an apt analogue for sub-Saharan Africa for a host of reasons: a turbulent colonial history (albeit a long time ago), divisions between indigenous populations and the descendents of settlers, a long and violent involvement by the military in politics, and poor development policy choices. Central America's countries also have small populations: Belize (300 000), Costa Rica (4.6 million), El Salvador (6.1 million), Guatemala (14 million), Honduras (7.5 million), Nicaragua (5.7 million) and Panama (3.5 million). Finally, in both regions, agriculture accounts for approximately 25 per cent of GDP.[1]

There are differences, of course. One international financial institution's regional representative notes that 'Central America has, unlike Africa, a tremendously wealthy segment of the population, comprising several hundred thousand people in each country, living alongside very poor people. And although there is a total lack of divergence in terms of national solidarity, there is still a strong intent to create generational wealth.'[2]

Both regions suffer from weak states where violence is a norm. Central America has long been a battleground for 'small' wars, civil wars, border skirmishes, insurrections, coups d'état, *juntas** – military and civilian – and even a football war. In modern history, colonial conquest and, more recently, foreign funding, interference and instigation have commonly been the sparks for violence. As one Guatemalan businessman has put it, 'We have long been the ham in the sandwich: between the Soviet Union and the United States in the Cold War, and now between the drug producers to our south and the drug-users to our north.'[3]

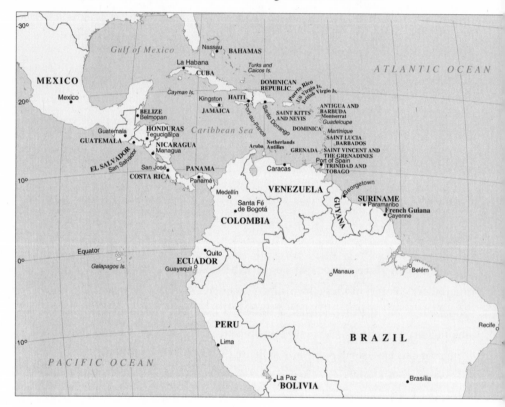

Figure 1: Central America[4]

From the Yucatán peninsula in the north to Panama at the southern end of the isthmus, few countries have been spared this malaise. Only Costa Rica and Belize's histories have been markedly different – the former largely on account of its exceptional pattern of colonial development, where smallholdings developed in the Central Valley rather than the typical Spanish pattern of large estates, coastal settlements and mining; and the latter reflecting its British colonial inheritance

---

* Spanish term, often used in connection with Latin America, denoting a military or political group that rules a country after taking power by force.

and support.

Contemporary Central America suffers from the worst excesses of consumerism in the form of the fast-food strips and malls offering everything from KFC to Pizza Hut to the neon signs of McDonalds. However, these offerings are far from the worst aspect of globalisation. The impact of drugs and criminality is being felt across the region. As the Costa Rican president, Laura Chinchilla Miranda, put it in September 2010, 'From being just a transit point, due to our geographical location between the great drug producers of the south and the great consumers of the north, ours have been becoming, with different degrees, countries that produce, traffic and consume drugs.'[5] In 2007, just one per cent of all South American cocaine sold in the United States passed through the Central American region. Now the figure is estimated to be between 60 per cent and 90 per cent.[6] As one Central American banker warned in 2011, 'If Latin America is not able to cope with the level of violence, this will affect at least medium-term growth and development.'[7] As Figure 2 reveals, criminal violence is prevalent in Africa too.

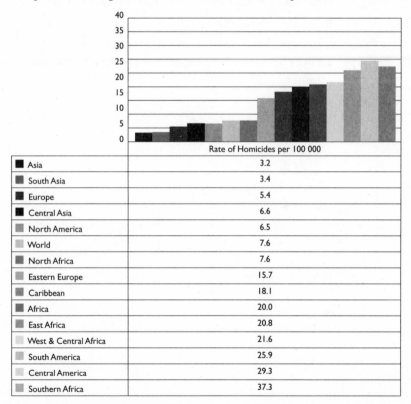

	Rate of Homicides per 100 000
Asia	3.2
South Asia	3.4
Europe	5.4
Central Asia	6.6
North America	6.5
World	7.6
North Africa	7.6
Eastern Europe	15.7
Caribbean	18.1
Africa	20.0
East Africa	20.8
West & Central Africa	21.6
South America	25.9
Central America	29.3
Southern Africa	37.3

Figure 2: Global homicide rates, 2004[8]

The resort to political populism is another common characteristic. Politics proffers economic shortcuts as a solution to the widespread plight of poverty – a case, as one Guatemalan businessperson observed about his region, 'of redistribution rather than growth'. The most recent incarnation of this response in Central America has been 'Chavezism', the threat to nationalise private business interests. As Pablo Schneider, a Guatemalan and former president of the Central American Bank for Economic Integration, puts it, 'Politics can be both a lever for development and a major restriction. Where living conditions are uncertain, complex and difficult for most people, invoking notions of radical change is attractive to the electorate. This is especially true for those politicians for whom the end justifies the means.'[9]

Since the end of the Cold War, however, the Central American region has slowly assumed a more positive development trajectory. And, just like every other region, it has its own taxonomy. In growth terms, circa 2011, there were the high performers of Panama and (if one wants to include it in a broader description of the region, given its orientation towards Central America) the Dominican Republic, growing at about six per cent annually; the next group, Costa Rica and Nicaragua, at four to five per cent; Honduras and Guatemala at two to three per cent; and the regional laggard, El Salvador, at around one per cent (though its growth averaged three per cent from 1960 to 2000).[10]

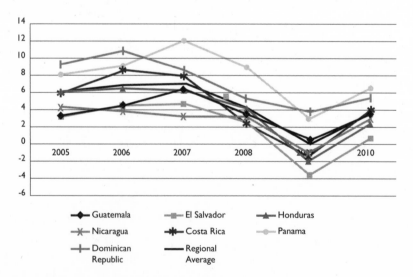

Figure 3: Central America: % GDP Growth, 2005–10

The recent high growth has raised income levels across the region, although there are, as Figure 3 demonstrates, significant divergences in regional wealth and economic drivers. For example, Panama's strengths are built on services, notably transport and banking. The Panama Canal gives it a special development advantage, though its industrial and agricultural sectors are weak. The Dominican Republic, on the other hand, benefits from having a failed state (Haiti) next door, which has offered it counter-cyclical opportunities in, for example, the delivery of humanitarian relief and accessing special preferences into the US market.

Costa Rica has benefited from large-scale investment in education, which, in combination with investor-friendly policies and an aggressive promotion strategy, enabled it to attract half of all foreign direct investment to the region during the 2000s, even though it has a relatively weak infrastructure (apart from energy) and its Doing Business indicators are within the same range as its neighbours.[11] The divergences in wealth and growth rates are partly due to the relative ease of doing business in each area.

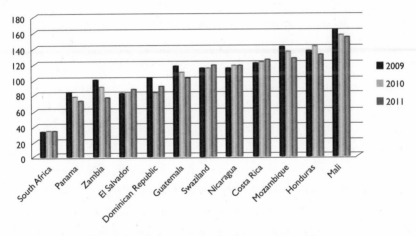

Figure 4: Ease of doing business rankings 2009–11 (higher score = worse)

However, Figure 4 suggests that while governance is important, it is only one of a range of factors encouraging growth and labour absorption. Labour productivity and natural resources are also key. Furthermore, the relatively good performance of some African countries according to these measurements suggests that there is a need to dig behind the facade of an effective state, to questions such as: the extent of state (or political party) involvement among monopolies in the economy;

the legal checks and balances and right of recourse; and the consistency of rules. As noted in Chapter 2, political economies characterised by graft, crony capitalism and rent-seeking are a significant hurdle to investment and growth, closing down the economic space and freedoms necessary for business to compete.

Of course, growth is not the only measure of performance, even though little development progress can be made without it. Costa Rica has benefited from other qualitative factors as well, including political stability, the relative absence of corruption, strong institutions and forward-leaning policies, including an aggressive approach to negotiating bilateral free-trade areas outside the Central American Free Trade Agreement (CAFTA) framework with a variety of partners including China, Singapore, Canada and South Korea.

As will be seen below, Nicaragua has progressed in spite of its Sandinista government's level of rhetoric and polemical links with Hugo Chávez's Venezuela. Indeed, the relationship between government and the private sector is today better than ever before, partly because of the opportunities present in the ties with Venezuela. It is also assisted by generous – moreso than the regional average – preferences into the US market on account of its least-developed status. Agriculture, *maquilas*** and tourism are the key drivers.

Guatemala and Honduras are in the next group. They share the same clear drivers – agriculture and *maquilas*˙ – although they are totally different countries. The former is comparatively sophisticated and developed, with industry comprising no less than a quarter of GDP and an economy six times the size of Nicaragua's. It has the advantage of tourism, from the beaches to the cultural tourism of Antigua and Tikal. It is also the most complex, with an extraordinarily violent civil war in its recent history that cost 200 000 lives, and issues of racial inequality (between Maya and settler) and economic access. As one regional expert put it, 'Guatemala's politics are shaped by clans – among the indigenous population and also among the "whites". Both have networks of association that transcend ideology and define the way business is done and decisions are made.'[12] This is amplified by the drugs phenomenon: in Guatemala the value of the transit drug economy is estimated by some to be as much as twice that of GDP (some US$37 billion).[13]

** *Maquiladora* and *maquila* refer to operations that have duty or tariff treatment. The terms originate with the practice of millers charging a *maquila*, or 'miller's portion', for processing other people's grain. These days they refer to duty-free export-processing zones.

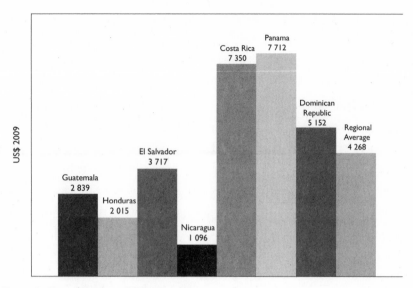

Figure 5: Central America GDP per capita

Honduras has the advantage of geographic location and a good Atlantic port, but, as explained below, the handicap of a poorly educated workforce. These countries have found it very difficult to diversify away from the *maquila* sector: for El Salvador, 70 per cent of exports to the US are apparel; for Honduras, 65 per cent; for Nicaragua, around 50 per cent; and for Guatemala, some 40 per cent. Only Costa Rica breaks the regional trend with less than five per cent of its US exports from this sector. In both Guatemala and Honduras, the institutional fabric is weak. In the former there has been little continuity in the political set-up: all the major parties have a short history, the legislature is very divided and dysfunctional, and a big feature is the political opportunism evinced by the *tránsfugas*, or aisle-crossers. In Honduras, the executive has an all-powerful role, so decisions are apparently taken very easily.

El Salvador is in a growth category all its own. Even though it has a history of strong institutions, it is small and densely populated and possesses few of the agricultural advantages of the region, a weakness exacerbated by the comparatively small size of the farming plots demarcated since land reform in 1980. With a poor natural resource endowment compared to Nicaragua, Guatemala or Honduras, El Salvador has battled to diversify into other service sectors, even though it has a solid banking sector. One reason for this challenge, bankers maintain, is that the highest percentage of loans have gone to private households and consumption, not into businesses. The country's attempts to diversify away from apparel have, as we explain below, also been complicated by a polarised society, defined by strong ideological positions.

Moreover, as in other countries of the region, El Salvador's heavy dependence on remittances has created a dependency and consumption culture, even though it may have cooled otherwise volatile political situations. A Guatemalan businessperson put it this way: 'That we have one million Guatemalans in the United States has helped probably to reduce crime and political violence. But it has also meant that people are less likely to want to get a job when they know that they can get the minimum wage from their cousin remitting money back from New York or wherever. Why should they bother?' he asks.[14] In El Salvador, remittance flows amount to around 17 per cent of GDP, in Honduras 20 per cent, and in both Guatemala and Nicaragua 10 per cent.

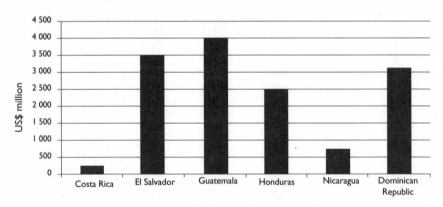

Figure 6: Remittances, 2009

The textiles and garment sector has traditionally been one of the first rungs, if not the very first rung, of the export-led growth strategies of developing nations. Across East (and later South) Asia and Central America, garments have provided the job intensity required both to stabilise societies and to provide a social, educational and financial platform for development. But the experiences are varied: some countries have used the sector as a stepping stone, while others have become stranded, or have even been forced to step backwards.

As noted above, Costa Rica is considered an 'exceptional' case in the region. It is also regarded as the most 'developed' of the Central American countries because it has a relatively high GDP per capita and the best indicators in the region for life expectancy at birth, infant mortality and adult literacy. These achievements are due, in part, because there was no large indigenous population in the area when the Spanish arrived. For all its social and political advantages, including mandatory and free education since 1870 and the disbandment of the army in 1948, Costa Rica did, however, suffer a widespread economic crisis in 1980. As with other performers in the region and beyond, it used the opportunity to implement significant business-minded reforms – it sought in essence to have a 'good' crisis.

The regional norm, a two-tier society with European settler descendants on top and an indigenous population at the bottom, did not evolve then in Costa Rica as it did in Guatemala, El Salvador, Honduras and Nicaragua. Indeed, throughout the Central American region, there has been extraordinary and often institutionalised feudal inequality between the ruling (usually Hispanic) elites, often clustered around a small number of exceptionally wealthy families and an *indigena* underclass.

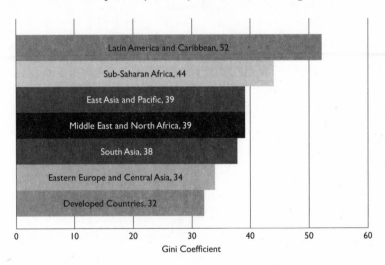

Figure 7: Measuring Inequality (higher = worse)

This difference has been exacerbated by corruption, historical dependence on single commodities (notably bananas and coffee), and relative regional impotence in global markets. In developed countries, the richest 20 per cent (quintile) of the population receives about six times more income than the poorest quintile. The ratio is 10:1 in sub-Saharan Africa and 12:1 in Latin America. In Brazil, the richest quintile receives in excess of 30 times more than the poorest quintile.[15] Africa and Central America rank first and second respectively in terms of inequality, though Africa's poverty levels remain higher, with nearly 50 per cent of the region living in conditions of extreme poverty. Figure 7 illustrates comparative regional inequality levels.[16]

What separates the winners from the losers in Central America?

Monopolies and *maquilas*

Guatemala looks a lot like an African country. Widespread poverty, deep-rooted conflict, a long history of military rule, an export profile historically based on raw materials, deep divisions based on race and violent crime all define its image and reality. Despite all the problems which have undercut its potential, Guatemalan business has competed successfully in specific industrial and services sectors, some of the very areas that Africa will need to engage in if it is to address its jobs crisis. Yet, the country still faces considerable challenges to institutionalising growth.

A drive through Guatemala City – which, by mid-2011, was teeming with nearly four million souls – on the campaign bus of Nineth Montenegro, a human rights activist and three-term congressional representative for Encuentro por Guatemala (the Encounter for Guatemala party), highlighted the problems faced by Central America's largest country. Nineth went into politics when her husband, Fernando Garcia, was 'disappeared' by state agents in February 1984. Just 25 years old at the time and with a young daughter, she took up his case and those of others in her 'struggle for justice' and 'against impunity'. Putting herself through law school and earning a master's degree, she was first elected to Congress in 1996.

Luis Pedro Álvarez, Encuentro's top congressional candidate for Guatemala City, went into politics, he says, because the 'situation is horrendous. Weak institutions are crumbling in the face of the narcos. Traffickers kill with impunity – district attorneys, assistant DAs, lawyers, witnesses. There is a lot of drug money in political parties.' He indicates a billboard from which a prominent leader gazes out over the heads of his electorate.

Luis should know. He has been a criminal lawyer for 12 years, not an occupation known for the longevity of its practitioners in Guatemala. Right behind us is an armoured vehicle with armed guards. 'It has been terrible for me. I have lived in a bulletproof environment all the time; in my car, wearing a vest, carrying a concealed weapon. My family – parents, brothers, sisters, brothers- and sisters-in-law – all live the same way.'

Guatemala's principal challenge is little different to that of other developing countries: how to create a positive cycle of development that promotes stability, attractive policies, and transparency and accountability, which entice investment-generating jobs, greater prosperity and government revenue, thus improving health, infrastructure and education facilities, in turn improving security, and so on. But this virtuous circle remains elusive. Unfortunately, Guatemala's politics is fraught and offers little comfort to business: corruption is a way of life, and government's tax income has hovered around just ten per cent of GDP; state institutions are weak, the education systems poor, skills limited, jobs hard to come by, wealth inequalities great, social cohesion fragmentary at best, and insecurity pervasive. And where the state is weak, others, including the 'narcos', have easily slipped into that ungoverned space. The narco-economy is estimated to be around 20 per cent of the formal economy of some US$38 billion.

This situation relates in part to Guatemala's two societies. Reputedly eight families 'own' the economy – referred to facetiously as the 'G8'. Put differently, 70 per cent of the arable land is in the hands of less than three per cent of the country's population of 14 million. As a result, it is among the world champions of wealth inequality and criminality. In 2006, 56 per cent of people lived below the poverty line, and 16 per cent in extreme poverty. Poverty is also predominantly rural, with 81 per cent of the poor living there, and higher among indigenous groups (76 per cent are poor). And while the wealthiest fifth of the population accounted for 54 per cent of consumption in 2004, the bottom fifth totalled just five per cent.[17] Guatemala ranks as the second-worst in infant mortality in Latin America, behind Haiti, a failed state. 'Yet we are just two hours away from the biggest market in the world,' says Luis Álvarez. 'It's absurd.'

Such inequities explain high levels of lawlessness and murder, lubricated by a battle against drug money and power. Guatemala City has become the murder capital of the world, with over 40 murders a week or more than 80 homicides per 100 000 people annually, more than ten times the global average.[18]

Guatemala has long struggled with the politics of inequality. In 1954, the US Central Intelligence Agency supported a coup out of Honduras led by two exiled Guatemalan officers, aimed at securing banana interests and preventing land reform. The protection of privilege explains, to a large extent, the scale of the upheaval during the civil war, which raged for three decades until a peace accord was finally signed between the government and the URNG (Guatemalan National Revolutionary Unity), a front of four guerrilla organisations formed in 1982. An estimated 40 000 people were killed, mostly civilians, and many by the armed forces, which, in the 1980s, adopted a scorched-earth policy, resulting in the extermination of the inhabitants of 400 villages.

High levels of inequality paralleled racial fault-lines and land distribution, exacerbated by foreign interference. An estimated two-thirds of Guatemalan Maya – broadly defined to include the indigenous population – remain marginalised by poverty, illiteracy and lack of access to medical facilities. As one official from an international financial institution has noted, 'It is still a country, in the rural areas, of owners and slaves.'[19]

As a result, Guatemala has battled to create a convergence around national identity, with wealth divides largely replicating ethnic differences, though there are more complex dynamics to the wealth equation. 'The biggest problem in Guatemala,' argues one observer, 'is that the political parties do not represent the real owners of the country – the sugar barons, the trade unionists and now the drug lords.'

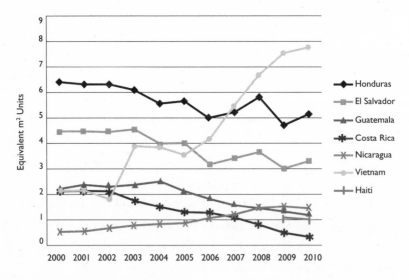

Figure 8: Textile exports to the United States

To this must be added further challenges: half the population is under 30, and only some 20 per cent are in formal-sector employment. As Hugo Maul, an economic analyst, observes, 'The roots of our problems are in Spanish colonialism – of crony capitalism, mercantilism and over-regulation. This makes it costly to comply with regulations for which there are few benefits – hence the preference for informality. But this does not provide a good environment for entrepreneurship to flourish beyond subsistence and survival.'[20]

Rising costs and increases in the minimum wage levels (to US$237 per month plus 60 per cent in benefits) have severely stressed the once-important *maquila* sector, job numbers declining to 90 000[21] by 2011 from a peak of 200 000 a decade earlier. 'We lost these industries,' says Maul, 'because the minimum wage policy is an income policy, not a competitiveness policy.' He maintains that a change in the wage rate and greater flexibility permitting piece rates (payment for production, not time) could create as many as one million *maquila* jobs within ten years.

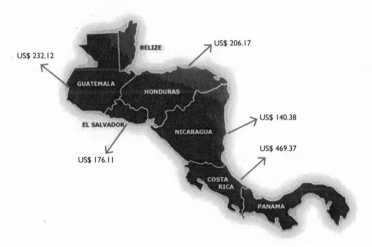

Figure 9: Central American minimum salaries (without benefits), 2011[22]

Guatemala has therefore lost market share to Vietnam and regional competitors, even though it has moved into the higher-end apparel market, producing what is known in the region as the 'full package' of spinning, dying, weaving, printing, designing, cutting, sewing and packaging. By 2011, there were 149 sewing and 37 textile plants, plus 260 associated industries. Two-thirds of sewing factories were Korean-owned and operated, and the bulk of the textile mills Guatemalan.

As a result, non-traditional exports (including services and manufacturing goods) by 2011 amounted to US$6.2 billion, with apparel comprising US$1.4 billion of this total, while traditional exports (coffee, sugar, cardamom and bananas) equalled US$2.3 billion.[23]

There would be more to come if domestic policies aligned to regional and global norms. 'For us,' says Sergio de la Torre, the head of Guatemala's industry body Vestex, 'Vietnam is an example of how fast one can create jobs – one million in just five years.'[24] The industry believes that rising demand in both India and China, coupled with the US market advantages supplied by CAFTA and rising unit costs in China, will produce a bright future. 'But like Vietnam, we need to make a decision as a country to go after the apparel business,' says de la Torre. 'We believe that we can increase direct job numbers in the sector to 125 000 and double exports to US$2.25 billion by 2015' – if Guatemala can improve security and labour flexibility, differentiate salaries (with lower salaries in poorer rural areas), maintain fiscal incentives and lower electricity costs. 'It's not rocket science to create jobs here. It requires security, competitive wages and some basic conditions.'

There have been successes. Annual tourism numbers are about 1.8 million, just below Costa Rica's regional benchmark of 2.1 million, and with some potential for further expansion. Call centres (now termed 'contact' centres) have grown rapidly, with about 10 000 jobs created in the past ten years. This has been on the back of 'wage arbitrage', with wages 35 per cent less than in the United States, Spanish–English bilingualism and low telecom costs.

The latter are the result of an extraordinarily successful liberalisation process that first ended the state telecommunications monopoly and then opened up the sector, contrary to the advice of international experts. With these reforms, Guatemala quickly grew from 300 000 landlines in 1995 to 18 million telephone connections in 2010.[25] The mobile phone experience has shown the importance of leadership, says Alfredo Guzmán who led the privatisation process under President Álvaro Arzú. 'To be in power means to make decisions and to live with them, no matter how unpopular they seem in the short term.' Whereas 80 per cent of telephone connections were in the metropolitan area of Guatemala City in the mid-1990s, today '65 000 rural coffee growers get the New York prices on their BlackBerrys up in the hilltops'.[26]

The greatest limit to the expansion of these centres, which handle everything from computer gaming enquiries to billing for Texas Energy, has been a shortage of English speakers. This constraint has been exacerbated by a high staff turnover (some 25 per cent), though this is an accepted norm in an industry where many of the operators are young, studying part-time and going on to other jobs, and lower than in other centres such as in India (where it is as high as 60 per cent). 'There are few limits to our growth,' says Nevres Genc of Transactel, the largest call centre in Guatemala, which employs 3 000 'agents'. 'We could grow like the Philippines which went from zero to 300 000 in eight years, apart from the number of English speakers.'[27]

Guatemala's challenges thus have similarities to those of some sub-Saharan African countries. These have included higher labour costs than their competitors, a lack of labour market flexibility, unions intent on protecting existing jobs at the expense of creating new ones (especially relevant to South Africa), and the exclusion of a large part of the local economy from both the formal sector and the global economy. Hugo Maul says, 'If you could repeal the labour laws, you would at least get rid of unemployment in the cities.' Others in politically influential positions have agreed on the need for 'very aggressive' investment incentives and a plan to promote them, including a waiver on labour laws for the *maquila* sector, and the need – according to Emmanuel Seidner, an adviser to President Otto Pérez Molina, a former general who took over power in January 2012 – to 'flexibilise' wage levels and institutions.

As a result, there has been a focus on developing the *encadenamientos productivos* – the value chains – of business, ensuring connectivity between businesses and external demands. The business community of Guatemala has, in this regard, worked closely with Harvard University's Center for Global Development to create the conditions to enable the spawning of new businesses. These would include not only new types of industries, but also more traditional sectors such as mining. In addition, reforms need to be aimed, at their core, at improving both hard and soft (especially educational) infrastructure. There is widespread agreement on the need to revamp the educational system, which has been very top-down (the state universities have consumed an extraordinary five per cent of the US$6 billion national budget). Improvements to the educational inspectorate regime are also high on the list of priorities, along with an aggressive approach to energy to bring down costs, which are among the highest in the region.

Monopoly interests, notably the family-run entities that have dominated the banking, cement (as demonstrated in Figure 10), beverage, sugar and even chicken sectors, also need to be confronted. Unsurprisingly it is usually these monopoly interests that preach openness of markets while ensuring their protection – without being aware of this contradiction, even as they express it.

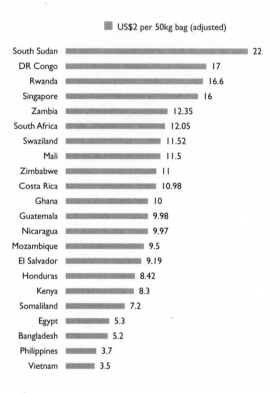

Figure 10: Cement spot prices, June 2011[28]

For progress to be made, it would be necessary to tackle the political-economy issues that have perpetuated Guatemala's two societies: the crony-capitalist cycle that has kept the vast majority outside the formal economy and the government's bias against legitimate business interests. Overall, the political class 'does everything it can to avoid creating employment – and this must be changed,' says Maul. Without these changes, he says, 'we will lose another decade'. Similarly, there is no getting around the need to create conditions of more inclusive growth. Without it, the country will remain two worlds, 'one poorer than Haiti, the other richer than Miami' – the difference on the ground between the classy hotels and restaurants of Zone 10 in Guatemala City and the grinding poverty on the flat highlands of the

Altiplano. Bridging these worlds demands political leadership willing to challenge vested interests and build a capable state. Otherwise, state institutions will remain weak and sections of the population jobless, marginalised and propelled into drug-fuelled criminality.

Peace is the best place to start

El Salvador has been through one of the worst civil wars in Central American history, the cost of thousands of deaths rivalled by that of the physical infrastructure destroyed. Even though economic growth has been lower than elsewhere in the region, the advent of leaders dedicated not only to ending the conflict but, as the cliché has it, also to winning the peace has made a significant difference to levels of poverty.

El Salvador's colonial history, like Guatemala's, is one of oligarchic economic control and the envy, anger, unrest and, ultimately, violence it generates.

In the 1700s, a small group of Spanish descendants – known as the 'fourteen families' – controlled the economy, especially the lucrative indigo trade. As synthetic dyes took over, coffee became the main export crop, accounting for 95 per cent of El Salvador's foreign income by the 20th century and controlled by an estimated two per cent of the population. Uprisings against such inequity occurred sporadically throughout the century, including the infamous *Matanza* (massacre) in 1932 of 30 000 political opponents, notably the opposition socialist politician Agustin Farabundo Martí, executed by firing squad. The Farabundo Martí National Liberation Front (FMLN), founded in 1980, bears his name.

In the 1960s and 1970s, the vehicles for leftist political mobilisation were the so-called mass or popular organisations, drawing their leadership from radical Roman Catholic groups. They sought to establish the conditions for a revolution through public demonstrations, strikes, property seizures and propaganda campaigns. By the 1970s, the civil conflict had developed into a struggle between anti-government guerrillas on one side and the government, paramilitaries and private 'death squads' on the other – the beginning of El Salvador's *tiempos de locura* or 'season of madness'.[29]

In October 1979, a reform-minded *junta* overthrew President Carlos Humberto Romero. The Revolutionary Government Junta (JRG) was inspired by a brand of left-wing politics. Under combined civilian-military leadership, the JRG devised a number of reforms during its tenure, which lasted until the elections of March 1982, including expropriating landholdings greater than 245 hectares. It also nationalised the commercial banking, coffee and sugar industries, while disbanding the Nationalist Democratic Organisation (ORDEN) paramilitary.

But even as these reforms proceeded apace, the war escalated. The assassination of popular opposition cleric Archbishop Óscar Romero while he was celebrating Mass in San Salvador on 24 March 1980 saw the country plunge into violent civil war. His funeral a week later ended in a bloody clash between demonstrators and security forces.

As the violence – which would cost 75 000 lives and displace 25 per cent of the then population of five million over 12 years – erupted, various peace initiatives reaped little reward. Then the 1989 poll ushered into power businessman Alfredo Cristiani, who received 53.8 per cent of the votes, starting 20 years of rule by the Nationalist Republic Alliance (ARENA). With business interests in cotton, coffee and seed, Cristiani had been drawn into politics at the beginning of the 1980s when the FMLN's *campesino* followers, the rural poor dependent on agriculture, began squatting on farms. The UN-supervised and monitored peace process began soon after, in April 1990. On 16 January 1992, the Chapultepec Peace Accords were signed in Mexico, under the terms of which the rebel FMLN became an opposition political party. Conservative presidents followed in the elections of 1994 (Armando Calderón Sol), 1999 (Francisco Guillermo Flores Pérez) and 2004 (Antonio Saca), before former journalist Mauricio Funes broke the run for the FMLN by taking power in June 2009.

Funes, whose brother was killed as a guerrilla in the civil war, was the first FMLN leader not to have fought in the war. He ran a moderate campaign, promising the retention of the US dollar as the official currency (dollarisation took place in 2001 under Flores) and more attention to health care and crime prevention. In spite of this moderation, however, relations with big business, long an ARENA constituency, quickly deteriorated.

El Salvador's accelerated industrialisation began in the 1950s, with government planning in the area around Soyapango down Boulevard del Ejército in San Salvador. These actions were the catalyst for industrial enterprises that grew through a combination of geographic location (being close to the US market) and policy initiatives, though such enterprises generally had their origins in El Salvador's agricultural production. Textiles were linked to the country's once burgeoning cotton production, though volumes declined significantly with land reform and the civil war in the 1980s, when cotton was an easy target for destruction.

The industrialisation process was accelerated with the introduction of *zonas francas* (free zones) in 1991, allowing duty-free imports to be assembled for export. The free zones radically increased the number of garment (or apparel) *maquila* enterprises, along with all the associated support industries such as packaging, in an era long before the term 'clusters' became common. By 2011, there were more than 15 such zones plus a further hundred or so *depósitos para perfeccionamiento activo* (inward processing establishments – DPAs), essentially factories given *zona franca* status.

In the free zones, businesses are exempt from all income taxes and duties, including property taxes, although electricity costs and rentals were charged at market rates. Until the advent of the Funes government, exports also received an incentive – known locally as a 'drawback' – of six per cent of their value as a cash payment, essentially a way of compensating for El Salvador's comparative production and transport inefficiencies. A small portion of the industrial workforce has been unionised.

The textile and garment sector has thus become the largest private sector employer, with nearly 100 000 direct jobs and 180 000 indirect (cluster) positions. It has grown from just US$160 million in exports in 1990 to over US$2.3 billion in 2010. It has sought to exploit all the advantages from El Salvador's proximity to the United States (three days by road and ship from Miami), low labour costs (the minimum monthly wage in the *maquilas* was US$187 plus benefits in 2011) and high productivity.[30] There has been some diversification, notably in electronics, food processing and back offices, though the expansion of the latter sector has been limited by the lack of competent English speakers. But there have been notable successes in the service sector, one of which is Aeroman.

Founded in 1983 as the maintenance arm of TACA, the Salvadoran-based airline, Aeroman has grown into a global service hub which, since 2006, has been owned by the Canadian Aveos group. Having carried out its first heavy maintenance 'D check' on a Boeing 737 in 1987, it executed its 1 000th in February 2011. Although all its work was for TACA until 1996, by 2011 it was a contractual service client of US giants US Airways, JetBlue and Southwest, with a demand beyond its capacity. What are the reasons for its success?

In a situation where a 'heavy' check takes on average 15 000 hours, a discount of US$10 per technician per hour compared to the Salvadoran workers' US counterparts certainly helps. But, said Aeroman CEO Ernesto Ruiz in June 2011, other things are more important for US customers, notably quality and turnaround time. 'For Third World customers, however, cost is the most important issue.' However, this does not explain how Aeroman got to its current market position. Success was ultimately due to a significant investment in training, recruiting technicians from technical schools and universities, and a cautious approach to growing the business – from 30 employees at start-up to 150 in 1987, 400 in 1991, 700 in 1996, 1 000 in 2006 and 1 800 five years later.

Fortuitous timing also played its part. Ruiz notes: 'The decision by TACA in 1998 to move from five aircraft types to a single aircraft type, the Airbus A320, left us with surplus capacity – in fact, 75 per cent surplus capacity. Thus we were forced to go out to the market to satisfy our capacity.'

The government has provided both direct and indirect assistance, the former by paying for the reinforced maintenance ramp in front of the hangars. But indirect assistance has been more important. The International Services Law, introduced in 2006, exempts the operation from VAT and from import and export duties and procedures, speeding up the delivery of parts and thus aeroplanes. Instead of customs holding up parts for three to five days, as in Mexico or Brazil, they can be delivered straight to the Aeroman facility at the airport.

Aeroman has shown that it is possible to move from a *maquila* low-wage export industry to a high-tech one quickly. But it does not happen overnight. It takes time and careful processes, not least international safety audits averaging one a week, to build customer confidence. And the company's competitiveness comes partly from El Salvador's strategic location, but also from being able to offer comparable skills at low prices. Even though starting technicians earn three times what they would in a *maquila*, US$600–US$700 monthly is well below the asking rates of their US counterparts. Adding just 150 workers annually has kept Aeroman's average experience level to about four years, while standards are kept high. Certification by a range of agencies and airlines does not come easily, nor does selection as one of 16 founder members of the Airbus MRO (Maintenance, Repair and Overhaul) network. As Ruiz reflects, 'It takes a long time to develop the skills we have, which are based on training, which, in turn, requires massive investment.' His Dutch chief operating officer comments on the work ethic and discipline of the workforce: instead of being unionised, they have 'a career plan with certain rules and promotion steps, and we pay above the market rate'. Aeroman's success is a lesson in building a business by taking a long-term view and not attempting to milk the operation for all its worth in a get-rich-quick scheme.

As president of a country 'coming out of war with a bad reputation', Alfredo Cristiani saw the need to get into 'high labour intensive industry, the *maquilas*, and agro-industry beyond just producing food'. He reflects: 'Although [global competitiveness guru] Harvard's Michael Porter told us that Latin American competitiveness could be found in the agro-industry, it has been difficult for us to get beyond traditional agricultural practices given the small size of our farms.' But these issues pale, he says, by comparison to what the country faced by the end of the 2000s. 'The reason for the war was a lack of political space, where the losers never left office or ever, in fact, lost. In the absence of electoral possibilities and with the violation of human rights by the army, people picked up weapons. Today, too, we need to promote political and economic space for the country to develop. However, this [FMLN] government is instead thinking of price controls, or bigger and stronger government, where government, not business, is at the centre, monopolising things. We are doing the opposite to what is needed to end our crisis: spending less and investing more.'

These dynamics translate into considerable contemporary problems for the industrial and services sector, notably the relationship between the government and the private sector, with the latter viewed by the former as inextricably linked to ARENA – and until now largely behaving as such. Tensions have been evident, such as in the summary manner in which the drawback subsidy of six per cent of exports was withdrawn, and in the challenge of getting the government to respond to business concerns – or even plans. For example, the National Association of Private Enterprise (ANEP) in 2011 outlined a plan to create more than 200 000 new jobs with US$4.2 billion of fresh investment in textiles, tourism, construction and other sectors, in return for which it asked the government for 'greater labour flexibility, better security, and "cleaner" rules'. However, the government's response was less than enthusiastic. There apparently was little trust and common ground.

El Salvador's low economic growth rate does not entirely square with the inroads made into poverty, which is less than half its 1991 peak of some two-thirds of the population.[31] This progress reflects, in part, the peace dividend – and also, in part, various government plans, including the emphasis on educational and health spending and, since 2004, the Solidarity Network scheme, which distributed between US$15 and US$20 monthly to the poorest households. The expansion of the *maquilas* has been part of the economic advances, as has the creation of other services such as Aeroman and the building of a tourism industry partly through the positioning of San Salvador's airport, with TACA, as the regional hub. The election of President Funes in 2009 has, however, illustrated the need for El Salvador's business community to keep a critical distance from the government, criticising it whenever its interests are threatened, and working with it regardless of political views.

From *maquilas* to charter cities

Honduras is one of the most violent societies in Latin America. Adversely affected by neighbouring wars, foreign intervention and, more recently, the drug trade, the stability of its economy has traditionally relied on the external pricing of agricultural products. In spite of this legacy, and the violence and the accompanying social division, Honduras has grown its textile industry to compete with Asian countries, a competitiveness based on labour productivity, legislation and infrastructure. It has not stopped there, and has ambitious plans to progress beyond this bottom rung of diversification by, among other things, building whole new cities that operate under a set of laws different from national rules and explicitly geared to attracting foreign investment.

The dead aircraft park at Honduras' Toncontín International Airport in the capital of Tegucigalpa hints at the rough history of this Central American country. Old propeller-driven Douglas DC3s, DC4s and DC6s mingle with ancient Fairchild C123s, some *sans* engines, the mould growing on their fuselages, hinting that most will never again take to the skies. Whatever the state of the hardware, the role of the military in Honduran politics has persisted.

Honduras is the original banana republic. By 1913, bananas comprised two-thirds of Honduran exports, dominated by the Vaccaro brothers (later to become

Standard Fruit) and the United Fruit Company (part of the multinational Chiquita brand). By the end of the First World War, not only did US companies hold three-quarters of Honduran lands, but their influence on local politics was pervasive. In 1911 and 1912 US president William Taft sent marines into Honduras to protect banana interests. The 17-year dictatorship of General Tiburcio Carías Andino ended in 1949, when US pressure forced him out. Military coups followed in 1956, 1963, 1975 and 1978, after which multiparty elections occurred in 1981.

But the military remained massively influential, especially since the country was surrounded by conflict in the 1980s – in Nicaragua, Guatemala and El Salvador. Power rested with the chief of the armed forces, General Gustavo Álvarez, who was responsible for increased US involvement through bases on Honduran territory to support the *Contras* in neighbouring Nicaragua, and for the formation of the notorious Battalion 3-16, which 'disappeared' domestic political enemies.

Although the bases and Álvarez were both gone by 1990 and civilian rule consolidated, the country remained beset by criminality and economic problems, and, in 2009, by political crisis. President Manuel Zelaya, who had gone ahead with his referendum plan on a constituent assembly despite a Supreme Court ruling to the contrary, was removed by the military on the Supreme Court's instruction in June 2009.

With Zelaya exiled to Costa Rica in his pyjamas, Roberto Micheletti, the former president of the Honduran Congress and a member of Zelaya's party, was sworn in as president by the National Congress on 28 June 2009. Amidst domestic and international outcry and threats of military action by Venezuelan president Hugo Chávez, the National Party's Porfirio 'Pepe' Lobo Sosa easily won the subsequent November 2009 election. A one-time left-wing student leader who had moved to the right, Lobo was sworn into office in January 2010 as Zelaya went into exile, ending seven months of political chaos. President Lobo promised to form a unity government, launching a national dialogue aimed at overcoming the crisis, and to boost investment, jobs and security for Honduras' eight million people.

Such political intrigue obscures the progress that Honduras has made over the past two decades in diversifying its economy. The second city of San Pedro Sula, housing 850 000, has become the centre of a giant *maquila* enterprise, creating over 130 000 jobs in 20 years. Honduras has become in the process Central America's largest textile and clothing exporter to the United States, and the third-largest worldwide (behind China and Bangladesh), making everything from designer clothing to parachutes and car seat belts. Exports have grown from US$113 million, when the *maquilas* first started in 1990, to more than US$3.6 billion in 2008. By mid-2011 there were 253 companies producing goods and services within these free zone 'parks'.

The *maquila* industry has been built on the advantages of location (being just 1 600 km, or two days' sail, from Miami), infrastructure (having the most modern Atlantic port in Central America at Puerto Cortés, linking the *maquilas* in a 45 km *canal seco* or dry canal – a road route, in other words – to San Pedro Sula) and a labour force of 2.8 million willing to work for competitive rates in the absence of other opportunities.

The *maquilas* have been completely exempt from all taxes, with no restrictions on capital repatriation or, unusually, on local sales. The minimum wage was, as at 2012, kept under US$200, and further discounted through the employment of up to 40 per cent of workers as 'part-time' – essentially with fewer benefits. The industry association also offered a cheap (US$1 000) and reasonably quick (two-and-a-half-month) registration process. And up to ten per cent of the workforce was automatically allowed to be foreign.

Honduras' manufacturing sector was small at the start of the 1990s, contributing just 15 per cent of GDP. From employing just 16 000 workers in 1991 in one free zone, 20 years later there were 17 such zones, the vast majority (80 per cent) of those employed being in textiles, garments or leather, with just under ten per cent in electrical goods, notably car wiring harnesses.

Honduras has also worked to position itself as being 'open for business', based around two strategic elements: first, positioning Honduras as the most competitive regional economy, and, second, identifying key areas for growth and directly targeting big-ticket foreign firms (and their principals) to set up operations in Honduras.

As part of the first element, Honduras has offered the lowest logistics costs in the region, actively using them to advertise and promote inward investment opportunities. Regardless, it has faced a major challenge common to many developing countries: there has been no quick-fix development solution, so considerable political resolve has been required to stay the low-wage steady upliftment course. 'Over the last 25 years,' says Helmis Cárdenas of the ESA Consultancy in

Tegucigalpa, 'the teachers' unions have been fighting government over salaries and for political reasons. This has resulted in some schools having 120-day class years, with people coming out of school in the sixth grade scarcely being able to read a paragraph. The government has attempted to establish a standard for the primary sector, but there has been no agreement. Instead, the standards have been left up to the teachers, many of whom have few skills themselves, and who teach subjects and curricula at their preference. The result is a disaster.'

In addition, attempts to diversify via agro-processing, for example, have had to deal with the shortage of cold-storage facilities, among other infrastructural constraints including electricity.[32] Yet these physical challenges are relatively easily overcome. Much more challenging has been the need to improve the quality of institutions and deal with corruption and violence. In 2010, Honduras had one of the highest recorded homicide rates in the world: 66.8 homicides per 100 000 people. This had climbed from 46.2 homicides per 100 000 people in 2006. From 2006 to 2010, 18 500 people were murdered in Honduras.[33]

Recognising the importance of creating the right legislative conditions, the Honduran government has actively pursued the 'charter city' concept, essentially making the legal and tax environment in Honduras – or parts of it – akin to Singapore or Hong Kong, the aim being to replicate 'the transformation of Hong Kong, from a small colonial outpost with little going for it, to a dynamic economy'. In August 2011, the Congress of Honduras amended its constitution and passed legislation creating a new legal entity, the special development region (RED). Under this framework, the citizens in a RED area could choose their own system of economic policy, becoming anything from a special economic zone under national rule to a semi-autonomous zone à la Hong Kong. Vital to the start-up of each RED was a nine-member transparency commission, empowered to hire and fire government, negotiate treaties and conclude cooperative agreements in these areas.

Those who point out the downsides of the *maquilas* for Honduras (and elsewhere in the region) have stressed the lack of loyalty owed by foreign manufacturers to any particular country site or commitment to the creation of permanent infrastructure and employment. They go where the wages are lowest and incentives the greatest. They also question whether new employment is enough to offset the loss of jobs in the more traditional manufacturing sector, given that the *maquilas*, allowed to supply goods locally, have undercut smaller Honduran producers. But this is, more positively, because the *maquiladoras'* relatively high wages (US$8 per day) have pushed up wages paid by the smaller firms.

Whatever the downsides, the US$3 billion in exports and 130 000 jobs which Honduras did not have before are a compelling argument in favour of the shift to low-wage *maquila* production. Honduras shows that attracting foreign investors requires the creation of an environment at least as competitive as others, including special economic zones. Without this approach, and with limited state resources in a difficult and violent environment, only future progress will be difficult.

Nicaragua's pragmatic schizophrenia

A Cold War liberation icon, Nicaragua has trodden the same path as many African countries, albeit with a greater stated antagonism to the market. Its leaders have learned, though, the cost of such choices, and while still romantically clinging to the rhetoric of the 1980s, operate with greater pragmatism today. Where there were once dreams of collectives, now there are textile factories with plans to diversify into services, and for greater private-sector-led linkages into the global economy. However, instead of socialist visions, the political economy has also degenerated into efforts by politicians to get rich.

An archway on the road from the airport into downtown Managua reads 'Bienvenido a Hugo Chávez'. There is little doubt that the Latin strongman is popular here, probably more than he is in his own country. His following harks back to the revolutionary days of the Sandinista government in the 1980s, when this small Central American state of just six million people was a centrepiece of the Cold War. The radical left-wing government was funded by Cuba and the Soviet Union, and the opposition *Contras* by the United States. Chávez's local popularity is also related to the US$800 million he provides annually (as a 24-year nearly interest-free loan) to the Sandinistas in the form of oil. The Nicaraguans sell this on, with half of the proceeds returning to Venezuela and the remainder being distributed by the Sandinistas in Nicaragua to various social projects for the poor, including housing, health, farming and electricity.

Still, it is a misleading banner. For the Cold War leftist icon has been, under the Sandinistas, making progress by adopting the very capitalist policies it once so reviled. As Bayardo Arce Castaño, one of three remaining Sandinista *Comandantes* (out of the original nine), and the economic and financial adviser to President

Daniel Ortega, says 'The revolution is not over. It is now happening by other means.'[34]

In the early 20th century, Nicaragua was known for America's military involvement, as the superpower installed and backed various regimes, focusing on control of the territory as a possible Atlantic–Pacific canal site. Direct rule changed to indirect control with the withdrawal of the US marines in 1933 and the seizing of power by the head of the National Guard, Anastasio Somoza Garcia, in 1937. Somoza removed all opponents (including, famously, liberal politician Augusto Sandino, by having him killed on the way home from a dinner they had had together). He amassed considerable personal wealth over the next 20 years, while the majority of Nicaraguans remained then, as today, poverty-stricken.

Somoza himself was assassinated in Léon on 21 September 1956 by the poet Rigoberto López Pérez, to whom there is a large monument in Managua displaying Jefferson's words: 'The tree of liberty must be refreshed from time to time with the blood of patriots and tyrants.' Somoza was replaced by his elder son, Luis. He, in turn, was succeeded in 1967 by his younger brother, Anastasio. At that time, the Sandinista National Liberation Front (FSLN) had been formed around students and other activists. By the mid-1970s, a campaign of retributive violence had taken hold. The January 1978 assassination of the editor of the *La Prensa* newspaper and head of the united opposition, Pedro Joaquín Chamorro, led to widespread strikes and street violence. Revolts were met with the shelling of major towns by the National Guard. On 17 July 1979, a war that had cost the lives of more than 50 000 people, ended as Somoza resigned the presidency and fled. Like his father, though, he was to be assassinated – shot in exile in Paraguay by a Cuban-trained Argentine agent.

After 40 years of steady economic growth under Somoza, a widespread failure to plant crops caused the economy suffer a traumatic 30 per cent decline in 1978 and 1979, from which it has battled to recover. By 2009, GNP per capita had only climbed back to the level of 1952. An already dire situation was compounded by across-the-board nationalisation and land seizures, leading to resistance among the conservative peasantry and giving rise to the *Contra* movement. The Sandinista government created, in the words of one of its close adherents, Dionisio Marenco, 'an economic earthquake'.

American president Ronald Reagan's strategy to stop Soviet influence in

America's backyard led him not only to suspend aid to Nicaragua but also to give financial support to the *Contras* operating out of Honduras and, later, Costa Rica. The trade embargo that followed forced the Nicaraguan economy into desperate straits. When the democratic option became available, a fatigued population voted Daniel Ortega's government out in February 1990. The damage done was considerable: when the Sandinistas seized power in 1979, the state made up just one-fifth of the economy; at the end of the 1980s, this share had increased to 80 per cent, while annual inflation was at 33 000 per cent, forcing the printing presses of the central bank to work overtime.

The chastened revolutionary was replaced by Violeta Barrios de Chamorro, widow of the assassinated newspaper editor. However, the subsequent 17 years of liberal economic reform still did not yield the hoped-for results. Shrugging off a family sex scandal, Ortega took over once more in the 2007 elections, this time recasting himself as a member of the new-wave Bolivarian Revolution led by Chávez.

Whatever the government and the polemic, the roots of Nicaragua's crisis have scarcely been addressed since the days of Somoza. Nicaragua has remained a traditional society with very low levels of productivity, and with the outlook of Nicaraguans mostly shaped by their immediate, rather than long-term, needs.[35] Even after continuous reforms and with greater openness to the global economy, poverty declined merely from 50 per cent in 1993 to 47 per cent in 2006. Growth has remained erratic and susceptible to external shocks, while 'people's expectations overwhelm the [state's] capacity to deliver'.[36] A further indicator of performance is the number of Nicaraguan emigrants: 900 000 (out of a population of seven million) departed between 1978 and 1999, and 700 000 from 2000 to 2006, mainly to neighbouring Costa Rica. Some chickens have come home to roost. In the brief interval between electoral defeat and departure from office in 1990, the Sandinistas redistributed land to political cronies, among others, in a process dubbed *La Piñata*, the grab-bag. Thus, some title is held by several different people, complicating long-term financing, even though it buoyed short-term, clientalistic support for the party.

But there has been a silver lining. The once arch-imperialist enemy, the United States, has become the key market for Nicaragua. Although foreign aid has become a social buffer, it has not been used as the principal tool of development.

Rather, the main sources of foreign income, for a country with a GDP of little more than US$6 billion, are, as of 2012, agriculture (mainly coffee, sugar, meat and bananas, some US$2 billion), garments (US$1 billion), tourism (US$500 million) and remittances (US$800 million). The *maquila* garment industry, which has benefitted from least-developed-country status, allowing access to the US market under CAFTA using third-country-supplied cloth, employs nearly 100 000 workers, and has proven itself to be, in the words of the head of the local business council, 'the most important formal employment generation tool. There is no place to go other than this sector for this number of jobs.' As Comandante Bayardo puts it, 'This sector generates employment, and that's what enables the economy to get on track. Sometimes we have to take bitter pills, and one of those is the *zona franca* (free zone) companies. They are like sparrows. They come and go. But they create employment.' Or, in the words of his Cuban-trained Sandinista colleague Dominisio Marenca, 'There is no choice. It is jobs in the factory or nothing in the street.' Less than one-quarter of the 2.5 million-strong workforce is employed in the formal sector.

Tourism has also grown at around 17 per cent annually over the past decade on the back of comparatively low costs (US$70 per tourist per day, about half Costa Rica's figure) and the rich variety of offerings, from the colonial city of Granada to the beaches and eco-lodges on the southern Pacific coast around San Juan del Sur. However, growth has required getting the basics in place. Mario Arana, the former minister of economy and head of the central bank under Enrique Bolaños, Nicaragua's president from 2001 to 2007, and, by 2011, head of the Nicaraguan Foundation for Economic and Social Development (FUNIDES), says that three issues had to be tackled during his time in government: reducing the high (six per cent) fiscal deficit, and improving both transparency and 'institutionality', which included depoliticising the bureaucracy.

Growth has also required changing the relationship between business and government. Under Somoza, the interests of the oligarchs were seen as inseparable from those of the regime. Under the Sandinistas, there was no relationship. In this new era there has been greater maturity, to good and bad effect. The business body COSEP (Superior Council of Private Enterprise) has met monthly with the president, and it has been possible to negotiate even the most difficult of issues, such as wage increases, in a consensual manner and for the long term. 'There is much greater engagement now with government,' says the head of COSEP, José Adán Aguerri. 'In 2008, I used to sit down with President Ortega to discuss issues including minimum wage negotiations. Even though we didn't get what we wanted, he changed the way he saw the private sector. Then we lost 25 000 *maquila* jobs in 2008. He then understood more than ever the need to collaborate with the private sector and protect employment, not wages.'[37] COSEP has even negotiated as part of the government team with the EU. Of course the ageing Sandinistas have also profited from their political access as the available vehicle for personal social and economic mobility.

Under Ortega, the government has skilfully played both sides. It has a long-term programme with the IMF, and meanwhile gets assistance from Venezuela. 'The government is much more friendly than its rhetoric suggests,' says one international observer. 'It meets regularly with big business, communicates with businessmen on first-name terms, and takes care not to compromise "the macro".'

However, Nicaragua's stability is fragile. 'The biggest source of employment in Nicaragua is outside Nicaragua,' Marenca contends. External support has depended on Chávez's generosity and longevity. The health of its main manufacturing sector hinges on continued US demand. With more than a million Nicaraguans in Costa Rica, any change in relations with or conditions in its southern neighbour could destabilise this source of income. Poverty, as noted, remains widespread. Whether the Sandinistas' contemporary pragmatism would survive an extreme external shock is moot.

Yet there are few alternatives to the Sandinista's 21st-century policy course. Poor levels of education make rapid diversification into other higher-yield areas of manufacturing problematic and probably long-term. 'We invest US$100 annually per capita in social spending while Costa Rica invests seven times that amount,' reflects Mario Arana. The high cost of energy has also been recognised as a developmental constraint by a government that is committed to turning round the ratio of thermal to renewable energy from its current 80:20. While some dream of recreating the Morgan Canal concept mooted in the 1800s as an alternative to the Panama route, linking the Pacific and Atlantic via Lake Nicaragua, more important (and realistic) is the prospect of opening up the Atlantic Mosquito Coast, where there is scarcely a road, let alone a port worthy of the name. Its isolation, along with the relatively effective Sandinista intelligence service, has helped ensure that the narcos have not so far, as in Guatemala or Honduras, threatened the state, but the area has paradoxically remained an untapped economic resource. 'The east is a world apart from the rest of Nicaragua,' says one international specialist based in Managua. 'The 400 km there will take at least nine hours. But there are other areas that need investment. The route to San José is only 350 km, but will take you also nine hours. There is only one viable port currently, Chinandega in the north-west on the Pacific, and that only handles 20 per cent of imports.'

Given Nicaragua's constraints, especially in education, the choices in dealing with the country's development challenges rest in practice rather than rhetoric; in improving the productivity of what it already does rather than looking for radical changes or new paradigms. 'We are not going to be Costa Rica. We are going to continue to rely on the rural sector,' says José Adán. 'But we need to increase productivity first rather than try to improve the extent of value we add.'

In the longer term, however, there are more profound choices, which resonate with many African countries. If growth is 'a necessary but insufficient' condition for development, the other factors have to include the more difficult process of building institutions, ensuring the rule of law, and realising that opposition is good for the country. 'The quality of spending remains very low in government, which requires regular auditing,' says one analyst. But most importantly, he adds, 'There is a need for consensus on how democracy works and the need for alternatives, otherwise there will inevitably be a crisis of succession, accountability and good ideas.'

Costa Rican exceptionalism

Costa Rica has long been the front-runner of diversification efforts in Central America, a performance that reflects long-standing civilian rule and a commitment to demilitarisation and spending on education. But this has been matched by brave and sound policy choices by politicians, and their attention to detail in the execution of these plans.

Costa Rica has shown what can be achieved in going from an agricultural to a high-tech and services base – from coffee and bananas to computer chips, medical equipment and high-quality services. Exports rose from US$870 million in the early 1980s to US$9.3 billion in 2010 – extraordinary for an economy of 4.5 million people. These achievements have been built on openness to trade and capital, by 'Ticos', as Costa Ricans call themselves, using their heads and good policy as the principal tools. The example of Costa Rica also shows how collaboration with experienced businesspeople is crucial to creating a supportive and mutually reinforcing business environment.

Costa Rica's success is built on its historical exceptionalism. In short, Spain largely avoided the territory, given its small indigenous population (and thus limited labour and slavery prospects) and lack of gold, despite its name, which means 'Rich Coast'. The small local population at the time of colonisation also resulted in far greater homogeneity. More recently, in 1949, Costa Rica's army was disbanded at the end of a short but brutal civil war. The region's subsequent travails with virtually endemic civil wars and military *coups d'état* ratified the wisdom of that decision. And since 1868, education has been both mandatory and free, which has led to the emergence of a large middle class, estimated at 80 per cent of the population. The country has far less obvious inequality and display of wealth than other countries of Central America. There is also a universal health care system.

The results are impressive. Bananas and coffee once made up 80 per cent of exports. By 2011, the country exported more bananas than ever for more money, but their share of overall exports had declined to just ten per cent. Costa Rica was exporting 4 255 different products to 148 countries by the end of the 2000s, and exports have grown at an average annual rate of 7.1 per cent since 2001, representing 26 per cent of GDP. Free-trade agreements with the United States (under CAFTA), Mexico, Canada, Chile, Peru, the EU and China have been a key strategic dimension of this expansion.

The economy has followed a steady progression from garment-producing free-trade zone *maquilas* in the 1980s to higher-tech back-office computer and electronic equipment production, starting in the late 1990s. As production climbed the rungs of industrial sophistication, the number of *maquila* sector jobs in the garment sector shrank to 10 000 by 2011, with US$200 million in exports, from a peak of 35 000 and US$900 million.

The signal event in getting out of *maquilas* was the investment by Intel in a computer chip factory in 1997, the result of a two-year wooing process, with the president at the forefront. In 2010, Intel accounted for ten per cent of goods and services exports, some US$1.4 billion. Similarly, pharmaceutical multinational Procter & Gamble (P&G) set up its accounting facilities for the Americas in Costa

Rica in 1999 with 200 staff. This led the way for the arrival of computer giants Hewlett-Packard (7 000 staff by 2011) and IBM (2 000). As Bill Merrigan, general manager of P&G's operations in Costa Rica, says, 'This track record shows the power of getting one good company to believe.'

The number of companies in the advanced manufacturing sector (notably in computers and medical technology) has grown from five (with 4 500 jobs) in 2000 to 59 (15 159) in 2010; and in services from five (1 061 jobs) to 113 (31 747) over the same period. Total foreign direct investment inflows have grown an average of 13.5 per cent every year since 2000.[38]

By 2011, the minimum wage was more than US$700 (including benefits), though wages have steadily increased well above this figure, given increasing labour demands and improving skill levels. Whereas P&G had 70 expatriates when its staff in Costa Rica numbered just 400, it had just ten by the time the local workforce reached 1 400.

However, success is not just down to the new arrivals. Existing companies have also transformed along with the business environment. The world's largest tyre company, Bridgestone, has had manufacturing facilities in Costa Rica for 44 years, under the Firestone brand until 1988. Its general manager, Oscar Rodríguez, is proud to point out that his plant has the lowest absenteeism and highest productivity across the group's factories in Latin America. The 1 056 workers at his 24/7 plant produce 12 500 tyres daily. Venezuela, from where he hails, produces 8 000 tyres with 1 300 workers.

The difference, he says, is due to the absence of unions 'which fight the company for the worker'. Costa Rica has instead 'solidarist associations', in essence unions of mutual interest between workers and management 'which fight for the interests of the company'. These organisations have, since their inception in the 1950s, eclipsed unions except in the public sector. They handle countrywide US$5 billion in redundancy funds, equivalent to a month's pay per worker per year. The funds are invested by the workers (not by management) and used for social tasks and, ultimately, payouts on retirement. Critically, they give workers and management (who are also members, but are not allowed to manage the funds), as well as the company, a vested interest in the company's well-being. The associations have transformed employee–employer relations in Costa Rica for the better in the past half century.

At the core of growth and prosperity has been the education system. For example, more than 60 per cent of Bridgestone's wage-earning workforce have a high-school or tertiary qualification; that figure rises to 79 per cent for the salaried staff. Indeed, the World Economic Forum's Global Competitiveness Index (measuring institutions, policies and practices correlated with growth) rates Costa Rica very highly. There are problems, of course, some of which are highlighted in the Doing Business indicators discussed earlier in this chapter. Powerful monopolies have remained in agriculture (especially rice), telecoms, and energy. The government has also recognised the need to increase the number of science and mathematics graduates. 'In Finland, 98 per cent of high school students go to university,' says Anabel González, the minister of external trade. 'In Singapore and Ireland this figure is 60 per cent. In Costa Rica it is just 20 per cent. But it is not just the volume. Some 30 per cent of students in Singapore, Ireland and Finland study maths and science. In Costa Rica it's just 12 per cent.'

As a result, Costa Rica has turned its attention to what sort of economy it needs to become within a generation in order to be competitive. In addition to the education and skills focus, the government intends to improve what it is already doing in back-office services, while moving into new areas of business processing, reducing inefficiencies in the economy, particularly in energy and agriculture, and expanding service activities with new partners, potentially in China and elsewhere in Asia. Costa Rica, Minister González points out, is thinking about the conditions that will enable a further generation of reforms and growth over the next 20 years.

Costa Rica's formula for diversification and success has served it well over the past generation. Those who favour the 'old model' of a closed economy and vested interests have lost the battle against supporters of the 'new model', which represent the global route to prosperity. In the process, a new middle class has been created in Costa Rica that is no longer dependent on the state for a job and intent on protecting that job at the cost of modernisation and growth. This success should prompt other states to think about the conditions necessary to attract such investment.

Overturning patronage politics

Whatever their challenges, Central American countries show that progress can be made by dedicated leaders who overturn the patterns and pathologies of patronage politics and state behaviour. In contrast to the pessimism about export diversification commonly found in Africa and among Africa's partners, these countries have all broken into new international products and markets, reducing their dependence on commodities and setting the stage for new elites to emerge with independent power bases. However, the Central American nations are not the first to have done this, and neither are they the most successful. That honour goes to the set of countries we turn to next.

Endnotes

1   Where other sources are not cited, this section is based on interviews conducted during a research visit to the region in June and July 2011: El Salvador (June), Honduras (June), Guatemala (June), Nicaragua (June and July) and Costa Rica (July).

2   Discussion, Guatemala City, 28 June 2011.

3   Discussion, Guatemala City, 27 June 2011.

4   Map No 3977, Rev 4, UNITED NATIONS, May 2010.

5   http://mexidata.info/id2821.html.

6   http://en.centralamericadata.com/en/article/home/The_Power_of_Central_Americas_Drug_Traffickers.

7   Discussion, Tegucigalpa, June 2011.

8   http://en.wikipedia.org/wiki/List_of_countries_by_intentional_homicide_rate.

9   Discussion, Guatemala City, 27 June 2011.

10 This figure is sourced from information supplied by Luis Membreno Consulting.

11 http://www.doingbusiness.org/rankings.

12 Discussion, Antigua, 26 June 2011.

13 http://en.centralamericadata.com/en/article/home/The_Power_of_Central_Americas_Drug_Traffickers.

14 Discussion, Guatemala City, 27 June 2011.

15 http://www.worldbank.org/depweb/beyond/beyondco/beg_05.pdf.

16 http://www.thedialogue.org/PublicationFiles/Social%20Policy%20Brief%20No%201%20-%20Poverty%20and%20Inequality%20in%20LAC.pdf.

17 Hela Cheikhrouhou, Rodrigo Jarque, Raúl Hernández-Coss, and Radwa El-Swaify, 'The US–Guatemala Remittance Corridor: Understanding Better the Drivers of Remittances Intermediation', *World Bank Working Paper No. 86*, 2006.

18 At http://www.fco.gov.uk/en/travel-and-living-abroad/travel-advice-by-country/north-central-america/guatemala.

19 Discussion, Guatemala City, 28 June 2011.

20 Discussion, Guatemala City, 27 June 2011.

21 As of June 2011, there were 59 043 employees in 149 apparel factories, plus 18 500 in 37 textile producers. These figures were supplied by Emmanuel Seidner of the Partido Patriota (Patriotic Party).

22 This was supplied by Vestex, Guatemala City, 28 June 2011. The benefits amount to: 59.23 per cent in Honduras; 62.06 per cent in Guatemala; 42.64 per cent in El Salvador; 52.47 per cent in Costa Rica; and 53.30 per cent in Nicaragua.

23 'Guatemala en la Encrucijada,' *El Economista*, 4(42), June 2011.

24 Interview, Vestex, Guatemala City, 28 June 2011.

25 Discussion, Alfredo Guzmán, Guatemala City, 27 June 2011.

26 Discussion, Lissa Hanckel, Antigua, 26 June 2011.

27 Discussion, Guatemala City, 27 June 2011.

28 This information was gathered during personal visits to stores in these countries in June and July 2011.

29 Todd Greentree, *Crossroads of Intervention: Insurgency and Counterinsurgency Lessons from Central America*. Maryland: Naval Institute Press, 2008.

30 In 2011, Salvadoran apparel workers produced an average of ten dozen items in an eight-hour shift. The equivalent figure for Guatemala was 60 per cent of that (though the price on the T-shirts produced at this rate in Guatemala was twice as high, given greater value addition, including pockets, printing, piping and collars).

31 http://siteresources.worldbank.org/INTPGI/Resources/342674-1115051237044/ oppgelsalvador.pdf.

32 Discussion, Helmis Cárdenas, Tegucigalpa, 24 June 2011.

33 http://www.hondurasweekly.com/ honduras-posts-highest-murder-rate-in-central-america-201004052479/.

34 Interview, Managua, 30 June 2011.

35 Discussion, Arturo Cruz, former Nicaraguan Ambassador to Washington, Conference on Economic Populism, Como, Italy, October 2010.

36 *Ibid.*

37 Discussion, Managua, 29 June 2011.

38 This information was supplied by CINDE, Costa Rica's investment promotion board.

4

WHAT CAN BE LEARNED FROM ASIA?

The comparison between Asian and African countries at independence is an old chestnut. In 1965, for example, Nigeria had a higher per capita GDP than Indonesia: by 1997, just before the financial crash, Indonesia's per capita GDP had risen to more than three times that of the former British colony. Ghana, the first British colonial state in Africa to acquire independence, had a higher GNP per capita in 1957 than South Korea. In 2011, according to the IMF, the average income of South Koreans (US$20 591) was about 16 times that of Ghanaians (US$1 312), the former well above and the latter well below the global average of US$9 218. When Malaysia gained independence in 1957, it had a per capita income less than that of Haiti. But at the end of the 20th century, when Haiti was the poorest country in the Americas (with a per capita income of US$673), Malaysia (US$8 423) had a standard of living higher than that of any major economy in that region, save for the US and Canada.[1] Comparisons between Asia and Africa are stark even in the case of countries with similarities in their economic make-up and political histories, such as Indonesia and Nigeria.

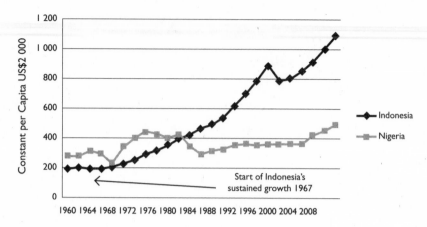

Figure 1: Where it went wrong[2]

For some, including Hans Rosling, this is a spurious comparison, given the differences in history. 'Korea was a unified nation, with a thousand-year history,' he says, 'which makes it very different to Ghana.'[3] Asia's success shows nonetheless that a commitment to pro-growth policy matters. Indeed, much of Southeast Asia follows the same pattern of growth: an agricultural revolution based on land reform segues into progressive industrial development through garments, light manufacturing and electronics, and then into services.

Crucial to all the success has been education for both boys and girls, which has had many consequences, some unintended. A sufficient quality of labour coupled with investment in primary and secondary education proved to be a cocktail for success. A surge of highly trained young people entering the economy at the same time provided the necessary kick-start for both higher rates of productivity and lower birth rates, particularly where girls were educated as extensively as boys and remain in the labour market. In turn, a decline in birth rates has reduced the number of people to be educated in East Asia, which has, in turn, allowed the provision of better than just basic education, with a substantial increase in per-pupil expenditure. A large number of young people coming into the market at the same time consequent upon a reduction in health and education demands produced the region's demographic dividend, though labour productivity in manufacturing has also been a critical element in GDP growth.

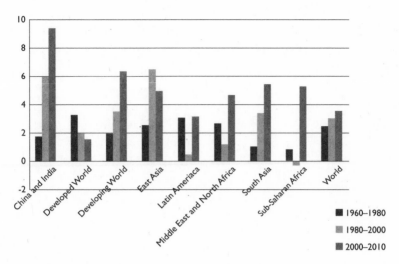

Figure 2: Per capita % growth rates by region

Of course there are some variations on these general rules. Singapore and Hong Kong did not, for reasons of size, have significant agricultural growth. Some aspects are not possible to replicate elsewhere, notably the extensive American presence in the region, which, although destructive in some respects, provided a security guarantee that allowed Southeast Asian countries to focus spending on productive investments rather than defence. In any case, the simple lessons from the region's economic transformation over the past half century illustrate the importance of efficient government as much as, in some cases, the cost of cronyism, and the benefits of peace as much as the cost of war. They highlight, too, the centrality of education and training to diversifying economies from light industry to services and knowledge-based activity.

These lessons are not universally accepted. There have been criticisms of the Asian approach to development, in terms of, on one hand, attitudes towards liberal concepts of democracy and human rights and, on the other, the sustainability of an export-oriented growth model. Those critical of East Asia's growth, such as Nobel economics laureate Paul Krugman, have argued that it was, like growth in the former Soviet Union, down to 'perspiration, not inspiration', and was therefore not sustainable since it resulted from heavy investment and a big increase in employment, rather than productivity gains. Once all spare labour was used up and capital employed per worker reached rich-country levels, it was argued, Asia's growth would slow. To an extent this has proven true, though East Asia still has a way to go to catch up with the capital intensity of Western economies. This might also explain why Singapore, for example, deliberately increased its population by 20 per cent during the period from 2007 to 2010.[4]

Figure 3: Asia[5]

Overall there have been several waves of regional growth: first Japan's post-war economic reconstruction followed by the development of the 'tigers' (Hong Kong, Singapore, South Korea and Taiwan), then the next wave (Malaysia, Thailand, Vietnam, Indonesia and the Philippines) and the comparative latecomers (Laos, Cambodia, Myanmar/Burma and Bangladesh), while China and India have cut remarkable growth paths of their own.

This chapter explores some of the patterns of growth in a number of examples among the more recent reformers. It illustrates reform in a post-Cold War context, where leaders have had to overturn policies and structures created by their predecessors. These examples therefore stand in contrast to the earlier Asian successes, which were often started in an environment of extreme militarisation, with high levels of external support and interference, on a political stage which was more tolerant of autocratic regimes and where many vested interests had been shredded in recent bouts of warfare.

Problems with picking winners

Malaysia is held up as an example of state-led capitalism, of the advantages of picking winners, and of the benefits of enforced wealth redistribution through indigenisation. Though the country has indeed developed at tremendous speed, in part through its natural resource dividend, its growth has, to a great extent, been in spite of government actions rather than because of them.

The express train known to the locals simply as the ERL (Express Rail Link) does the 57 km from central Kuala Lumpur to the Malaysian capital's impressive international airport in just 28 minutes of air-conditioned comfort for only US$12. The journey takes one down the Multimedia Super Corridor through the purpose-built government city at Putrajaya and Malaysia's aspirant Silicon Valley, Cyberjaya, both centrepieces of the country's desire to become a developed economy by 2020.[6] Leaving the main station, one is greeted immediately by the fast-changing and growing skyline of 21st-century Kuala Lumpur, the glinting modern high-rises overshadowing the few remaining 'bungalows'.

At the one end of the corridor is the spectacular Petronas Towers, at the time of completion the world's tallest buildings; at the other end, the airport and the Formula One Grand Prix circuit, which annually hosts the Petronas-sponsored Mercedes team, among others. The area around the airport is a giant construction zone, oil palm trees giving way to high-rise accommodation, swathes of sand carving away the crust of deep green, and an old natural-resource economy making way for the new – or so it seems.

Malaysia's economic recovery and policy of social upliftment have been the result of the government's recognition of two priorities: economic growth alongside improving social and racial equity. An extensive national affirmative action scheme for indigenous Malays, the *Bumiputra* ('sons of the soil'), was developed in the 1970s, involving preferential access for the Malays (by 2012 around 55 per cent of the population of 28 million) to state finance, contracts, government positions and educational opportunities. The aim was to create a Malay capitalist elite and redistribute wealth between the races. The government introduced its New

Economic Policy (NEP) in 1970 shortly after race riots in the capital in May 1969, which claimed the lives of 196 Malaysian Chinese. The NEP was designed to achieve national unity by eradicating poverty in all racial groups and by restructuring society to achieve inter-ethnic economic parity. These plans have been most successful in reducing poverty, with levels falling from 50 per cent to five per cent since 1970. Success has been achieved fundamentally not through redistribution, but through high GDP growth, averaging 6.8 per cent annually from 1971 to 2002.

Malaysia's approach was formulated in a succession of five-year development plans from 1955, in which it progressed through a number of key stages. One was the boosting of agricultural development in the 1950s and 1960s. Exports were diversified and palm oil production was expanded to the point that Malaysia has become the largest supplier worldwide, while the traditional export of natural rubber (in which Malaysia has fallen from first in the 1950s to fourth by 2012) was consolidated.

As Malaysia reached the point of maximum agricultural land utilisation, this growth stage was followed in the 1960s by a period of light-manufacturing industrialisation, initially focusing on textile production. At first this growth was enabled by the imposition of higher tariffs to spur import substitution. As the domestic market was soon saturated, from the 1970s the industry was reoriented to cater to external markets.

Additional growth came via the development of the petro-industry in the mid-1970s, followed later by an emphasis on the IT sector, though mainly assembling rather than manufacturing. State-led heavy industrialisation occurred in steel mills and, notably, the car industry through Proton (the *Perusahaan Otomobil Nasional*, or National Automobile Enterprise), though with mixed results.

Indeed, one oft-criticised feature of the Malaysian experience has been the attempts to 'pick winners', notably in the automobile sector. The first Proton car rolled off the assembly line in September 1985, an initiative of the then prime minister, Dr Mahathir Mohamed. The aim behind the establishment of Proton was to drive the automobile industrialisation process, which would enhance international competitiveness and act as a technology catalyst. The earliest model, based on Mitsubishi components, was officially called the Proton Saga – the saga, in Malaysia, being a tree with seeds so uniform in weight they were once used to measure gold. However, it became known as 'Potong Harga', Malay for 'cut price'. Despite a rough and ready finish, within three years the Saga – Proton's only model, but 20 per cent cheaper than anything comparable – had grabbed three-quarters of the 400 000-strong Malaysian passenger car market.

In August 2008, Proton produced its three millionth vehicle. By that time, the majority of its equity was held by a government-owned investment company, Khazanah Nasional Berhad, and the government pension scheme, while Petronas increased its stake in 2000. Mitsubishi disposed of its minority share in 2004, the partnership deemed a failure by the Malaysians because of the lack of technology transfer, something that Proton's purchase of high-tech Formula One engineering firm Lotus in 1996 aimed to address. In January 2012, Khazanah Nasional Berhad disposed of its 43 per cent holding to the Malaysian conglomerate DRB-Hicom for $412 million in an effort to boost competitiveness and declining market share.[7]

The Proton has only been competitive in the Malaysian market because of high import tariffs on other makes. Duties on completely knocked-down cars for assembly in Malaysia have averaged 30 per cent. There has also been a 75–150 per cent excise duty on new car imports, reducing dependence on local content rebates. Malaysia has so far managed to avoid implementation of the 1992 Association of Southeast Asian Nations (ASEAN) Free Trade Area agreement, which came into effect on 1 January 2008, preferring to maintain duties while paying any penalties applicable. As a result, ASEAN-made cars have cost 30–60 per cent more than equivalent Malaysian-made vehicles, protecting Proton's market share despite its outdated designs.

Mahathir, who had first dreamed up the idea of a local car on a visit to New York in 1964, defended these tariffs based on historical experience. 'I grew up with the British Empire's Imperial Preference,' he says, 'which was a blatant and unscrupulous protection policy for British products. Today developed countries apply tariff and non-tariff barriers to shield their products from competition.' On the other hand, he goes on, 'Malaysia needed to protect its infant industries if it was to industrialise. Accordingly the national car was shielded by a lower excise duty than import duty on foreign cars. Clearly developing countries cannot industrialise without some form of protection.'[8] But at what price – and did Malaysians want the product and the cost?

Proton has defended the extent of the capital investment (US$5 billion) and the cost passed onto Malaysian consumers in higher vehicle purchase prices due to tariffs by citing the number of direct and indirect jobs created. (Direct jobs numbered 12 000 in 2011, including 1 227 at Lotus in the UK, and 100 000 indirect jobs were created through more than 140 domestic subcontractors, and 236 sales and 293 service outlets.) Additionally, Proton says it contributed US$7 billion in taxes between 1985 and March 2011.[9]

With plans to drop duties by 2016, Proton aims to target high-growth markets in China, India and the Middle East, while investing in new technologies including range-extended electric vehicles (hybrids) and drawing on its Lotus links, both in the production of new engines and through offering a range of engineering consultancy services.

Although it is claimed that 'Malaysia is only one of 11 countries worldwide with a full-scale automotive capability', Proton's local content has been only 60 per cent. Moreover, despite the scale of investment in the automotive process and education, there are still only 400 automotive engineers countrywide, a relatively small figure that reflects the use, still a quarter century on from Proton's creation, of imported major components in the cars, including the gearbox.

Proton was conceived as one leg of a three-pronged strategy, the others being the creation of a raw material industry in the form of the state Perwaja Steel company (which went on to rack up debts[10] estimated at over US$2 billion in five years from 1988) and new infrastructure such as the construction of the North–South Expressway. Not only can you 'not build a car industry in isolation', say Proton, but they have also learned that the 'differentiating proposition' between success and failure 'has to be knowledge'. Without knowledge, 'we would just be in a business competing for the lowest wages. Yet we need 1 000, not 400, engineers today.'[11]

Despite the subsidies and the protection, Proton's share of the domestic car market had slid, by 2011, to just one-third, with the other national car maker, Perodua (formed in 1992), having another third, and the remainder made up of imports. As a result, its three manufacturing plants were running at about 50 per cent of their 380 000 annual capacity.[12] Whatever 'pride, passion and progress' the company may claim, the result of Proton's 25 years is mixed, at best. The Malaysian public have, despite the comparative cost saving, voted with their wallets, illustrating that the consumer – rather than business or finance or government – is the ultimate driver of capitalism. Mahathir, however, puts this view and the lack of pride down to 'the old inferiority complex again',[13] rather than the quality of the Proton product.

The 'mixed results' verdict also applies to other mega-projects such as the Petronas Towers, the administrative capital of Putrajaya and the Multimedia Super

Corridor. By the mid-1990s, before the Chinese manufacturing boom took off, Malaysia was the largest exporter of electrical and electronic products worldwide. Since then Kuala Lumpur has concentrated on the development of a service-based 'knowledge' economy. In reality, this means expanding tourism, building biotech and logistics industries, and positioning the country as a service centre for the 550 million-strong ASEAN region, especially the 220 million people in nearby Indonesia, which regional analysts view as the next boom country. It is also banking on benefiting from 'China fatigue', as multinational companies embark on a 'China plus one' investment risk hedging strategy, the 'one' destination for investment being low-cost manufacturers in ASEAN including Thailand, Indonesia and Malaysia. Another growth sector is palm oil processing, including biofuels.

The idea of an information technology (IT) city came from a study by McKinsey consultants commissioned by the Malaysian government in 1995. It was hoped that a centre with excellent infrastructure would attract world-class multimedia and IT companies. Although this was supposed to be based on private investment, the government took over the real estate Cyberview company following the 1997 Asian financial crisis. Has it worked?

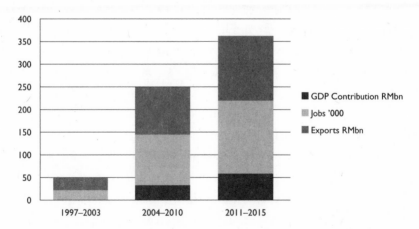

Figure 4: Multimedia Super Corridor performance

The activities of the Multimedia Super Corridor (MSC), opened in May 1997 by Mahathir, have been categorised in three phases: first, setting up Cyberjaya as an 'intelligent city' from 1996 to 2003; second, creating a 'web' of such corridors from 2004 to 2010; and third, aiming to establish Malaysia as a global ICT hub from

2011 until 2020. Revenue, given here in Malaysian ringgit, has increased from RM26.1 billion (US$9 billion at 2012 values) in the first phase to RM103.8 billion by the end of the second, and exports from RM1.2 billion to RM33 billion. The original aim was to create 100 000 jobs by 2010. By the start of 2011, 111 367 IT jobs had been created (92 per cent of them filled by locals), with some 2 800 MSC-status companies involved. By 2011, investments totalled over RM27 billion, with a 68:32 split of domestic and foreign money, though the latter had doubled in the second phase.

As with Proton, the government has thrown a lot of money at this project. It has also been very aggressive in offering preferential 'free zone' type conditions involving a five-year tax holiday, research and development grants, and duty-free importation of multimedia equipment. Such incentives apply to Business Process Outsourcing (BPO) operators.[14] Furthermore, it set up the Multimedia Development Corporation as an aggressive one-stop shop window for investors.

Yet, across the region, countries have done a bad job of picking winners. The billions spent on Proton and its battles to win over a sceptical Malaysian public parallel the attempt to create an Indonesian aerospace industry under the steward-ship of the renowned Messerschmitt aerospace engineer (and later Malaysian president) Bacharuddin Jusuf ('BJ') Habibie. Jakarta has written off at least US$500 million as cash injections into Indonesian Aerospace (formerly Industri Pesawat Terbang Nusantara, established in 1976 as a state-owned company), which at its peak employed nearly 10 000 people, though this had fallen to 3 700 by 2011. However, it has a poor record in delivering on its aim of mastering aircraft design, development and manufacturing.

Barry Desker, dean of the S Rajaratnam School of International Studies in Singapore, and a former Singaporean ambassador to Indonesia, notes: 'Poor choices reflect that government choices tend to be the result of internal negotiation which results in something that everyone can agree on – where projects are the lowest common denominator.' Desker points to the failure of Thailand to develop its natural air hub in the 1980s as a result of military control over the ancient airport facilities at Don Muang in Bangkok. This allowed Singapore to take the gap and build its own hub at Changi in 1980. However, by concentrating on its premium service, Singapore overlooked the opportunities present in the budget segment of the market, a space that was quickly filled by the entrepreneur Tony Fernandes with AirAsia, the Malaysian-based low-cost airline. Founded in 1993, by 2012 AirAsia was operating 142 routes to 78 destinations, and had won Skytrax's award for the world's best low-cost airline in 2009, 2010 and 2011. It carried 25.6 million passengers in 2010, up from 22.7 million the previous year.[15]

This, Desker says, shows the difference between those who favour a government-led industrial policy and those who argue that governments should rather set the conditions for growth without favouring particular sectors at the expense of others. It demonstrates the difference between making the arguments for business case by case, on individual merit, and having the government decide policy according to sector. 'The difference is that if you are in a bureaucracy making decisions, your life does not depend on it,' says Desker, 'whereas if you're a businessman, it does.'[16]

The difference between Asian and other regional failures from poor choices in their industrial strategies is, however, not as pronounced simply because of administrative efficiencies. As Mahathir bluntly argues, most countries know what they have to do to reform, but 'there's quite a wide gap between learning about and doing something. In Africa, while most leaders are well educated, ways of administrating their countries seem to escape them.'[17] Malaysia has not, however, escaped the worst excesses of rent-seeking that characterise government-led intervention in the economy, from industrial policy to redistribution. On the plus side, Malaysia has moved to become one of the most attractive destinations for doing business in East Asia, ranking 21 in 2011 (up from 23 the previous year) on the World Bank's Doing Business indicators, and 26 out of 139 on the 2011 World Economic Forum's Competitiveness Index.

Mahathir is closely identified with the diversification of Malaysia's economy away from natural resource dependence, while at the same time ensuring redistribution to the Malay majority. The colonial legacy, he notes, was poor: 'The British did not encourage industrialisation in their colonies, so Malaysia missed out on the "Industrial Revolution". It was more convenient for the colonial masters that Malaysia produced raw materials like tin and rubber to feed Britain's own industries.' Mahathir wanted Malaysia to develop its IT capability by offering certain advantages to businesses within a defined area, hence the MSC. But as he noted in 2011, 'it is sad that our journey into the Information Age seems to have stagnated ... We threw that chance away.'[18]

All this intervention has not been funded through increasing individual and corporate tax rates and revenue, however, but rather from the windfall of oil. One-tenth of GDP and more than half of Malaysia's government revenue of US$60 billion annually has reputedly been sourced from Petronas, the state oil and gas company. As Mahathir himself has admitted, '[Petronas'] profits in 2005 were bigger than our total collection from income and corporate tax,' that is, over RM70 billion (US$23 billion).[19]

Official estimates have put the volume of annual subsidies to the Malaysian economy in the 2000s, including those on food and fuel, at US$8 billion.[20] That some of its revenue from natural resources has been invested in infrastructure and not simply consumed is, however, also a plus. Whether it has been spent wisely, and the extent to which Proton and other schemes are little more than vainglorious and sophisticated forms of rent-seeking, can only be gauged on their ability to survive without this life support. Picking winners is, at best, a risky business.

English, incentives and ethics

The Philippines has often been considered the 'odd man out' in the Asian growth and development variable, a country that, in spite of high levels of aid, has underperformed. Its politics have often more resembled Africa's, with a long-standing dictator, family aggrandisement and dynastic politics, political assassinations, ethnic strife and insurgency, and problematic democratic transitions. However, the Philippines' performance as a services leader has, surprisingly, been overlooked. Its record of success has been dependent on the use of special economic zones, its stress on English, and keeping wage and other costs low.

The obviously inebriated middle-aged Japanese visitor staggered noisily out of the lift in our Shangri-La hotel in Manila, an attractive local escort cooing on his arm. A hotel security guard, showing his concern, ushered him towards his room and presumably a memorable hangover. The Philippines has shown remarkable character in putting recent historical grievances behind it.

During the Second World War, the islands fell under a brutal Japanese occupation. More than a million Filipinos died during the struggle to regain control. Their sacrifice and that of the Americans they fought alongside is remembered at the American Cemetery, just ten minutes ride from the Shangri-La. Nearly 17 100 headstones surround a wall of remembrance bearing the names of 36 286 missing in action. Another 3 000 American and Filipino prisoners of war who died in captivity are remembered at the site of their incarceration, the former Cabanatuan prisoner-of-war camp 135 km north of Manila. In the city, the iconic Manila Hotel on the capital's waterfront, once the home of General Douglas MacArthur and, during the Second World War, the headquarters of the occupying Japanese, is the preferred accommodation of the rich and famous, from Bill Clinton to the late Michael Jackson and Nelson Mandela – and the prime minister and royal family of Japan.

Of course, the US has its own bloody history in the region. The Filipino–American war, in which an estimated 600 000 locals died, raged for three years from 1898, with skirmishes continuing for a further seven. Although the Philippines only acquired its full independence from Washington in 1946, and the latter only departed its bases at the Clark airfield and Subic Bay in 1992, relations are close.

Despite this history of conflict, the US and Japan ranked first and second as the Philippines' trade partners in 2010. The US was the largest foreign investor, with close to US$6 billion in total foreign direct investment as of 2010. The Philippines has also been among the largest beneficiaries of the US Generalized System of Preferences (GSP) programme for developing countries. In 2010, the Philippines ranked as eighth-largest exporter under the GSP programme, with nearly US$913 million in US-bound duty-free exports.

However, despite its location in an economically dynamic region, and possessing both sound infrastructure and a large, educated population of 94 million, the Philippines has remained a comparative regional economic laggard – termed the 'sick man of Asia'. Once the second-largest economy after Japan's and the chosen site for the training of South Korean public officials in the 1960s, it has not kept pace with most of its East Asian neighbours in reducing poverty – or in growth. Between 1980 and 2000, the Philippines' economy grew at 2.5 per cent, well under the East Asian average of 6.6 per cent.[21] The result has been high levels of poverty. The proportion of the population living on less than US$1.25 a day in 2006 was 23 per cent, representing around 20 million people. Some 40 million Filipinos were living on less than US$2 a day then.[22]

Although formal unemployment is just seven per cent, the vulnerability number is above 40 per cent.

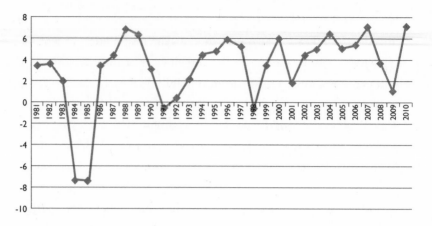

Figure 5: Philippines GDP growth: % change

One of the reasons for this poor performance is geographic dispersal: the Philippines archipelago comprises 7 100 islands totalling 300 000 km². Another is weather, with regular typhoons worsening the already poor performance of the agricultural sector. The favouring of import substitution policies over export-oriented ones has compounded the challenges, as did the slow implementation of agrarian reform and low investment in infrastructure. Although the country is ranked as one of the most mineral-rich in the world, with an ore wealth at US$1 trillion, investment has been discouraged by excessive and slow regulatory procedures, along with laws that give local governments significant power over the exploitation of mineral resources. There is inequality – the poorest 20 per cent of the population account for five per cent of total income – and growth has been primarily based on consumption rather than on the creation of employment opportunities for the poor. In part, limited economic growth is also due to high population growth, averaging two per cent annually, which puts strain on basic services. And poor growth performance is also linked to the turbulence in Philippines' politics over the past 50 years, itself a result of the excesses of colonial and post-colonial government. Twenty years of rule by Ferdinand Marcos ended in 1986, when a 'people power' movement in Manila known as 'EDSA 1' (named after Epifanio de los Santos Avenue, a major road in Manila) forced him out and Corazon Aquino was installed. She was the widow of opposition senator Ninoy Aquino, assassinated at Manila airport on his return from exile in August 1983. Her presidency, punctuated by no fewer than seven coup attempts, failed to make inroads into pressing issues of land reform and widespread poverty. She left power after the election of Fidel Ramos in 1992. Tough-guy former film actor Joseph Estrada, elected president in 1998, was put on trial in 2001 on charges of receiving illegal gambling pay-offs and forced to leave office by the 'EDSA 2' movement, which involved protests by half a million people.

Similar allegations plagued his successor, Gloria Macapagal-Arroyo, who, having taken over for the last three years of Estrada's term, was elected to a further six years as president in May 2004. She managed to survive two coups in 2003 and November 2007, bringing the number of attempts to about a dozen over two decades.

The government of Benigno Aquino III, elected in May 2010, continues along the general path of economic reform followed since the presidency of his mother, Corazon Aquino, while facing down threats from several groups named on the US's list of designated terrorist organisations, as well as from ethnic Moro insurgencies in the southern Philippines and the Maoist-inspired New People's Army insurgency.

Given limited job prospects for young Filipinos (young adults under 25 comprise about half of the unemployed), many migrate overseas to find work, with an estimated 9–11 million classified as Overseas Filipino Workers. In 2010, remittances from the US and Canada alone amounted to nearly US$10 billion, and those from the Middle East came to a shade under US$3 billion, out of a total of nearly US$19 billion.[23] (Sub-Saharan Africa has around the same figure for a population nearly ten times larger.) Remittances account for at least ten per cent of the country's GDP. While these flows support many families, they have also created a demotivating dependency culture among those who remain behind.

Long-term domestic economic growth remains threatened by inadequate infrastructure and education systems, and barriers to foreign trade and investment, often a reflection of cronyist leanings. It is said that six families 'own' more than half of the economy. They have diversified from large *hacienda* land holdings into real estate, industry and other sectors.

As a result, international competitiveness rankings have been poor. For example, the Philippines was ranked 148th out of 183 economies in the World Bank's 2011 Doing Business indicators, down from 146th in 2010, and 85th out of 139 countries surveyed for the World Economic Forum's Competitiveness Index.

More recent economic performance has, however, been more impressive: GDP growth during the 2000s averaged over five per cent. The growth has been on the back of continued political stability – and increasing diversification. The most notable development has been Business Process Outsourcing – better known as 'back-officing'. The global BPO industry was valued at US$32 billion in 2002, and quickly grew to between US$105 billion and US$125 billion in 2010, with growth predicted to reach US$256 billion to US$268 billion in 2016.[24] It can be divided into the sectors of engineering and information technology, voice (call or contact centres) and non-voice (back offices for administration, publishing, banking, etc). India is the overall global leader with 350 000 voice and 1.4 million non-voice full-time employees (FTEs). The Philippines overtook India in 2011 in BPO voice services, with 370 000 voice and 200 000 non-voice FTEs. Total revenue generated in 2010 touched US$9 billion and the industry has consistently grown annually at over 20 per cent. Those present in the Philippines' BPO world read like a who's who of international business – including J.P. Morgan (25 000 employees), Procter & Gamble (2 400), ANZ (2 300), IBM (8000) and Hewlett-Packard (4 000) – and contributed no less than 4.5 per cent of GDP in 2010.

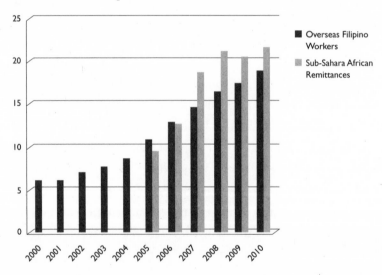

Figure 6: Comparative remittance flows, US$ billion

Government has assisted in growing this industry by providing export processing zone (EPZ) status for BPO centres. These EPZs, numbering no fewer than 225 by 2011, can be proclaimed over a piece of land, or just certain floors of a building. Their provisions include (income) tax-free status for between three and six years, permanent residence status for foreign investors, exemptions from duties and taxes on capital equipment imports, VAT exemptions on all utilities, and the facilitating role of the Philippines Economic Zone Authority, which functions as a one-stop shop, obviating bureaucratic runaround.

Celeste Ilagan, formerly director for investment promotion at the government's Board of Investment (BOI), part of the department of trade and industry, and subsequently with BPO operator SPi Global, recalls that the government's role came about as a result of Dakila Fonacier, then head of the BOI, reading in a 1999 article in the *Far Eastern Economic Review* that AOL had set up a Philippines-based call centre. He then took on championing these centres as a cause, one which was pursued also by his successor, and later transport secretary, Manuel Roxas. The government went on the offensive, targeting likely customers in visits to the US, 'where we tried to meet with them face to face and get them to visit'.

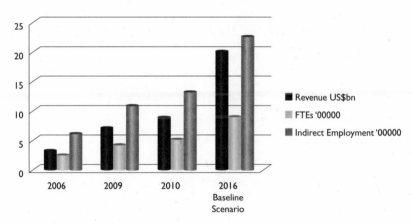

Figure 7: BPO growth in the Philippines

Many competitors offer similar incentives, while comparative telecoms costs[25] are assumed as a given for those vying in this sector. However, four additional reasons for the Philippines' BPO success, as displayed in Figure 7, go beyond the government's role and to the heart of Filipino history and people.

First, the price has been right. The maximum salary has been between US$200 and US$300, and US$100 more for those in the financial sector. Jaideep Pradhan of EXL, the largest insurance BPO, with 18 000 employees in India, the Philippines, Romania and the Czech Republic, observes that 'in today's world, wherever there is global competition, if you cannot compete on the price, you're out'.

Another reason concerns the Filipino skill set. As one Indian entrepreneur who has run BPO centres in his home country and in the Philippines notes, 'They lucked out with English.' English is widely spoken in the Philippines, and without the heavy accents of some other regions. BOI assistant secretary Felicitas Agoncillo says that 'Filipinos are great mimics. Many can master languages in six weeks, and accents change to suit the market.' Even though the average Filipino BPO salary was, in 2011, about 15 per cent higher than in comparable Indian outfits, says Pradhan, 'customers are willing to pay the differential given that Filipino front-line staff are much better in communicating.'

Third, the Philippines enjoys a relatively high level of education, with no fewer than 500 000 university graduates seeking work each year. The typical profile of a worker is a single female between 25 and 28 years old. The presence of large numbers of graduates plus the prospect of returning *émigrés* thus offers a 'scalable talent pool'.

And finally, the Philippines, for all of its insurgent problems and the scourge of entrenched corruption, has paradoxically been perceived to present minimal risk of changes to the investment climate and any failure to respect the rule of law.

Building on this success, the government and the Business Processing Association of the Philippines have moved to develop the 'next wave cities' outside Manila with lower costs, spreading the benefits of this industry. Even so, given the rates of joblessness, vulnerability and inequality, it is clear that more will have to be done than just developing the BPO sector. The country faced, at the end of the 2000s, what Renaud Meyer of the United Nations Development Programme describes as 'extreme demographics', with the majority of the population under 25 and a throng of young people coming into the job market simultaneously. Until now, he observes, migration and the resultant institutionalisation of the Overseas Filipino Worker have offered a social and economic safety valve.

Progress in developing other sectors has been patchy. During the 1980s, the Philippines attracted auto and other industrial production. For example, the anti-lock braking systems (ABS) used in Mercedes, BMW and Volvo vehicles are made in the Philippines, while Ford, Toyota, Mitsubishi, Nissan, Isuzu, Kia and Honda have all produced vehicles locally. In electronics, Intel has been present since 1974, investing over US$1 billion, while Texas Instruments, Nokia, Ericsson, Toshiba and Lexmark have set up manufacturing facilities on the islands.

The electronics industry in the Philippines has essentially been what Asian Development Bank chief economist Norio Usui describes as 'a "clean-up" assembly industry – you get the parts from Japan and Korea and assemble them using your cheap labour advantage'. But, he observes, the Philippines has lost market share to Thailand and other Asian countries, and has not been able to make the progress into higher value-addition that countries such as Malaysia, which started in the same space, have managed. Such diversification, he argues, is necessary, since inevitably the lower-wage sector will increasingly be filled, if not by China, by 'Asian latecomers', including citizens of Laos, Cambodia, Burma and Bangladesh. As a result, 'middle-income Asian countries like the Philippines will have to be very strategic, and this likely cannot happen through the market alone'.

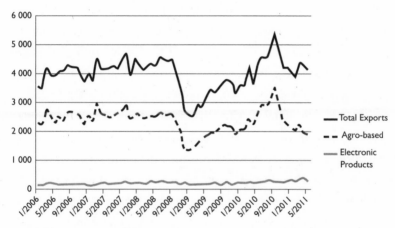

Figure 8: Philippine exports (US$ billion)[26]

Yet, as we observed in the Malaysia discussion, picking winners has proven a hit-and-miss affair. In education, the government picked nursing, with the result that the Philippines is the largest exporter of nurses worldwide, with more than 160 000 working abroad.[27] But there is still a surplus of workers and jobs are limited, with some nurses having to go into medical BPOs. Less productively, the country is awash with lawyers. This illustrates, as the head of the Manila ILO office, Jeff Johnson noted, in 2011, 'a failure to link the needs of business with the supply side'.

There have been other economic policy challenges. Inadequate infrastructure, lack of financing and government policies have also limited productivity gains in agriculture, the sector employing more than one-third of the workforce but providing less than a fifth of GDP. These statistics reflect, too, the relative labour intensity of this sector.

The country is rich with mineral and geothermal energy resources. In 2003, it produced 1 931 MW of electricity from geothermal sources (more than one-fifth of total electricity production), second only to the United States. Its gold, nickel, copper and chrome deposits are among the largest in the world, while there are significant oil and gas deposits. However, high production costs, lack of investment in infrastructure and a challenge to the mining law have contributed to the industry's overall decline.

Tourism presents the greatest lost opportunity. Although numbers have increased from a little over one million visitors in 1995 to two million in 2000 and more than 3.5 million in 2010, with revenues climbing to around US$5 billion, the sector is still seen as performing below potential. Politicians regularly profess their commitment to promoting tourism, among other sectors, but comparatively little has happened, says Maria Ela Atienza at the University of the Philippines, 'in translating their ideas into actions'. In part, therefore, the answer to the Philippines' growth and development conundrum lies in what Meyer calls 'human governance: oversight, human rights, transparency around political campaigning and financing, integrity, dealing with corruption, improving access to justice, and citizen participation in these processes beyond just creating an NGO'.

Some aspects of the tourism agenda have received attention: for instance, most tourists do not need a visa to stay in the country for up to 21 days. However, other aspects have lagged. The government has failed to implement an open-skies regime. There are infrastructure bottlenecks at airports, and the roads need much investment. Moreover, the banning of Philippine carriers from European skies and the downgrading of their status by the US Federal Aviation Administration on safety grounds have proven further significant hurdles.

Yet the overall trajectory has been upwards. The Philippines is currently the world's 32nd-largest economy. Its growth and job-creation record suggests that Goldman Sachs' projections that it will rise to the world's 14th by 2050 is credible.[28] Many improvements have been the result of a change in attitude and increasing openness. The government has consistently signalled its pro-business stance. It has opened the power generation sector to foreign investment, introduced competition in telecommunications and in the sea and air transport sectors, and become a member of the World Trade Organization. Major obstacles to be addressed include the prohibition on foreign ownership of land, cronyism, and restrictions on majority foreign ownership of public utilities.

As the BPO success illustrates, these changes have to come from inside. It's appropriate to quote what General Douglas MacArthur, the American most closely associated with the Philippines, for good or bad, once said: 'The best luck of all is the luck you make for yourself.'

Spinning in the mausoleum

If ever there was a country that had more excuses than any African state not to develop, it is Vietnam. Destroyed by successive wars with China, Japan, France and the United States, divided by colonialism and imposed foreign administrative systems, and dogmatically committed to socialism, it should be one of the poorest countries in the world. Instead, having started from essentially nothing, it has surpassed most African countries in per capita income. The moment of its transformation was when it abandoned rigid adherence to communism in the mid-1980s, at which point the energies and aspirations of its people supplanted those of the state. As a result, it set out, and remains, on a sharply higher growth and development trajectory than Africa.

The Number Three Factory of the May 10 garment factory outside Hanoi is, in some respects, the epitome of a state socialist enterprise. And it's not just the name. Above the entrance of May 10 is inscribed a saying by veteran nationalist leader Ho Chi Minh: 'A clear mind makes good work.' Pictures of the bearded icon smile down on the chattering sewing machines of the 3 000-strong 'May 10 Number Three working class'.

May 10 – literally 'Sewing ten' – was founded in 1946 to make military uniforms. But things have really taken off since the Vietnamese *Doi Moi* (renovation) economic reforms were implemented in the mid-1980s, and especially since the manufacturer's partial privatisation in 2001. Since then, exports have been growing at 15 per cent per annum. The 15 May 10 factories employ 8 000 people, by 2012 annually exporting shirts, trousers and suits worth US$40 million, mainly to the EU and United States.

This growth parallels what has happened elsewhere in Vietnam's garment sector, and in other sectors. Spurred on by the end of the US embargo in 1995 and the global quota regime a decade later, along with Vietnam's accession to the World Trade Organization in November 2006, the garment industry grew by one million jobs between 2005 and 2010, by which time there were 3 700 companies employing 2.5 million machinists and other workers. The sector generated US$11.2 billion from exports in 2010, up 23 per cent from the previous year.[29]

It was not as if the sector did not face significant challenges, internal and external. China has been a major competitor, despite the high productivity and low wages of Vietnamese workers. Monthly salaries averaged US$150 in 2011, and productivity was exceptionally high. At May 10, workers have owned 62 per cent of the company since its partial privatisation in 2001, with the state retaining a 38 per cent share. As a result, an annual dividend payment per worker has averaged around 20 per cent of their annual salary.

Another challenge is the shortage of domestic spinning, weaving and dying facilities. As most materials have to be imported from China and elsewhere, differences in wages and productivity leave little scope for making profit.

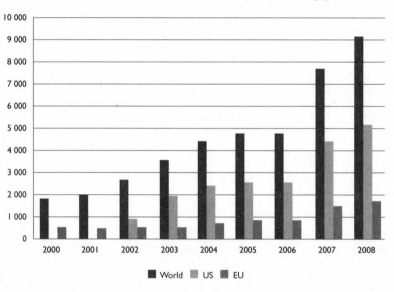

Figure 9: Garment and textile exports from Vietnam (US$ million)

And there has been a dearth of available workers because of competition from other higher-paying domestic sectors, including services and electronics manufacturing. As a result, May 10 offers its machinists a hospital, kindergarten (80 per cent are women), accommodation and training college, though management remains concerned about what it considers a high labour turnover rate of three per cent annually.

The rapid expansion in garments parallels what has happened in agriculture and electronics. From 1990 to 2005, Vietnam's agricultural production nearly doubled, transforming it from a net food importer to the world's second-largest exporter of rice.[30] In 2011, Vietnam exported an estimated two million tonnes of rice, most of it to Asia (54 per cent) and Africa (31 per cent).[31] Although coffee was introduced by French colonists in the middle of the 19th century, the industry withered through a combination of war and central planning. Following *Doi Moi*, the introduction of private enterprise caused a surge of growth. By 2000, from virtually nowhere, Vietnam became the world's second-largest coffee producer after Brazil, with annual production of 900 000 tonnes. By 2010, coffee production exceeded 1.1 million tonnes, second only to rice in export value. Cashew has seen a similar expansion: Vietnam has built up an industry from the roots in the past decade, shifting quickly from exporting the raw nut to developing its own processing techniques.

As a result, despite myriad problems including rickety infrastructure, inflation and overheating, Vietnam has been one of the fastest-growing economies in the world since 1990, averaging eight per cent GDP growth from 1990 to 1997, 6.5 per cent from 1998 to 2003, and more than seven per cent between 2004 and 2010, notwithstanding global financial travails. Foreign direct investment has climbed sharply, with disbursed capital totalling US$11 billion in 2010 alone. That same year, Vietnam's exports (US$71.6 billion) were up 25 per cent.

The country has moved up the industrialisation ladder rapidly, too.

Hanel (Hanoi Electronics) was created by government decree in December 1984, the first ever electronics business in the capital. Starting with black and white TVs, it progressed quickly to manufacturing colour sets, DVDs, refrigerators, car wiring looms and laptops. While the main holding company was 100 per cent state-owned, from 2004 four joint ventures were created involving foreign entities, including Daewoo, with 70 per cent foreign ownership. Hanel has also enjoyed partnerships with a range of leading firms including Intel, Microsoft, Cisco, IBM, LG, Canon, Acer, Dell and Sony. Indeed, Hanel has operated essentially as a component assembly plant, with around 70 per cent of items imported for the higher-tech products.

Employing 6 400 workers, Hanel is only one of several electronics firms to have sprung up, especially since 1990. Total employment in the sector in 2011 was 100 000 in both the greater Ho Chi Minh (Saigon) and Hanoi areas. Hanel cites the key restraints on continued growth as the availability of more skilled workers, along with the challenge of creating a vertically integrated system of production, and the competition presented by China.

However, Hanel remains keen to stress the advantages of Vietnamese production: low labour costs (around US$150 monthly per worker in 2011), a special dispensation on land costs for investors, a stable legal framework and political system, a large internal market and trade preferences into developed markets. As Hanel's Nguyen Dinh Vinh puts it, 'We have the technology, the supportive industries and, most importantly, competitive human resources.' Moreover, transition up the value chain from garments to electronics has been facilitated by two additional factors: regional production throughout Southeast Asia and high levels of education (all the machinists at May 10 have finished secondary school). Vietnam's growth is also driven by domestic demand. In July 2011, Honda Vietnam announced its intention to build a third motorcycle plant in the country, expanding production in the world's fourth-largest (behind China, India and Indonesia) two-wheel market by 25 per cent. Its two existing plants in Vinh Phuc province north-west of Hanoi already produce two million bikes annually in a market totalling 2.69 million units in 2010.[32]

Tourism has been another growth area, increasing employment from 1.3 million to five million jobs between 1995 and 2010. In 2010, Vietnam received 4.4 million international visitors, an increase of two million over ten years.

The garment sector has ambitious aims, too. Vitas, the Vietnam Textile and Apparel Association, an association body with 700 of the larger firms as members, has predicted that exports will rise to US$18 billion in 2015 and US$25 billion by 2020. Productivity aside, foreign investors, who comprise one-quarter of this sector, have been incentivised by a number of tax breaks, including up to 50 per cent on income tax from exports.[33]

The direction of the Vietnamese economy might have Ho Chi Minh – 'Uncle Ho' to the locals – spinning in his nearby mausoleum, given his professed communist aims. But the Vietnamese remain steadfastly pragmatic. A decade before the US withdrawal from Vietnam, Ho reportedly said to the Americans: 'We will spread a red carpet for you to leave Vietnam. And when the war is over, you are welcome to come back because you have technology and we will need your help.'

Vietnam is a country of contradictions. Members of the ruling 2.5 million-strong Communist Party (joining whom requires a process of selection involving careful scrutiny of three generations to check applicants' ideological purity) openly question what it means to be a contemporary Marxist. As one party member put it: 'Vietnam has a lot of bamboo. Its people too are very flexible, though they remain very strong. After all, Ho said that we must be flexible.'

What is officially termed a 'planned market economy' has been driven less by ideology than the search for margin and access to global finance and markets. With half of the 12 000 state-owned enterprises privatised by 1995 and a further 1 300 merged, sold or closed by 2010,[34] the private sector has become, for all the statist rhetoric of bureaucrats, increasingly dominant. 'All the government had to do was to create more favourable conditions for foreign investment,' said one garment industry specialist. 'The private sector did the rest.'

Struggles of a crowded nation

Bangladesh has been a poster child for poverty, war and natural disaster. Swamped with people, the country has found poverty alleviation not through aid, but rather through low-wage employment. Such growth is not pretty, but the alternatives are uncertain and could be worse, as evidenced by its former other half, Pakistan.

George Harrison anticipated Live Aid by more than a decade when he organised the Concert for Bangladesh on 1 August 1971 in Madison Square Garden, New York. Featuring rock superstars including Bob Dylan, Eric Clapton and fellow Beatle Ringo Starr, the event raised more than US$240 million for refugees affected by the 1970 Bhola cyclone and the 1971 liberation war with Pakistan.

Bangladesh's population was, at that time, 70 million. Forty years later it exceeds 160 million. This growth partly explains why, although Bangladesh's economy has grown faster than six per cent for much of the 2000s, more than 40 per cent of Bangladeshis remain poverty-stricken and engaged in low-wage and low-productivity agriculture, notably rice, wheat and jute. Yet agriculture is responsible for less than 20 per cent of GDP, with industry (nearly 30 per cent) and services (over 52 per cent) leading the way.[35]

Independence in December 1971 did not solve problems of domestic political fractiousness. By 1975, Prime Minister Sheikh Mujibur Rahman (Mujib) had initiated one-party socialist rule, including the nationalisation of all industries. Coupled with poor education standards (a legacy of British colonial policy towards what had been part of imperial India), this resulted in most workers being illiterate and unskilled. Economic growth stuttered in this environment, and critical shortages of food and other items soon ensued.

In the following years, there were periodic political interventions by the military, an institution that still remains 'a force of last resort to sort out the mess', in the view of one former senior military officer. Along with most of his family, Mujib was assassinated on 15 August 1975. Following a series of coups and counter-coups, General Ziaur Rahman took over, founded the Bangladesh Nationalist Party, and reinstated civilian rule. When he was assassinated by military elements in 1981, General Hossain Mohammad Ershad took power. After he resigned in 1990, Bangladesh resorted to a parliamentary democracy, with leadership coming from the families of Mujib and General Zia.

The economy has followed a similar pattern. By the mid-1980s, with greater scope and space for private sector enterprise, things began to turn around, though these advances were subject to periodic, politically induced reversals. For example, as a result of a slowdown in reforms in the late 1990s, the country experienced a significant drop in foreign direct investment. Since that time, IMF assistance, coupled with about US$1 billion in annual aid flows, has stabilised the economy, while pro-growth policies have led to a rapid rise in employment, notably in garments.

By 2011, about five million people, mostly women, were working in Bangladesh's garment and related textile industries. With Bangladesh-based factories making clothes for international brands such as JC Penney, Walmart, H&M, Marks & Spencer, Zara and Carrefour, the sector accounted for more than 80 per cent of annual export earnings and was worth US$18 billion annually, including more than US$2 billion in exports to the US. The next biggest 'export' sector is remittances, mainly from workers in the Middle East, worth an estimated US$12 billion in 2010.

The reasons why the garment (and textile) sector took off were quite simply low wages, a change of government policy towards private enterprise, and the end in

2004 of the Multifibre Arrangement quota, which had limited exports, especially to the US market.

Although there was a traditional handloom textile sector in Bangladesh and a fledgling ready-made garment export industry, originally set up in the 1970s, the big impetus for growth came with the development of the government's New Industrial Policy in 1982, which turned back the socialist clock, 'denationalised' industry, and encouraged private enterprise. Until the late 1980s, much of the garment industry still relied on imported textiles mainly from China and India, not least since the pressure on farming land discouraged cotton farming. By the 2000s, the local textile industry supplied 80–90 per cent of the knitwear and 40 per cent of the woven export goods of Bangladesh', according to the chairperson of the local industry organisation, which has 1 250 members including 356 spinning mills employing '1.4 million directly and another 2 to 2.5 million indirectly with home businesses'.

In comparison, the ready-made garment sector has 5 310 registered companies, of which about 3 000 are said to be functional. High productivity has encouraged investment in the garment sector and an annual growth of around 15 per cent. Although industry officials say this growth is due to the fact that 'our women, our workers, are by nature good stitchers', social commentators note the irony that malnutrition may have contributed to making Bangladeshi women more dextrous 'as their fingers and hands are smaller'.

Wages undoubtedly have also played their part in this equation. In 2010, the stipulated monthly minimum salary almost doubled to 3 000 taka (US$43). Salaries had already been increased in 2006 from Tk950, about US$15, where it had stayed for more than 12 years. The industry argues that the average salary, however, is around US$100, given pressures on the availability of skilled manpower, though a more accurate gauge of wage sensitivity came in the form of misplaced industry fears at the time of the 2006 increase that 'over 50 per cent of factories would be ruined within three months'.

Bangladesh's textile sector is concentrated in EPZs in Dhaka and Chittagong. These zones, which are administered by the Bangladesh Export Processing Zone Authority, aim to offer 'a congenial investment climate, free from cumbersome procedures'. The EPZs also offer ten-year tax holidays; duty-free import of capital goods, raw materials and building materials; exemptions on income tax on salaries paid to foreign nationals for three years; and dividend tax exemptions for the period of the tax holiday. There is no ceiling on investment in the EPZs and full repatriation of profits is allowed. The formation of labour unions within the EPZs is prohibited, as are strikes.

In reality, however, these zones have had limited success in attracting investment, partly because the industry has deliberately not encouraged foreign businesses into the textile sector. This could be put down to a fear that foreign firms will be forced to raise worker standards – or perhaps locals prefer to keep the current system as a 'closed shop'.

Despite the wage advantages, investors have expressed frustration with the 'politics of confrontation' of local authorities, the level of corruption, the slow pace of reform and of privatisation and deregulation in the public sector, and the lack of basic infrastructure, especially roads. Bangladesh was ranked 137th out of 183 countries surveyed in the 2011 Index of Economic Freedom, and 107th, also out of 183, on the World Bank's Doing Business indicators. According to the Corruption Perception Index of Transparency International, the level of corruption in Bangladesh was perceived to be the highest in the world from 2001 to 2004. There has been some recent improvement, to 139th out of 180 countries in the 2009 index, and 134th out of 178 in 2010.[36]

The government's role in facilitating industrial development has been limited, and its most constructive contribution has been simply to get out of the way of investors. Two important pieces of policy, however, have made a difference. The first relates to the provision of back-to-back letters of credit, enabling loans against orders; and the second is permission to import textiles and other necessary goods as duty-free bonded goods for processing, thus freeing up capital.

But much more needs to be done if Bangladesh is to provide for its burgeoning and poverty-stricken population. Even though the economy has grown over five per cent per year since the mid-1990s, 'Bangladesh remains a poor, overpopulated, and inefficiently-governed nation'.[37] Political chaos aside, its transport system remains in a shambles, the result of a rapid growth in personal transport and a lack of government response. SUVs and cars compete on the roads with bicycle rickshaw taxis, battered green 'CNG' (compressed natural gas) mini-taxis scurrying in and out of impossible spaces, and belching battle-scarred commuter buses. This gridlock is the result of a combination of political apathy with the disappearance of a fair chunk of money through the corruption that defines the behaviour of Bangladesh's political class. In 2011, for example, it took five hours to travel the 55 km northwest from Dhaka to the campus of Square Pharmaceuticals, a domestic market leader. Outside was a confusion of squalor, garbage, disintegrating tarmac, honking buses and people.

There are many, many millions of people everywhere. Aside from the unique city states such as Macau, Hong Kong, Bahrain, Monaco and Singapore, Bangladesh is the world's most densely populated country, with 1 000 people per square kilometre. By comparison, sub-Saharan Africa's average density is just 35 per square kilometre and the world's, 47. On average 4 500 people arrive in Dhaka every day looking for work, and at least 2 000 of them have a secondary education.

Inside Square Pharmaceuticals' facilities, it's a different world. Established in 1958, by 2010 the group encompassed health care, textiles, fast-moving consumer goods (mainly toiletries, snacks and spices) and IT interests, employing 33 000 and with a turnover of US$781 million. Of this revenue, pharmaceuticals turned over US$200 million, comprising a 20 per cent share of the domestic market. Inside the high-tech environment, equipment of British, Italian and German origin combines with Bangladeshi management to produce what is known as 'GMP', or good manufacturing practice, which involves not only technical excellence, but also the clear audit and testing trail necessary for certification.

The spur for the expansion of the domestic pharmaceutical industry in Bangladesh was the 1982 government ordinance which stipulated that essential drugs had to be made available at affordable prices, fixed the prices of certain drugs, and stopped multinationals from manufacturing basic products such as vitamins and analgesics. This approach wasn't so much picking a winner as driving profits down for the benefit of the impoverished masses. In 1981, multinationals provided 75 per cent of drugs used in Bangladesh; by 2011, the 194 local pharmaceutical manufacturers in Bangladesh supplied 90 per cent of needs.

Square, for example, manufactured a range of products in 2010 that included top-end antibiotics, insulin, painkillers and anti-ulcer medication, totalling five billion capsules and tablets. With a planned US$100 million expansion under way and new, imported production and packaging equipment due to arrive, production was slated to rise to ten billion tablets and four billion capsules by 2013. Firms like Square are deliberately taking advantage of Bangladesh's least-developed-country status, by which they are deemed exempt from requirements of the Agreement on Trade-Related Aspects of Intellectual Property Rights (TRIPS) until 2015.

Yet Square's progress, like that of companies in the textile and garments sector, has again been largely in spite of government. Bangladesh not only faces extraordinary difficulties with logistics and basic services, including potable water, but energy has been an increasing constraint. With a national demand for 5 100 MW and a regular supply of only 3 800 MW, businesses have had to install their own gas- and diesel-powered systems. For the garment industry, local generation consumes 250 million litres of diesel annually, a huge foreign exchange loss for the country and a significant hurdle for the industry to overcome. Square, for example, has 6 MW of gas capacity installed, and a further 3 MW of diesel for its 24/7 operations.

Despite the challenges, the only way, for both the textiles and garments sector and pharmaceuticals, appears to be up. The total size of the world apparel market in 2010 was US$300 billion, and it has been growing at an average of ten per cent per annum. With Bangladesh's slice of this market just five per cent, and given the potential for greater value addition, 'the sky is the limit', in the words of the industry association president Shaiful Islam.

Similarly, in pharmaceuticals, the cost of Bangladeshi products has been some 25 per cent less than that of Indian rivals, mainly as a result of lower salaries. Yet Bangladesh's share of the US$2 trillion global pharmaceutical business is just US$1 billion, or 0.05 per cent. By comparison, India's slice is US$100 billion, including 60 per cent of the generics market. With firms like Square seeking and obtaining international approvals, there is great optimism about the future, even without government assistance. With it, the pace of change could be faster. 'What government needs to do,' says one chemist at Square, 'is to build a city like Putrajaya in Malaysia, to start afresh on new infrastructure.' But as a social commentator notes, 'Our governments have no vision and no desire to use their political capital to make change. They are only good at fighting with each other and feathering their own nests.'

Bangladesh has had the worst of colonial inheritances and subsequent violent separation, its people live in intolerable conditions, its domestic politics are familial and fraught, and its services are hard pressed by one of the highest population densities in the world. These could easily be taken as reasons for failure, as they have been in many African settings. But in Bangladesh, a combination of government policy and the government getting out of the way has enabled industry to prosper, albeit in the lowest-paid rungs. Nevertheless, it is no longer the basket case it once was and could easily still be.

Conclusion: grandmothers and children

Each of these examples – Malaysia, the Philippines, Vietnam and Bangladesh – highlights the fact that rapid change is possible. The living standard of children now is dramatically improved compared to that of their grandparents, just as the circumstances of employees of later generations will be different from those of today's workers. For countries on the road to industrialisation, sweatshops are a first step, however socially and politically unpalatable they may be. What is good enough for a grandmother, however, does not have to be good enough for her granddaughter, but it can be a starting point. Bangladesh's challenge is to ensure that its granddaughters do not have to do what the grandmothers are doing today, particularly not for less money.

Unlike the Central American countries that sought to reform their inherited political systems, Asians have overthrown the constraints of the past. This success is partly is due to the fortunes of history and good leadership, but this is not ubiquitous in the region. Asia has also shown much greater willingness to change economic systems than either Central America or Africa, where leaders have sought to work around structures rather than radically reform them. This determination to reform reflects a true commitment to popular welfare as opposed to elite interests and survival, imperatives that drive many governments to perpetuate systems intent on distribution rather than inclusive prosperity through jobs. Good regional examples also serve as models for others to follow.

Endnotes

1   This point was made by Malaysian Prime Minister Mahathir: Dato' Seri Dr Mahathir bin Mohamad, *The Asian Values Debate*. Kuala Lumpur: ISIS Perdana Papers, 1997.

2   This figure was kindly supplied by Roel van der Veen.

3   Speech at SIDA Africa Day, Stockholm, 19 January 2012.

4   http://www.economist.com/node/115063.

5   Map No 4365, Rev 1, UNITED NATIONS, March 2012.

6   For a comprehensive survey of the Malaysian economy since independence, see 'Malaysia in Economic Development: Policies and Issues.' Kuala Lumpur: Institute of Strategic and International Studies (ISIS) with The PROGRAM, 2011.

7   For details on the sale, go to http://online.wsj.com/article/SB10001424052970204555904577163900500194864.htm.

8   Mahathir was interviewed in Kuala Lumpur in March 2007. See also Mahathir Mohamad, *A Doctor in the House*. Salangor: MPH, 2011, pp. 516–517.

9   This information was gained during a visit to Proton's Multi-Vehicle Factory at Shah Alam outside Kuala Lumpur in August 2011.

10 On the corporate excesses and mismanagement that led to this, see http://xbrain.biz/2007/06/26/the-politics-of-perwaja-steel/.

11 Discussion, Proton, KL, July 2011.

12 Sales in 2005/6 were 166 156 domestic and 17 168 exported; in 2006/07, 80 635 and 21 753; and in 2009/10, 148 968 and 25 512.

13 *A Doctor in the House, op cit*, p. 520.

14 http://www.mscmalaysia.my/topic/12073025559425.

15 http://www.etravelblackboardasia.com/article.asp?nav=2&id=73065.

16 Discussion, Sentosa, Singapore, August 2011.

17 Personal interview, Kuala Lumpur, March 2007.

18 *A Doctor in the House*, op cit, pp. 633–640.

19 *Ibid*, p. 651–653.

20 http://malaysiasdilemma.wordpress.com/2011/06/13/malaysia-cutting-back-on-subsidies/.

21 Institute for International Economics at http://www.piie.com/publications/chapters_preview/348/2iie3489.pdf.

22 http://www.ausaid.gov.au/country/country.cfm?CountryID=31.

23 At http://www.abs-cbnnews.com/business/02/15/11/remittances-reach-record-188-b-2010. For the African figures, see http://web.worldbank.org/WBSITE/EXTERNAL/NEWS/0,,contentMDK:22757744~pagePK:64257043~piPK:437376~theSitePK:4607,00.html and http://www.un.org/esa/desa/papers/2011/wp102_2011.pdf.

24 Jon Messenger and Naj Ghosheh (eds.), *Offshoring and Working Conditions in Remote Work*. New York: Palgrave Macmillan/ILO, 2010, p. 1.

25 The cost per dedicated line today is US$2 000. At the take-off of the industry in 2002 it was US$20 000.

26 Figures supplied by the Asian Development Bank, Manila, July 2011.

27 Fely Marilyn E Lorenzo, Jaime Galvez-Tan, Kriselle Icamina and Lara Javier, 'Nurse Migration from a Source Country Perspective: Philippine Country Case Study', *Health Services Research*, Vol 42(3.2), pp. 1406–1418, http://www.ncbi.nlm.nih.gov/pmc/articles/PMC1955369/.

28 'BRICS and Beyond', Goldman Sachs study of BRIC and N11 nations, 23 November 2007.

29 http://moeaitc.tier.org.tw/idic/mgz_topic.nsf/0/54f372825f4887ac4825676a002abac9.

30 http://www.state.gov/r/pa/ei/bgn/4130.htm.

31 *New Age (Bangladesh)*, 27 July 2011. See also http://www.vccinews.com/news_detail.asp?news_id=23604.

32 *The Independent* (Dhaka), 26 July 2011.

33 For details of the 'Law on domestic investment encouragement' 03/1998/QH10 passed in Hanoi on 18 May 1998, go to http://moeaitc.tier.org.tw/idic/mgz_topic.nsf/0/54f372825f4887ac4825676a002abac9.

34 http://www.pep-net.org/fileadmin/medias/pdf/files_events/ngoc.pdf.

35 The poverty data is as of January 2011, and is sourced from the *CIA World Factbook*, at http://www.indexmundi.com/g/r.aspx?c=bg&v=69.

36 http://www.guardian.co.uk/news/datablog/2010/oct/26/corruption-index-2010-transparency-international.

37 http://en.wikipedia.org/wiki/Poverty_in_Bangladesh.

5

LESSONS FROM
THE MIDDLE EAST

Some countries are blessed with an abundance of resources, and some have few. This is not the determinant of success or failure, however. Learning to manage whether or not there is an ample natural resource base is especially important for Africa, where more than 70 per cent of exports comprise mineral products.[1] Indeed, the differentiation of African growth rates has largely been structured according to the extent of this resource dividend: the top performers (Angola and Equatorial Guinea, for example) have been entirely dependent on the revenue from oil.

But such flows have proven historically to be no guarantee of development success. That more Nigerians lived in poverty during the 2000s than in the 1960s is evidence of the corrosive effect of oil on both governance and attempts at diversification. This fate is due not only to the resultant demotivation and the distortion of currency values, important as these effects are, but also to the impact these resources have on politics. Instead of being used as a development tool, they become the goal of political victory: the ambition of leaders is not to reap the reward of investments in terms of development, but rather to prosper from cutting deals with investors. This is the lesson of the Democratic Republic of Congo, for example, which functioned in this way before independence in 1960 and has continued to do so ever since.

The African resources challenge extends into their use as a tool of diversification. Even better-governed and consistently performing mono-economies in Africa – such as Botswana, which has prospered through careful management and use of its diamond resource – have battled to diversify into other sectors, partly because of the comfort their single resource offers. 'Resource-rich countries wake up in the morning with their stomachs half-full,' says Alberto Trejos, Costa Rica's former minister of trade. 'We don't have that luxury.'

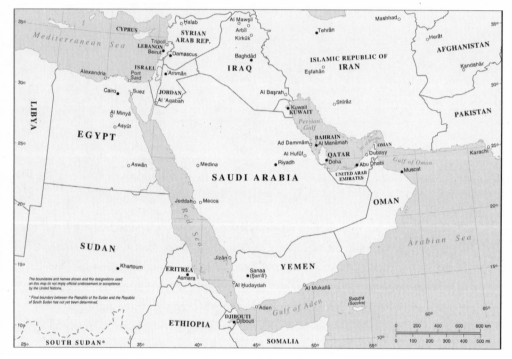

Figure 1: Middle East[2]

Exploring and contrasting the experience of Qatar, Abu Dhabi and Dubai with that of Israel makes the limits of government-supported economic activity clearer. These are important lessons for Africa, because the 'Dubai model' of government-fostered service diversification has been much discussed on the continent. Ironically, Israel's path is less understood, but may also be more relevant, especially given its success in job creation by home-grown entrepreneurs.

The Dubai model

The answer to the challenge of diversifying an oil-rich country with a small population is, at least according to the consultants, to try to do much the same thing as other, similar countries: focus on services, infrastructure, duty-free zones, the attraction, retention and creation of skills, and the hosting of premier events, sporting and cultural – even in the same region and even, in the case of Dubai and Abu Dhabi, among neighbours.

In the case of Qatar, this advice has translated into the hosting of the air-conditioned 2022 FIFA World Cup, along with bids for the Olympics in 2016 and 2020. The kingdom has created a world-class airline (Qatar Airways) virtually overnight from nothing, like Dubai (with Emirates) and Abu Dhabi (with Etihad), and has also established Al Jazeera as a leading satellite broadcaster. These developments have been coupled with a more adventurous approach in the political domain, notably the government-funded peacemaking missions to Sudan and Afghanistan, extensive military involvement in the overthrow of Colonel Muammar Ghaddafi in Libya, and the hosting of large Western military bases. With a population of just 300 000 nationals (plus 1.4 million expatriate workers), Qatar seems to be successfully punching above its weight.

Cynics would say this is all about oil and, especially, Qatar's vast gas reserves, about 15 per cent of the world's total. Qatar also has investments of over US$100 billion and the world's second-highest (behind Luxembourg) per capita GDP of US$110 000. Such wealth has funded Qatar's various initiatives.

Whatever the motives, Qatar has been following an economic diversification path first trodden in its region by Dubai, and pursued with vigour by Abu Dhabi, among others.

Dubai's transformation is enviable in many respects. For one thing, its rulers could simply have spent its oil money on themselves rather than invest in real estate and services. In other ways, the model is flawed. Between 2000 and 2005, Dubai's economy grew at 13 per cent, even more than China. Dubai's free zones, by 2012 numbering more than 30, attract international capital and visitors, and their names alone challenge the imagination: Internet City, Media City, Knowledge Village, International Financial Centre, Multi Commodities Centre, Gold and Commodities Exchange, Studio City, Silicon Oasis Authority, Biotechnology and Research Park, Cars and Automotive Zone, Outsource Zone, Airport Free Zone, Academic City, Healthcare City, Logistics City, Maritime City, Energy and Environment Park, Textile Village, Carpet City, Textile City, Al Awir Free Zone, Jebel Ali Free Zone and Dubai Sports City.

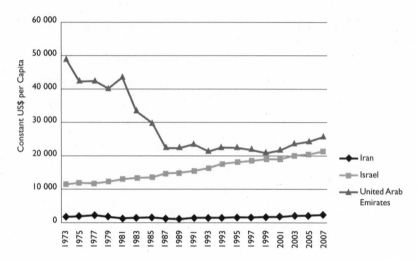

Figure 1: GDP per capita

By the mid-2000s, US$100 billion worth of construction projects were under way in Dubai. Three palm islands were envisaged (Jumeirah, Jebel Ali, and Deira). So too was a 'world' island complex and even the 'universe' – all of them, like the innumerable high-rises dotting the emirate, intended to attract *nouveau riche* footballers and their 'wags' (wives and girlfriends), Russian oligarchs and others fleeing taxation and other regimes. The Al-Maktoum Airport at Jebel Ali, with six runways, was planned to accommodate up to 150 million passengers annually – which would make it the world's largest such facility, with four times the capacity of the existing Dubai International Airport. The world's tallest building – the US$4 billion, 160-storey Burj Dubai – was to be the centrepiece of a planned US$20 billion 'downtown Dubai' development, surrounded by the Dubai Mall, six-star hotels and a signature lake.

But the dream ended with the global financial crisis in 2008, when the emirate had to be bailed out with US$20 billion from Abu Dhabi. Dubai's escape route was symbolised by the renaming of the Burj Dubai to the Burj Khalifa after the

United Arab Emirates (UAE) president, Khalifa bin Zayed Al Nahyan, as a gesture of gratitude for Abu Dhabi's support. In November 2009, Dubai World – which includes the property giant Nakheel, Dubai Port, DP World and the private equity firm Istithmar – had to apply for an extension on repaying a US$3.5 billion bond as part of its US$59 billion debt. This amount was just part of an estimated debt overhang for the emirate that officially stood at US$80 billion, though the IMF put it at US$109 billion,[3] or 130 per cent of GDP, and perhaps even higher, given other, 'hidden' debts. The total borrowings made Dubai's citizens the most indebted in the world, with over US$400 000 of debt each.

Real estate speculation and unrestrained short-term borrowing lay behind this crisis. As one indication of the bubble, the value of land had dropped by half by the end of 2009. At the end of 2010, a year after its opening, more than 800 of 900 apartments in the flagship Burj Khalifa remained unoccupied, their owners preferring to hold onto them and try, over time, to recoup their investment. While the construction of many residential apartment blocks remained incomplete by 2012, occupancy of the finished properties was estimated at only two-thirds. Real estate prices had fallen by 60 per cent from their pre-crisis peak, the focus being on filling up existing properties rather than embarking on new ventures.

Dubai's debt situation has been compounded by a pernicious culture of entitlement in a state where locals comprise less than 12 per cent of the population and for whom the state is a source of generous welfare. Most skills and labour are imported.

The pace of development in Dubai reflects both the realisation that its oil reserves and revenue are running out and the desire of its rulers to keep ahead of its much wealthier neighbour, Abu Dhabi. 'This was why Dubai,' says one analyst, 'threw caution to the wind and adopted a strategy of "supply first and demand will come".'

The most populated of the seven emirates making up the UAE, Abu Dhabi, has nine per cent of the world's proven oil and five per cent of its gas reserves, but it has become a byword for diversification from hydrocarbons. Generating nearly two-thirds of the UAE's GDP and functioning as the seat of the country's federal government, Abu Dhabi has been putting together its own diversification plan, at the same time (though its government is loath to acknowledge this) learning from Dubai's successes and mistakes.

The regional mantra of diversification is expressed in the Abu Dhabi Economic

Vision 2030. The plan suggests that Abu Dhabi's economy will not be dependent on any one facet or source of revenue and that the non-oil portion of income will increase from about 40 per cent to 60 per cent by the target date. The tangible outputs of this vision can be seen in a variety of ways, such as Abu Dhabi's international airport and Etihad Airways, along with US$1 trillion in infrastructure development in the city, including high-rise buildings, tourism infrastructure, a new port and a mooted rail link with Dubai. It has also created five 'free zones' including the Industrial City of Abu Dhabi and Media City.

This quest for diversification is fuelled by and also recognises a projected increase in population numbers. According to the 2030 plan, Abu Dhabi's gross population will surge to 3.1 million.[4]

The general secretariat of Abu Dhabi's executive council was the main author of Vision 2030, in a process that included as many as 70 agencies sitting down together to discuss the coordination, alignment and integration of plans into the Vision 2030 targets. Abu Dhabi, like the rest of the Middle East and North African region, is all about top-down government planning. In this model the private sector is consulted, foreign consultants are hired, and benchmarks and country role models are selected – for instance, Norway, as a developed oil economy, along with other knowledge-based economies such as Ireland, New Zealand and Singapore.

There could be little argument with any of the Vision 2030 targets from an African perspective. They include the need to build a 'sustainable economy ... primarily through diversification ...enlarging the economic base, encouraging entrepreneurs, small business and foreign direct investment ... developing National Champion enterprises to act as economic anchors' and the need to 'enhance competitiveness and improve productivity.'[5] Neither would there be much argument over the mechanisms: building an open, efficient, effective and globally integrated business environment; adopting a disciplined but responsive fiscal policy; establishing a resilient monetary and financial market with manageable inflation levels; driving significant improvements in labour market efficiency; developing a sufficient and resilient infrastructure; developing a highly-skilled workforce; and enabling financial markets to become local financiers of growth and progress.

The key enablers, too, could be replicated in a number of settings: energy and gas, petrochemicals, metals, aviation and defence, pharmaceuticals and biotechnology, tourism, health care equipment and services, trade (transportation) and logistics, education, media, financial services, and telecommunication services.[6] Government officials have been keen to differentiate Abu Dhabi's model in this regard from Dubai's, putting greater emphasis on energy-dependent areas, such as aluminium-smelting and petro-chemicals. The government aims to increase GDP more than fivefold by 2030 (and GDP per capita by more than 50 per cent) and reduce unemployment among the national population to less than five per cent by essentially doubling non-oil sector GDP (to 64 per cent) by 2030 while reducing reliance on the oil component from 60 per cent to 36 per cent.[7]

It is the government, rather than the private sector, that has been behind much of this development. The Abu Dhabi Tourism Authority and the Tourism and Development Investment Company have spurred growth with several large-scale development projects. The Abu Dhabi Investment Authority – its sovereign wealth fund – was estimated at US$875 billion in 2012, making it the world's wealthiest, generating a reported US$500 million per day in earnings. This centrality of the government's role reflects the enormous oil and gas reserves, of which Abu Dhabi owns the majority, intended as the wellspring for its development needs. With plans to increase oil production to three million barrels per day, revenue for the plan will not be a problem as long as oil prices remain high.

Overall, however, Vision 2030 has proven a lot easier to draft and propagate than to implement. Identifying models from around the world and studying and visiting them can easily be arranged, but replicating or applying them is far trickier. And it is necessary to break away, too, from the diversification 'template' of a world-class airline, real estate, infrastructure, a logistics *entrepôt* with free zones, and a Formula One track and race. The fingerprints of foreign consultants are everywhere, ensuring problems of originality, specificity, prioritisation and ownership. As one foreign observer based in Abu Dhabi has put it, 'They do such a cut-and-paste job on these plans that I have seen them use slides with Qatar's name on them when referring to Abu Dhabi.' Moreover, while there has been little that one would take exception to in the vision, putting it into action is another matter altogether.

There are more problems with such schemes.

First, investment in increasingly outlandish infrastructure schemes has seldom been productive, as other country examples show, such as Dubai's 'world' and 'islands', or Malaysia and other Southeast Asian countries' problems during the Asian debt crisis in 1997 and 1998. It is very difficult to justify the existence of one, let alone three or four, regional airport 'hubs': Qatar, Bahrain, Dubai *and* Abu Dhabi. Some consolidation must inevitably be necessary, though Abu Dhabi has even found it difficult to agree on merging its bourses and the aluminium smelters.

Second, human resource development has been the weakest link, along with changing mindsets. When Emiratis cannot be fired for poor performance (but are instead put on 'special projects'), the buck apparently does not stop anywhere. Partly as a result of this environment, the first five-year development plan had already been five years in the manufacture by 2012, and yet there was little sign of it. The same lack of urgency applies to the creation of specific sector incentives. There was little reason for Emiratis to go into the private sector when life was so cushy in government. 'The greatest curse of resources,' says a member of the government, 'is that it demotivates our people, and creates a sense of entitlement.' As a result, observes another, 'things move at glacial speed because people are not hungry for change when the oil price is where it is.' Or, as one foreigner who has lived and worked in the region for 35 years, notes, 'Unless this work ethic changes, Emiratis will never replace expats.'

Third, the relevance of the Dubai/Qatar/Abu Dhabi type of case study is questionable outside of oil-rich territories with small populations. True, the money has been well spent in some areas, but there has been a lot of it to go around. There has been little need to create employment in Abu Dhabi, for example, where foreigners outnumber the local population by 1.24 million to 406 000. By 2015, Emiratis will, it is projected, comprise less than ten per cent of the total population. In fact, the Dubai model has done best in creating jobs for foreigners.

Some aspects of the Dubai model are, however, worth closer study and even imitation by some African states. The creation of Emirates, the airline, has been a remarkable success, and it was, by 2012, not only an extraordinary brand for the tiny country, but also registering a positive cash flow. The emirate has capitalised on its location, openness and relative liberalisation to become the *entrepôt* of choice. As Western economies wobbled in the wake of the 2008 financial crisis, Dubai's role has shifted eastwards, with an increasing focus on business logistics and services for Chinese and Korean companies, including those operating in sub-Saharan Africa; while at the same time Africans, notably from Nigeria and Angola, have supported property investments in Dubai.

Overall, there has been a critical element of planning and setting visions and targets. Performance contracts have to link individuals with projects, and outputs with the vision. It is impossible to achieve this, however, without possessing – or importing – the skills necessary for service delivery, infrastructure development and diversification. And it is essential for the government and its citizens to have ownership of these plans, and not leave them to be worked out by others from outside.

Here it may be more helpful, as with Israel's bottom-up venture capital experience, for governments to avoid drawing up complex yet largely banal visions and development plans, and instead to identify paths in which the roles of their citizens as active participants can be identified, where their actions and choices matter, and where the private rather than the public sector is at the centre of growth. Without private sector dynamism, as has happened in both Abu Dhabi and Dubai, leaders focus on a vision of where the territories should go and not, as one analyst based in Abu Dhabi suggests, 'where its people might go'. As a Dubai-based foreign correspondent notes, 'Why would Africa want to copy the Dubai or Abu Dhabi model? It has created tensions to the way of life, with foreigners completely outnumbering local nationals, with the economy funded essentially by the import of talent and export of services. While the elite has done well, most locals, if someone bothered to ask them, don't like the outcome of Russians in bikinis walking around their malls.'

Finally, Dubai's post-2008 problems illustrate the cost of weak institutions and regulatory opaqueness, and the absence of checks and balances. As the boom progressed, Dubai's rulers got involved in every part of the economy, especially in real estate schemes, and rash decisions followed. Such are the costs of a lack of accountability and transparency. 'If this was Singapore,' says the correspondent, 'debtors would have been dealt with equitably, where the rule of law would have prevailed. In Dubai, individuals are jailed while the government does its level best to "forget" about US$70 billion of the US$100 billion worth of debts. This has left a very bitter taste.'

In Abu Dhabi, similarly, before the oil boom, there was a balance of power between the royal family and those with wealth, notably the pearl harvesting and trading elite. Today the commercial sector is vulnerable to the government and dependent on its largesse. A political economy where choices are not regulated by the market and business is vulnerable to political whim contains many dangers, as

Dubai's collapse and countless African examples show.

Components for high-tech success

For many years, Israel's defining economic characteristic was a lack of oil or any other natural resource. Instead, especially noticeable in recent years, it has grown an entrepreneurial class that has driven new, dramatic economic activity. While the education of Israel's human talent base makes it different from that in African countries, it does offer lessons on how people can drive economic change. This approach should not be foreign to African countries, where it has been demonstrated that the right economic incentives can induce entrepreneurial activity – as it did, for instance, in the late 19th century, when hundreds of thousands of peasant farmers quickly adopted cocoa and coffee and made West Africa a leading producer of both, in spite of the fact that neither crop is indigenous to the region. Examination of the Israel model has sometimes been clouded by regional politics.

A drive down the West Bank of the Jordan Valley is a journey through a pop-up Bible. Here, there, everywhere are historic sites, from Jericho to Jerusalem, the Dead Sea to Tiberias on the Sea of Galilee, the road north to Nazareth and that to Nablus, the home of the Samaritans.[8]

With so much history and not a little emotion, it is small wonder that this patch of earth has been so fought over. As one descends lower than 300 m below sea level south from Jerusalem, there is little greenery in sight. Caramel hillsides rise up like giant blobs of ice cream slowly melting in the baking sun, the landscape broken only by the odd camel, a few Bedouin, and Route 90 snaking up from the Negev. Pass the road to Qasr el Yahud, where John baptised Jesus in the Jordan, today little more than a stream, and the opposite turn-off to Jericho, and suddenly the desert comes to life, greenhouses and shade cloth hiding tomatoes, grapes, peppers, herbs and melons, where Arab and Jew work side by side for the European table.

Just 20 per cent of Israel is arable. Yet since its independence in May 1948, the country's agricultural output has increased 16-fold, many times the rate of population growth. The productivity gains have been thanks to a lot of perspiration and, more importantly, a large dollop of innovation and cooperation. And they are nothing new. Close to the Desert Plant Research Station in Be'er Sheva are the remains of a farm cultivated by the Nabateans, the earliest desert farmers. Using sophisticated terracing, they would collect every drop of run-off water and divert it to the fields and orchards.

Fast-forward 2 000 years and Israel is producing over two-thirds of its food requirements. Agriculture exports were, in 2010, worth more than US$2 billion, more than half of which was fresh produce, including flowers, vegetables and exotic fruits.

While Israel's external image has been dominated by pictures of conflict and perceptions of injustice, internal progress has been due to smart development. In agriculture, for example, Israelis have used technology to reduce water usage and increase output, and higher-yield crops to increase both volumes and financial sales values. Drip and direct-feed computerised irrigation systems are the norm, saving water, increasing yields and improving returns. Just 40 per cent of the amount of fresh water used for agriculture in 1950 is being used 60 years later, and half of that water is recycled.

It's all a far cry from 1948, when the Jewish state seemed to have little going for it. Not only was it a dry, rocky territory, contested both theologically and militarily, but it had neighbours who wanted to erase it from the map, enemies within and outside the domestic population, and a citizenry of just 800 000, many of them traumatised from their experiences in the Second World War.

Despite rapid population growth (to more than 7.5 million by 2011), Israelis enjoy a per capita income of US$29 600, putting them in the top 30 worldwide, between Spain and Italy. Their direct neighbours – Egypt, Jordan, Syria, Lebanon and the embryonic Palestinian state – have per capita incomes, respectively, of US$6 400, US$5 700, US$5 100, US$13 950 and just US$2 800.

There are many other indicators of transformation and success. Israel possessed the 24th-largest economy in the world in 2010, ranking 15th out of 169 nations in the UN's Human Development Index and therefore classified as a 'very highly developed' country. Since 2010, it has been a member of the Organisation of Economic Co-operation and Development (OECD) group of higher-income countries. It has also struck free trade agreements with, among others, Europe, the United States, Mexico, Canada, the Latin American Mercosur trade bloc and even its more complicated partners, Jordan, Egypt and Turkey.

Although it depends on imports for nearly all of its raw materials, from oil to diamonds, Israel has become a global industrial hub. Not only has it been a world leader in diamond polishing and cutting, processed foods, electronic and medical equipment, and, more recently, software, semiconductors and telecommunications, but the concentration of high-tech start-up industries has given it the monikers 'Silicon Wadi' and 'Start-Up Nation'.

By the end of the 2000s, Israel boasted the highest density of start-up ventures by population in the world, one for every 1 844 Israelis.[9] After the US and China, Israel had more companies listed on the NASDAQ than any other country, and more than Europe. Put differently, by 2008, per capita venture capital investment in Israel (some US$250 per person per year) was 2.5 times greater than in the US, 30 times more than in Europe, 80 times more than in China and 350 times greater than in India. Israel attracted close to US$2 billion in venture capital, about the same as the UK (which has nearly ten times the number of people) or France and Germany combined (20 times Israel's population).

It's a long way from grainy images of farmers on *kibbutzim* as the pioneering, rural ideal of happy socialist cooperation in the Jewish homeland.

The easy, shorthand explanation of Israel's success is that it is down to a concentration of educated, motivated, brighter-than-average people facing an existential threat in a small geographic space – at 370 people per square kilometre, about the same density as Rwanda, Holland and India.

Performance driven by adversity is important, though Israel is not unique in this regard. US assistance, some US$3 billion annually, is another oft-cited reason. Not only has much of this *tranche* been spent on military equipment, but Egypt has a similar chunk under the 1977 Camp David peace terms, and that income has seldom been used to define the country's circumstances positively. Moreover, the aid amounts to 1.5 per cent of both Israel's and Egypt's GDP, even though the latter has more than ten times as many people. While Israel's trade deficits have traditionally been covered by large transfers from abroad and by foreign loans, such imbalances and mechanisms are not uncommon in Africa and other developing regions. And while the fragility of African countries too has often been explained by their difficult inheritance and regional circumstances, such factors seem to affect them more drastically than they do Israel.

The explanation for Israel's success in the high-tech field lies in a combination of human and other factors, one of which is the very high level of civilian and military research and development (R&D) expenditure. Israel's civilian R&D is

4.5 per cent of GDP, while Japan's is 3.2 per cent, the US's 2.7 per cent, the UK's 1.9 per cent and China's 1.4 per cent.[10] To this research stock has to be added to military R&D. It is a difficult component to quantify, but the military has historically accounted for as much, in the worst security years, as 40 per cent of the national budget. By 2010, military spending was down to 6.3 per cent, but that still placed Israel in the top six worldwide – behind North Korea, Eritrea, Saudi Arabia, Oman and the United Arab Emirates. The military, the regional threat and limited international friendships have combined to drive innovation in military technology. As the first Israeli prime minister, David Ben-Gurion, was reportedly fond of saying, 'In the army it is not enough to be up to date; you have to be up to tomorrow.'[11]

A more important contribution from the military, perhaps, than money, has been the culture it has engendered, one of accountability no matter the rank, of agility, questioning and problem-solving rather than uniform rigidity, as well as a 'can-do', risk-taking attitude. Major General Aharon Ze'evi-Farkash headed up a variety of units during his 40 years in the armed forces, including the elite Unit 8200 signals intelligence unit (the equivalent to the US National Security Agency or Britain's Government Communications Headquarters, GCHQ), and, from 2002 until his retirement from active duty in 2006, the Military Intelligence Directorate (known as 'Aman'). 'It is also a bottom-up process,' he says, 'since it is dependent on taking young, brilliant soldiers who are highly motivated because they understand what is at stake, and we give them a budget, a target and a short time-frame.'

He cites the way in which Israel confronted the suicide bomber challenge as an example of this ingenuity. 'I met [Prime Minister Ariel] Sharon just one month after I was appointed. He let me find a solution to the suicide bomber challenge. In 2002 we lost more than 430 people to the bombers in 66 acts. By 2005 we had reduced this to just six acts and 15 people were killed. In 2007, four and three people, and in 2008, zero. We – myself and Avi Dichter of the Shabak [the internal security agency] – convinced the prime minister to build the security fence. We convinced him that if we could build peace with the Palestinians it would have to be like peace with Lebanon and Egypt, where we minutely defined the borders. This idea came from young minds working in intelligence, thinking about the problem and the solution in a different way.'

This motivation comes also, Farkash maintains, 'from the Jewish DNA'. Born in Romania, he emigrated to Israel with his parents at the age of 14. 'We survived in the diaspora by being the best. Israel was not formed as a result of the Holocaust, even though it may have been the catalyst. This helps to explain why immigrants do so well. We have 800 engineers in the army each year, and 400 of these are from this "periphery".' Education and a social infrastructure where 'everyone shares a sense of direction and of the future' are important, he says, and can be imitated by others 'with the right leadership'.

Oded Distel of the ministry of trade and industry's Newtech section agrees. 'The notion of distance is very limited in Israel. Combined with a questioning attitude, we are used to having open, direct discussions, where we are always looking for something new, something which others have not thought of before.' Part of this is attributable to the melting-pot nature of Israeli society and, especially, the number of skilled Soviet *émigrés* who arrived in the late 1980s and early 1990s, which 'offered certain technological opportunities'.

Of course money and even technology are not enough. To be effective, they have to form part of a system of skills and funding to translate ideas into business ventures. The system must have, to use academic terminology, a 'cluster' of universities, and companies large and small: suppliers, talent and capital in close proximity.

Here the Israeli government has offered a funding bridge through the chief scientist's office in the ministry of trade and industry, which provides US$450 million in annual grants to 1 200 worthwhile projects from as many as 2 000 applications. Much of this money is given to projects in the 'proof of concept' and 'pre-seed' phases. The money is paid back in the form of royalties (with nominal interest), though as many as half of the original projects fail to deliver, ensuring that winners are not so much picked as tested. It has been a high-risk, if high-return, system for Israel, but it was designed as a bottom-up process, in that, as Gil Shaki in the office of the chief scientist says, 'it is what the market throws up, where excellence and competitiveness win out. We are not picking winners and directing things top-down.'

Israel's services and high-tech edge has been linked to a dynamic venture capital market, formed originally with government intervention around *Yozma* (meaning 'initiative' in Hebrew) in 1993. This development, says Gaddy Weissman in the ministry of trade and industry, 'opened the floodgates and created a venture capital industry'. Ten *Yozma* 'drop-down' funds with US$200 million in funding were set up by 1996. By 1999 a second fund was listed on the NASDAQ. By 2011, the Israeli venture capital market was worth more than US$5 billion.[12]

But the government does not provide all the answers. Take Orni Petrushka. A former Skyhawk A4 pilot in the Israeli Air Force, he studied electrical engineering at the prestigious Technion Institute for Technology in Haifa, followed by a master's at Cornell. He served as the head of systems engineering at the ECI Telecom optical communications line, after holding various positions at Telcordia (formerly Bellcore). In 1993, at the age of 35, he started his entrepreneurial career by co-founding Scorpio Communications, which USRobotics acquired in 1996 for US$72 million. In 1997 he and his partners founded Chromatis, an optical networking firm, which was purchased in just 26 months by Lucent for a whopping US$4.75 billion and then, within 12 months, shut down in the wake of the dot.com collapse in 2001.

Orni divides his time between his alternative energy firms and philanthropic ventures. Although Scorpio took 20 per cent of its US$10 million start-up funding in the form of a loan from the chief scientist's office, he questions the utility of such a support system from the state. 'A good company and product,' he says, 'does not need the support of government. I would advise them not to use that route as there are strings attached, especially with the export of intellectual property. Also, government does not understand the business world and its dynamics and the pressures of time, where business can't wait until the next committee meeting for an answer.' People, rather than government interventions, are all-important in entrepreneurship. He questions Israelis' ability to run large businesses rather than excel at start-ups. 'Israel is small and Israelis are entrepreneurial in their spirit – the fight for survival is part of the Jewish DNA. But we don't operate in a way that a large company requires. We cut corners. We don't do things by the book. And we get upset by tedious processes.'

Gili Raanan worked for ten years in the elite Unit 8200 once commanded by General Farkash. There, aged just 24 and armed with a bachelor's degree from Tel Aviv University, he was put in charge of 'one of the largest software projects in Israel in terms of budget and manpower'. When it was completed in time and within budget, he was awarded the presidential Israel Security Medal, the nation's highest non-combatant military honour. This, he says, 'tells the story of a country that believes in talent and not in experience – and while it makes terrible mistakes, also achieves a lot by giving young guys the chance to prove themselves'.

After leaving the military at 27, Gili joined the business support giant Amdocs for a year, and then started a company with a friend from the same unit, working also with a retired general. 'That also tells its own story. Just as colleges are for the American entrepreneur, military service is for the Israeli entrepreneur, where your profession is moulded and you acquire your network for the rest of your life.' He later moved to California for six years, where he started and ran, first, a web security operation (which was sold to IBM) and a 'data centre automator' (sold to EMC). Having returned to Israel in 2008, he now runs the local Sequoia venture capital business, a US$1 billion fund.

In addition to the military dimension, like his former boss Farkash, Gili highlights several other factors in Israel's start-up success: 'the immigrant society where no-one feels comfortable, yet they possess the desire to prove themselves'; the 'Jewish mother syndrome, where they are never happy with their son's achievements'; and the government's early role in supporting the start-up business model with funding. 'The typical Israeli entrepreneur,' observes Raanan, 'is 25, from a first or second generation immigrant family, and has an unsatisfied mom!' The 'first driver of entrepreneurship,' he notes, 'is security – and financial security in particular'. Unlike China and India, he adds, Israeli entrepreneurs 'have to think from day one what foreigners and not their small domestic market wants.' Saul Singer, co-author of the best-selling *Start-Up Nation* says that this is 'why the Israeli high-tech entrepreneur is geared for the US market, to go through Silicon Valley.'

High-tech business is, however, not the whole Israeli economy. For all its earning power, this capital-intensive sector, comprising more than 50 per cent by value of Israeli exports, provided employment for only nine per cent of the workforce by 2011. The bulk of jobs were still in more traditional sectors and in services. While these areas are not as high-profile as start-ups, Israel has continued to exploit its comparative advantages there too. Indeed, the same lessons of fusing technology, capital and skilled labour apply also to other sectors. For example, Israel remains a major tourist destination, with 3.5 million annual visitors in 2010, bringing in US$4.4 billion.

And although agriculture accounts for less than three per cent of GDP and employment, it is still a major export earner, as Israel has moved away from farming low-value grain to higher-value fruits and vegetables for European consumers. It's not only the yields but the number of varieties that growers have increased dramatically in the search for market advantage. 'Fifty years ago there were just 15 types of vegetable. Today there are more than 70 grown,' says Yitzhak Kiriati, the director of Israel's Export and International Cooperation Institute. 'But there have been lots of failures along the way.'

However, such failures are part of the job, since 'modern agro-business is not about what are the right crops to grow in a particular region based on tradition, but rather what will sell – what the market wants'. Technology has been crucial in this, much of it of a systemic rather than revolutionary nature. Israel has held the world record for the amount of milk produced by a single cow in a year: 12 000 litres. But this has been achieved, smiles Kiriati, 'by knowing the performance and yield of every single cow in the country. That way breeding and feeding is carefully controlled and improved.' The improvements are best summarised by a single statistic: in the 1950s, one farmer supplied food for 17 people; by 2012, this number was more than 100.

The lesson from agriculture, he maintains, is the same as that from start-ups. 'If you want to succeed, you need to take care of the whole food chain: producer, market and post-harvest – and, critically, to find the right model to integrate the farmers with each other and the market.'

Israel did not, of course, start with high-tech. Industrialisation initially followed the creation of a textile industry, itself based on cotton growing, a sector that comprised around 12 per cent of merchandise exports in the 1960s, second to diamonds and agriculture. However, with competition from Southeast Asia, many enterprises relocated to Jordan and Egypt. By the end of the first decade of the 21st century, industry accounted for 33 per cent of economic output and services for two-thirds.

Israel's agriculture growth in the face of severe water shortages has been no accident. Again, it has involved close cooperation between researchers, farmers, university and other research centres, and extension officers. It has been based on extensive market research about customers' needs and wants, in Israel and outside. And new products have created additional business opportunities. Improvements in yields and crop quality have demanded innovation in irrigation and 'fertigation', machinery, automation, chemicals, cultivation and harvesting. As a result, the country has ten major companies producing irrigation and filtration equipment, while Israeli agro-specialists ply their trade across the world.[13]

Rather than leaving behind these old industries, Israel has forged ahead in related new areas: water, biotechnology, nanotechnology and clean energy. But it's not all been plain sailing. While the first two post-independence decades enjoyed high growth of over ten per cent annually, a combination of the 1973 Yom Kippur War and the banking crisis of the early 1980s demanded a stabilisation plan in 1985 to curb runaway inflation (which touched 450 per cent). Market-oriented reforms put in place the conditions for contemporary economic success and started a second phase of growth.

During the period from 1996 to 2010, for example, Israel's economy grew at an annual average of nearly four per cent, faster than other developed nations in spite of its security dramas, including the 'second *intifada*', which kicked off in 2000. Of course, if Israel had failed to develop and had remained aid-dependent, all of the factors listed above – a difficult region, nasty neighbours, fraught internal politics, little water and so on – would have been a recipe for failure.

Israel's innovation success is not easily replicated. It is a product of circumstance (the existential threat and the fight for survival), government policy and systems (including sponsorship for start-ups), linkages (between research centres, government and business), and education and skills (related also to the military dimension), all of which is sometimes explained by the term 'culture'.

However, it is important not to overstress the cultural aspect. While culture is an important unifying factor, it does not explain why others have done well or badly. As Singapore's first prime minister, Lee Kuan Yew, has reminded, the value of culture in development is only determined by history, not by argument. Culture should also not be used as an excuse to cherry-pick the importance of all the lessons from Israel's experience, or from that of others. It is possible to learn lessons from Israel, but not if you only look at the bits that are palatable.

Gili Raanan believes that the Israeli experience is replicated in some other centres, notably California and New York, where there is a high percentage of immigrants along with a geographic concentration of educated people 'enabling the exchange of ideas'. 'But,' he notes, 'you need something to ignite this process – the government, a critical mass of guys or women, an event, whatever.' Since technological solutions exist to most problems, the challenge is twofold: ensuring that the governance and ownership issues standing in the way of its adoption are removed, and also changing the incentives – so that, for example, if African farmers produce more, the means exist for them to profit from this, to get the surplus to market at a fair price.

Many have incentives to play down Israel's achievements and use it as a scapegoat and whipping boy for the failings of others. And with nearly half the West Bank's and 80 per cent of Gaza's population under the poverty line, the conditions don't only exist for deprivation, unemployment and radicalisation, but they provide ample grist to the mill of Israel's opponents. For the awful circumstances that gave rise to Israel's creation, read about the Palestinian *al-Naqba* ('the catastrophe'), which robbed them of their territory. Some see Israel's spectacular agriculture technology revolution, for example, as a cover for land and water grabs.

There have been other problems, not least the over-concentration of wealth in the hands of a few tycoons, the 15 or so families that control conglomerates which dominate the Israeli economy. Growing wealth inequality is widely discussed, with one-quarter of the population living near or below the poverty line,[14] though this includes some of the 30 per cent of the population who do not work, most for religious reasons. An estimated two-thirds of ultra-Orthodox men in Israel (the group comprising about ten per cent of the overall population) study in *yeshivas* and do not work, relying on government stipends to support their (usually large) families, in the process costing Israel's economy as much as US$4 billion annually.

The difficulty of translating start-ups into producers has also been problematic, though a number of large manufacturing companies have emerged, including Teva, a market-leader in generic pharmaceuticals, Amdocs, web publisher Conduit, and IT security firm Check Point. Increasingly, Saul Singer believes, Israel will have to gear its technological solutions not exclusively to the US, but to developing world markets, where big, long-term opportunities lie.

None of this should obscure and diminish Israel's accomplishments, a case of development performance through adversity, in part, but fundamentally catalysed by Israelis not pretending that their fate was someone else's responsibility. The bottom line is that the Jewish state's progress has been down to having a system which encourages and caters for entrepreneurship.

Africa: differences and parallels

There are many differences between Dubai, Israel and Abu Dhabi, on one hand, and African countries on the other. For one, the former are very small territories with relatively developed systems of governance and governments capable of extending authority across them. Additionally, they have small populations; indeed in the Arab examples, the national population is outnumbered by expatriates providing everything from unskilled manual to highly skilled labour. The state has provided welfare, but for all the reasons highlighted above, job creation for locals has lagged.

But there are, too, certain parallels with some African countries. The challenge of living in difficult regions engulfed in fraught religious, sectarian and ethnic settings is one. Dubai, Qatar and Abu Dhabi also illustrate how diversification from a considerable natural resource endowment might be planned – or, in some respects, as with Dubai, squandered. This could have similarities with Angola, Equatorial Guinea and other commodity-rich African nations, especially those with hydrocarbon endowments.

There are positive aspects, too, in terms of the appetite to import skills and good, efficient management where this cannot be found locally, and of leaders' commitment to popular welfare. Israel's uniqueness makes comparisons problematic, though certainly its transformation from a water-scarce, insecure territory to a major agricultural exporter offers lessons for some African countries, though not all. Similarly, its development of a venture capital market enabling financing for start-up industries and the application of technology to solving problems can be replicated. But not much will be done without a willingness on the part of leaders to make these moves, including allowing some ventures to fail despite government support. And as countries move up the wage ladder, there is no way to get around the importance of education and innovation.

Endnotes

1   Simon Freemantle, *Africa's Macroeconomic Outlook*, presentation to 6th Africa Economic Forum, IMAX Theatre, Cape Town, 6 March 2012.

2   Map No 4102, Rev 5, UNITED NATIONS, November 2011.

3   http://www.thenational.ae/business/economy/imf-estimate-puts-dubai-debt-at-109bn?pageCount=0.

4   http://www.uaeinteract.com/docs/Abu_Dhabis_population_set_to_grow_to_3.1_million_by_2030/26936.htm.

5   *The Abu Dhabi Economic Vision 2030*. Government of Abu Dhabi, November 2008, p. 18. See also Joe Bennett, *Hello Dubai: Skiing, Sand and Shopping in the World's Weirdest City*. London: Simon & Schuster, 2010; and Jim Krane, *Dubai: The Story of the World's Fastest City*. London: Atlantic Books, 2010.

6   Vision 2030, ibid, p. 113.

7   Vision 2030, ibid, p. 127.

8   This section is based in part on a research trip to Israel in October and November 2011, when the interviews cited were conducted in Tel Aviv, Nazareth and Jerusalem, and to Dubai and Abu Dhabi in February 2012.

9   Dan Senor and Saul Singer, *Start-Up Nation: The Story of Israel's Economic Miracle*. New York: Twelve, 2011, p. 11.

10 Ibid, p. 13.

11 Ibid, p. 226.

12 http://www.yozma.com/overview/.

13 http://www.mfa.gov.il/MFA/History/Modern%20History/Israel%20at%2050/Israeli%20Agriculture-%20Coping%20with%20Growth. See also Israel Export & International Co-operation Institute, *Israel's Agriculture*. Tel Aviv: 2009.

14 See, for example, 'What's wrong with Israel, à-la Yaron Zelekha', *Haaretz*, 3 November 2011.

CONCLUSION: A MODEL FOR AFRICA'S THIRD LIBERATION

Africa is a rich continent. Thirty per cent of the globe's natural resources are vested in its land mass, as is 60 per cent of the world's arable land. But little of this has benefited the people of a continent where some 400 million still live near or below the poverty line. The current political environment in Africa offers the possibility – but it is not an inevitability – that leaders will develop the kind of productive economic policies that have led to growth and development elsewhere. Accordingly, there is finally the possibility of transforming the wealth in the ground into prosperity that will benefit many, especially young people looking for jobs. However, this hopeful scenario will not materialise without a fundamental commitment on the part of governments to a set of policies that shift political economies from an emphasis on distribution to a laser-like focus on growth.

Some African leaders, as we have discussed, have simply reinvented the patronage politics of the past, with elections added. However, others have promoted change, and it is possible that still more will use the more liberal environment to overturn entrenched elites and patronage politics. Smaller countries may have an advantage in this regard, because it is easier for them to govern themselves, as has been seen from the cases in this study, both African and non-African. They have an easier geography. But what is clear from the Vietnamese case, if nothing else, is that inheritance is no arbiter, and no country is destined to be poor.

The stakes are extremely high. If sub-Saharan Africa grew at more than five per cent for a generation, its people would have the same wealth levels as Argentina today; growth at three to four per cent would bring them up to Brazil's levels.[1] At the same time, failure to follow a substantial growth trajectory will mean no end to the extraordinary poverty that currently afflicts so many of Africa's citizens.

These case studies reaffirm what we have learned about growth over the past century. Trade, open markets, macroeconomic stability and prudence, fiscal conservatism, and the centrality of entrepreneurs and human capital constitute the necessary package for economic advancement. What is perhaps less well understood, especially in Africa, is that, with suitable alterations for specific circumstances, this general model can be applied to a wide range of countries.

Yes, despite the numerous successes throughout the world and the unprecedented reduction in global poverty, many in Africa still want to reject the main tenets of the conventional model. Often, the rise of Asia and the BRIC countries (Brazil, Russia, India, and China) is seen, at least in much of Africa, as a counterbalance to the 'Western' way and to those traditional markets, offering not only greater opportunities to African countries but an alternative path for development, one less constrained by external conditions and mores. To a degree this is understandable. The hurt to pride, person and fortune inflicted by colonialism still lingers across much of the continent. Any positive developmental effects of what the Harvard historian Niall Ferguson describes as the 'white plague', the emigrants from Western Europe, have largely been overshadowed by the political consequences. African governments take solace from those offering easier, ideologically more palatable alternatives. The 2001 Nobel laureate Joseph Stiglitz, for example, the former chief economist of the World Bank, was appointed to the advisory panel of South Africa's economic development minister Ebrahim Patel in March 2010 and, in 2012, was representing the South African government on a three-person panel conducting a 'supply-chain study' of the impact of the aforementioned Walmart-Massmart merger. Among his bits of advice to the South African government during this time was to become more interventionist in the currency market so as to weaken the currency and to import rather than export capital. Poster-child for

220

the left he may be, but these bits of advice were contradictory. Preventing South Africa from exporting capital would, among other things, strengthen the currency, while ignoring that the roots of South Africa's net capital deficit lay not in the volume being exported but deeper maladies: The lack of an investment and savings culture among government and citizens and rampant consumerism is one, as is the absence of a less-than-benign and attractive regime for foreign direct investors, including Walmart and especially the mining sector, which is why the $2.5 trillion's estimate of natural resource wealth remains under-developed. Stiglitz's suggested range of politically palatable counter-interventions would also produce a range of inflationary and other consequences demand yet further interventions, creating jobs only for those intervening.[2] The heart of his suggestions is not just a statist reflex, though, but an attempt to avoid dealing with the growth dilemma. Without higher growth, faster and more widespread development is not possible.

The search for alternatives to the 'Western way' is no doubt also influenced by the insensitivity of Western development and aid practitioners in their clumsy attempts to impose conditions on Africans for how aid could be spent, in the hope that this would steer bankrupt governments onto a more fiscally prudent and managerially sound path. Of course, this approach conveniently forgets that the donors themselves had not developed in an externally directed manner through the charity of others. The aversion to the 'Western model' is especially topical in the context of the global economic crisis of 2008, and the wounding of the United States' influence and prestige as the beacon of capitalism as a result especially of the misadventure of the finance industry.

In part, the search for a model that Africa can call its own is desirable. Local ownership of development is, in spite of what donors have attempted, crucial for progress. The case studies have demonstrated that in the most successful countries leaders take full responsibility for their country's economic destiny. In Africa, there remains, in particular, an aversion to the public embrace of markets, let alone capitalism, even if that is precisely what some African countries are doing. It does not matter, of course, if they call their economic strategy 'the embrace of the free market' or anything else recognisable to Westerners. What is important is that African states should have a rigorous vision of how to grow, how the proceeds of growth are to be employed, and how growth will be used for the benefit, overwhelmingly, of people, not a tiny elite.

The bigger the market, Adam Smith reminds us, the easier it is to produce what people can make cheapest and best, and that is where the bigger profits and jobs lie. Trade agreements, stable currencies, and improvements in transport and telecommunications facilitate this exchange; protectionism and anti-competitive practices are its converse. Hence attempting to build domestic industries behind protectionist tariffs bucks market logic and sacrifices external opportunity to political urges. Similarly, frustration over the scale of benefits apparently accruing to external rather than local actors in the harvesting of African (and other regional) natural resources, while understandable (it explains the tendency to resource nationalism), ignores both the commercial risks wagered and the technical skills required.

The opening up of markets in the form of 'globalisation', Ian Morris points out in his magisterial and entertaining account of *Why the West Rules – For Now*,[3] also has other desirable consequences, not least because it places the individual at the centre of development, less constrained by traditions of class, ethnicity, religion or gender, where they might work and what jobs they might do. Globalisation is also expedited by the media revolution – and it's a digital revolution, with the cost-effectiveness of information technology by 2000, according to Moore's Law, a billion times greater than 100 years before – and the fact that consumerism is what people desire. The 'vision' documents that African countries have developed do not, in general meet these needs. These works, often composed at the behest of donors for donors, do not seem to be directed at the citizenry. Indeed, it is relatively rare that an African election centres on government economic policy, not least because no one can summarise it in a way that can be sold to the public (or criticise it in order to turn the public against it).

African countries face two challenges in particular. First, they must transform their wealth in minerals and other natural resources to benefit their entire society. Given that commodity prices will be relatively robust in the foreseeable future due to demands from Asia, it will not be that hard for many African countries to achieve reasonable (four to five per cent) growth that compares favourably to what they had in the past. However, such growth will not necessarily yield jobs and other developmental benefits unless these countries undertake to transform their patronage-based systems. Indeed, increased revenue from natural resources might simply reignite the old distributional systems that we describe in the case studies.

Second, many African leaders need to end their public and private animus towards business. This posture may have its origins in colonial rule and perceptions of 'them and us', but its perpetuation is often grounded in self-interest. Either business is kept very close, and therefore evolves into a client of government rather than a source of dynamism, or it is regarded with hostility, a prey to be devoured if circumstances demand. In this environment, politicians have limited understanding of the private sector, how it works and grows. They seem to understand more about the public sector, the other economy, which is why the policies they advance seldom positively incentivise the private sector. They spend on people and industries that are dependent, and always will be, on public budgets, not those connected to the most dynamic and competitive private sector industries. This approach infuses a statism, but one that is seldom undergirded by a competent and efficient public service. Rather than the private sector orbiting the public sun, in reality it has to be the other way round – that is, if the intention truly is to grow. Selfishly, of course, it is in the political leadership's best interests to keep things as they are, maintaining dependence on their largesse and ensuring that sectors of influence outside remain weak or under their control.

We have seen throughout our case studies of Asia and Central America that successful leaders work hard to develop a modus operandi with business. Success can come in a variety of forms, but those who successfully develop a friendly posture toward business are often able to accelerate development. How well countries manage their politics so as to put the lessons of reform into practice will determine their development outcome. Some of these truths are politically problematic and difficult to digest.

A search for an African model

Of course it is not enough just to try to replicate the lessons of others. Direct mimicry is ill-advised, as are attempts to reinvent the wheel. The challenge of institutionalising change is illustrated by the World Bank's *World Development Report 2011*. It took, according to the Bank, the 20 best-performing countries an average of 17 years to get the military out of politics, 20 years to achieve a 'functioning bureaucratic quality', and 27 years 'to bring corruption under reasonable control'. Many of these countries – Portugal and South Korea, for example – had a much better starting point in terms of literacy and state capacity than others, including the Democratic Republic of Congo and Haiti, do today.[4]

Many policy successes are not, therefore, simply about replication, even though there are best technical practices worth emulating. In *The Origins of Political Order*, Francis Fukuyama highlights the origins of legal systems as reflecting local people, habits and customs, which vary among countries and the contexts in which they operate. But, as Fukuyama argues, today's dynamic conditions mean that societies are not doomed to be 'trapped by their histories'.[5]

This volume does not argue that change and development are a linear phenomenon, or that there is only one path. And while it acknowledges that growth is but one aspect of development (along with, for example, governance rules and capacity), it is a necessary feature of the development 'story', impossible to do without.

While there is little gainsaying the desirability of East Asian-type rates of economic growth over a sustained period, it is unlikely that Africa can follow the development route of rapid industrialisation. It is true that some African countries (such as Mozambique and Sierra Leone) have been able to achieve high growth (seven per cent or above) coming out of conflict, but that is because they have many unused assets that idled along during the wars. Oil-producing countries can also experience bursts of high growth, given the role that hydrocarbon plays in those countries, but worldwide experience demonstrates that such oil-propelled growth is not sustainable and may, over time, actually lead to significant economic problems. Despite increasing unit costs in Asia, there is plenty of scope for low-wage producers in that region who can move, for example, from Singapore to Bangladesh. African skill levels, while improving, remain below those in Asia in terms of their relative availability and cost.

And the foreign direct investment that Southeast Asia has been able to attract is largely unavailable to Africa for several reasons: first because of the 'halo' or country-club effect of Asia, where peer groups invest on the basis of each other's choices and actions; second because many investors, especially those outside the natural resource sector, are uncertain about the scale and predictability of African corruption, whereas it is regularised in Asia; and third because of the state of African infrastructure, especially electricity.

The Africa growth model, if countries adopt the necessary reforms and manage their infrastructure problems, is thus likely to be less Asian than European or American: rates of economic growth above the population growth rate for sustained periods, resulting in economic development that takes far longer than the single-generation 'jump' that Asian countries experienced from poverty to relative affluence. The four to five per cent annual growth that many African countries could achieve, compared to population growth rates of three per cent, would actually be quite impressive by world standards, as this scenario implies significant gains in consumption over time. Such as growth would, in fact, be higher than in large parts of the Western world during their formative periods.

Given that the economic transition in many countries will take longer, there will be a premium on good governance as it unfolds. Setbacks, such a return to violence or sharp deteriorations in governance, can quickly wipe out years of good growth.

Of course, in light of the scenario we sketch, there are possible game changers. Conflict and terrorism is one, as is a significant reduction in external demand resulting from a sustained global downturn, where demand from Asia no longer compensates for a slowdown in Western markets.

On the other hand, we cannot rule out the possibility that if an African country broke out with sustained higher growth rates grounded in good governance, it could serve as an exemplar for the continent. It would then play much the same role as first Japan and then the first round of 'tigers' did in showing other Asian governments, and perhaps more critically other populations, that it was possible to grow quickly if the right policies were adopted.

Until now, Africa has had no such exemplar because the two highest-growth countries (Mauritius and Botswana) are regarded as exceptional. Many do not see island Mauritius as 'African' anyway, and Botswana, the other African country to experience sustained growth, is dismissed, unfairly perhaps, as dependent on a single commodity, a characterisation cemented by its difficulty in diversifying away from diamonds. A robust growth record by a country widely seen as representative – Ghana comes to mind, given its record of both growth and democracy – might set up a dynamic that encourages citizens of other African nations to demand the same growth that they see in others whom they can relate to and who are not that far away. If anything, this is an incentive to the international community to be as accommodating as possible to Africa's winners, especially in providing trade concessions that will allow them to sustain their upward progress while motivating others.

Challenges that must be met

By and large, what African countries need to do is evident from the case studies. In particular, they must enhance and extend the emphasis on macroeconomic stability and good governance that is the hallmark of high-growth countries worldwide and a feature of Africa's high performers. A focus on the fundamentals is all the more necessary in those countries emerging from conflict, such as Côte d'Ivoire, Zimbabwe, Liberia, Sierra Leone, Congo, Burundi, Somalia and Somaliland. In these environments, the establishment of national peace through negotiated agreements, reconciliation processes and elections has to parallel the pursuit of local, human security, enabling citizens to go about their lives and seek livelihoods free, at least, from fear.

As a country progresses from short-term stability to development, there is an overall challenge to change its operating system and political economy from one based on elite-driven interests characterised by consumption rather than longer-term investment, towards a more inclusive system, even though this may not necessarily be the elite's short-term preference. This is a special quandary for donors and other external agents as they seek to change an incentive structure that contributed to stagnation in the first instance. Such change is particularly difficult in countries where one party is dominant and its own governance structures are top-down, helping to preserve the culture of elite impunity.

African governments have learned at least one lesson from the two decades of lost continental growth: the importance of education. From South Africa to Côte d'Ivoire, government officials routinely state their intention to make education a priority. But as the high proportion of South Africa's national budget allocated to education (20 per cent of spending and more than five per cent of GDP) and the huge emphasis placed on education and literacy – now declining – by Côte d'Ivoire's first president Felix Houphouët-Boigny show, education by itself is not enough. *Quality* education must be extended and improved if African countries are to improve the extremely low productivity of the average worker.

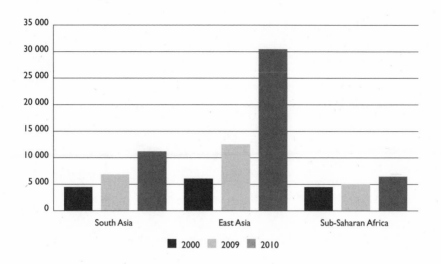

Figure 1: Output per worker (US$)

For most African citizens living in abject poverty and lacking even basic skills, sweatshops are an attractive option – possibly the only option – with the prospect of industrial development, diversification away from natural resource production and agricultural subsistence, and formal jobs. As Figures 1 and 2 illustrate, however, African countries are falling behind their counterparts in East Asia and Latin America, reflecting, among other things, very low primary school completion rates of less than 70 per cent, compared to over 90 per cent for North Africa and East Asia. Also, where some have managed to obtain an education, the quality of students and levels of employment preparation remain rudimentary at best. While Asian scores in maths and science outperform those of developed nations, Africa lags.[6] Countries cannot get rich without exporting goods, and widespread sustainable employment is unlikely with only a commodity or resource base to live off.

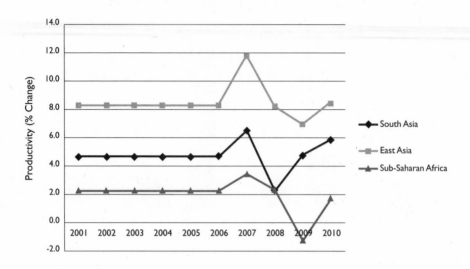

Figure 2: Africa's productivity challenge

The next stage, of progressing from a low-income to a middle-income country, is even more difficult. While there is no fixed model for growth, some elements are not negotiable. Much Chinese growth during the 2000s, for example, has been attributed to 'total factor productivity'.[7] Neither improvements in capital nor labour productivity were critical; what were decisive were increases in the quality of institutions, governance and management. This requires not only a higher level of efficiency in government, imposition of the rule of law, the safeguarding of land rights, the ending of monopolies, and the (de)regulation of labour and credit markets, but also the establishment of an environment that spurs an innovative and transformational culture. The creation of an additional 400 million African private bank accounts between 2010 and 2020, as has been mooted,[8] would change for the better the human and commercial investment prospects of the continent. But these changes will only happen if politicians incentivise savings, institutionalise macroeconomic stability, and permit technology (including mobile telephone technology) to act as a banking facilitator.

And here technical progress should not be confused with innovation. More than anything, it depends on a far more basic and prosaic element – politics.

Improving government and working around it

There is a role for the state in these stages of growth, of course. In some respects it needs to get out of the way, such as in the importation of the equipment required to manufacture specialist parts, where regulation is not only predatory but suffocating. In other ways, government can incentivise and speed up the pace of technological innovation and application. The US space programme in the 1960s is a good example: the Cold War and the threat of totalitarian communism was the spur, then, for a focus on research and development rather than today's emphasis on health and safety and other entitlements.[9] As countries move up the value chain, the need for innovation, as opposed to replication, is important, given former Singapore prime minister Lee Kuan Yew's observation that competitiveness, like courtesy, is a marathon with no finishing line.[10] Technological innovation has helped produce the global economic surge enjoyed since the Second World War. And the reason why some countries, such as Britain in the motorsport sector, have been successful in going the high-tech manufacturing route is simply that it is one where costs matter less and skills and innovation more. That much is a lesson to everyone contemplating routes to employment and prosperity in the face of China's low-tech, low-wage challenge.

Throughout this volume, we have shown that many countries attempt to get around some of their governance challenges by carving out special areas with different rules. One example is the promotion of special economic zones (SEZs) – essentially geographical regions, buildings or specific sectors that have economic and other rules more conducive to investment than the host country's national laws, usually involving tax incentives and lower tariffs. The establishment of such zones – including free trade zones, free zones, industrial parks or estates, free ports and enterprise zones – became popular in Africa in the 2000s, though few countries have been able to successfully implement them as a growth-generation strategy.

What the SEZs do, essentially, is suspend 'politics as usual' in a particular part of a country. They are therefore an important start, but whether their good results spread to the rest of the country depends on political and economic reforms taking hold nationally. Indeed, formal SEZ creation by itself is not enough. The zones have to be linked to policies on the whole gamut of skills creation, from literacy to R&D, and to an infrastructure network. Not only must this network be there physically, but the monopolies and bureaucratic inefficiencies that make services costly and time-consuming have to be eliminated. Governance, education and a desire to liberalise trade are prerequisites for success, which is why zones in Congo and Angola (two of many African countries that have optimistically established SEZs) are going to struggle to succeed. As the Asian Development Bank has noted about the success of China's Shenzhen SEZ, 'A key factor in facilitating the industrialization and urbanization processes [necessary for development] is the provision of open and liberal economic policies. Industrialization and urbanization have taken place in the PRC [People's Republic of China] in parallel with its transition from a planned to a market economy.'[11] While the SEZ tool has been credited with much of the extraordinary success of China's ascent, providing places where taxes are low and infrastructure reliable, replication of this success does not allow cherry-picking only the aspects that are most politically digestible.[12]

The opportunity

Africa's turnaround early in the 21st century shows, fundamentally, that growth matters. A five per cent annual increase for a decade does make a difference: it begets stability and, in turn, further growth. Little wonder that the number of African conflicts have decline from their peak in the mid-1990s, although an increasing number of African peacekeepers are being deployed in the remaining conflicts.

This economic upswing has little to do with charity. In a decade when Western leaders were urged to double aid to the continent as the only way to help it out of its seeming morass, growth is related not to external donations but improving commodity prices, better and cheaper telecommunications, and making African government policy more responsive, through democratisation, to the ballot box and to private sector needs. This does not mean that aid does not have a role, especially in fragile or post-conflict countries. It has not proven that successful, however, where the key metrics are the volumes spent rather than the results achieved. Aid needs to be better aligned to promote economic activity in these environments.

Sub-Saharan Africa's capital inflows in 2011 were \$36.8 billion, with 75 per cent of this figure comprised foreign direct investment and one-quarter portfolio money. Not only did this signal a 12 per cent drop in FDI on the previous year (mainly due to South Africa's poor performance), but much of these flows (two thirds between 2001–10 for example) was into natural resources (specifically mining and oil), and still was also under five per cent of such overall flows to developing countries.[13] Taking a leaf out of the examples presented in this book, shifting from vainly attempting to develop Africa through aid (driven ostensibly by charity) to instead through increased investment (which is exactly how the aid givers themselves developed) could involve establishing an African venture capital market – an 'African Third Liberation Fund' – aimed at rewarding those entrepreneurs and countries open to business and competition, and offering development prospects (and formal sector jobs) outside of raw materials. With the right focus, such a Fund could reinforce the trajectory of reformers, and achieve what the New Partnership for Africa's Development (NEPAD) set out but failed to do, not least because it aimed at soliciting more aid rather than investment flows. The fund should be a patient form of capital, but one that otherwise imposes the same disciplines and expectations on its firms and countries that a private equity fund investing in India, Turkey or Brazil would do. Only, its ultimate returns may be far higher, reflecting the process of catch-up of which well-managed African countries are now capable.

Of course growth alone is not enough for development, even though sustainable progress is impossible without it. That it has taken sub-Saharan Africa until 2007 to exceed the per capita income levels of the early 1970s indicates, too, how difficult and painstakingly slow it is to undo the effects of collapse.

Africa remains an exceedingly poor continent, with an annual per capita income level of approximately US$600. This requires lifting economic growth rates above sub-Saharan Africa's margins in the 2000s of five per cent per annum. At that rate, Africans will double their average incomes in 15 years. But even then they will still be very poor. At ten per cent real growth rates, this 'doubling duration' will reduce to seven years, ensuring greater political support for the difficult policy choices involved. The patterns of growth, moreover, have been highly differentiated between states: some have got richer, while others have failed. This is, however, a positive phenomenon, showing that African countries no longer fall into a single category, but, as in other developing regions, are of all kinds: performers and failures; big and small (which usually perform much better in Africa); landlocked and littoral; autocratic and democratic (by now the overwhelming majority). In particular, Africa's larger countries (think of the DRC) have generally had a poor development record since independence, which in part is due to the extent of territory and the complex make-up of their societies, consisting of many nations within a single state.

The biggest challenge of all remains the gulf between those who favour the distributional model of growth over the model based on enterprise through entrepreneurship and the creation, by government, of an enabling environment. Until now, African entrepreneurs have made progress by circumventing their governments. To truly succeed, governments must be enthusiastic about creating an environment where business will prosper. This demands, too, a change in mindset prevalent especially in traditional societies, where there is a lack of interest in new business and investment opportunities because of a perception of the world as a zero-sum game. In terms of this outlook, there is only a limited amount of good to go around: That if someone profits, someone loses, fuelling hostility to outside investors and immigrants alike. This is contrary to both the nature and reality of modern, liberal societies, where if the economic pie grows, everyone profits, even if at different rates.[14]

In this and other ways, Africa's third liberation, bringing freedom from the yoke of poverty and unemployment, will, like liberation from decolonisation and liberation from dictatorship, be political in nature.

Endnotes

1   Cited at 'Africa's New Era' conference, SAIS, Washington DC, 1–2 March 2011.

2   See Ethel Hazelhurst, 'Stiglitz punts cut and paste intervention for economy,' *Business Report* (South Africa), 30 April 2012.

3   Ian Morris, *Why the West Rules – For Now*. London: Profile Books, 2010.

4   World Bank, *World Development Report 2011: Conflict, Security and Development*. Washington DC: World Bank, 2011, pp. 108–109.

5   Francis Fukuyama, *The Origins of Political Order: From Prehuman Times to the French Revolution*. New York: Farrar, Straus and Giroux, 2011.

6   These figures were presented by Ben Leo, then of the Center for Global Development, at a series of workshops on youth unemployment hosted by the Brenthurst Foundation in Zambia, Mozambique and Swaziland in May 2011, and are based on International Labour Organization data.

7   This is partly drawn from the presentation 'Uprising: Will Emerging Markets Shape or Shake the World Economy?' by George Magnus at the Bankinvest Emerging Markets Investor Conference, Hotel D'Angleterre, Copenhagen, 10 March 2011.

8   This projection was made by Standard Bank economist Simon Freemantle at the 6th African Economic Forum at the IMAX Theatre in Cape Town on 6 March 2012.

9   Niall Ferguson, 'The Pessimistic Billionaire', *Newsweek*, 20 February 2012.

10 Lee Kuan Yew, *From Third World to First: The Singapore Story, 1965–2000*. Singapore: Marshall Cavendish, 2008, p. 583.

11 ADB, 'Special Economic Zones and Competitiveness: A Case Study of Shenzhen, the People's Republic of China', *PRM Policy Note*, November 2007, at http://www.adb.org/Documents/Reports/PRM-Policy-Notes/Special-Economic-Zone-Shenzhen.pdf.

12 For a comprehensive survey of SEZs, see Thomas Farole and Gokhan Akinci, *Special Economic Zones: Progress, Emerging Challenges, and Future Directions*. Washington DC: The World Bank, 2011.

13 http://data.worldbank.org/sites/default/files/gdf_2012.pdf.

14 We are grateful to Johnny Clegg for this point. See also George M Foster, 'Peasant Society and the Image of Limited Good', *American Anthropologist*, Vol 67, Issue 2, 1965, pp. 293–315.

INDEX

ACKNOWLEDGEMENTS

The mission of the Brenthurst Foundation is to strengthen African economic performance. The foundation, set up by the Oppenheimer family in 2005, focuses its energies on identifying development solutions from around the world and applying them to African circumstances, notably through its various high-level strategic dialogues.

Our book reflects this methodology. It is partly based on research undertaken in Honduras, El Salvador, Costa Rica, Guatemala, Nicaragua, Argentina, Bangladesh, Vietnam, the Philippines, Malaysia and Singapore during June and July 2011, and in various African countries in late 2011 and early 2012. Research was also undertaken in Israel in October 2011, and Dubai and Abu Dhabi in February 2012.

Tim Gray brought to our attention the African proverb 'We are people because of other people', one frequently used by Archbishop Desmond Tutu, among others, to describe the notion of *ubuntu*, which highlights the advantages of kinship rather than individualism. This book is no different in that regard, and has relied on the support and cooperation of a large number of people and communities.

Paul Theroux reputedly observed that travel is only glamorous in retrospect. However, it is an imperative requirement for researchers, and their job is made much easier by the hospitality and helpfulness of their peers. We have been blessed in this regard.

Luis Membreno and Professors Arturo Cruz and Alberto Trejos helped to organise the research itinerary in Central America. Luis was kind enough to act as organiser, supporter and translator in Guatemala, Honduras and El Salvador.

Giancarlo Ibárguen and the staff of Universidad Francisco Marroquín were gracious hosts in Guatemala, as were Domingo Cavallo, Tony Leon and Florencia Achcar in Argentina; Professor Do Duc Dinh in Vietnam; Major General Muniruzzaman and the staff of the Bangladesh Institute of Peace and Security Studies in Dhaka; the staff of the South African embassy in the Philippines, especially Ambassador Agnes Nyamande-Pitso and Hugo Lamprechts; and Ambassador Barry Desker in Singapore. Asher Susser, Daniel Pinhassi, Or Pearl and Ya'akov Finkelstein all helped to facilitate a jam-packed schedule in Israel. Linda Low and Eddie O'Sullivan offered insights and contacts in the Middle East, while Thomas Nziratimana was immensely obliging in arranging various African excursions, as was Leila Jack at the foundation. Manuel Barros and General 'Ita' helped to open up Angolan debates; Christopher Kiptoo and Ahmed Kassam were the organisational muscle behind a policy seminar with Prime Minister Raila Odinga and his team in Kenya in December 2011; Eric Kacou, Guy Mbengue and Serge Amissah assembled an extraordinary schedule in Côte d'Ivoire, where Daniel Pinhassi was a generous and enthusiastic guide and companion; Johnny Lin of the Lesotho Export Textile Association facilitated various contacts in the mountain kingdom during 2011, as did Jonathan and Larry Schewitz in the Eastern Cape. Zodwa Mabuza, Robert Young and Robert Sithebe were always on hand to assist in Swaziland.

Thanks are expressed to both the Oppenheimer family and the Danish government for their financial support, which made much of the research behind this volume possible. Special mention should be made in this regard of Mary and Rachel Slack, and Nicky, Jonathan and Jennifer Oppenheimer. Christopher Clapham, Barry Desker, Arturo Cruz and Alberto Trejos offered useful editorial advice, Dianna Games, Jacqueline Sheasby and Sharon Polansky spotted all manner of editorial *faux pas*, and Anthony Arnott helped dig out obscure bits of information, while the Penguin production team was not only professional but graciously tolerant of our errant timekeeping.

All views expressed here remain, of course, ours alone.

This volume is dedicated to our ever-supportive partners, Sharon and Janet. We could never have attempted this without them. Happy Valentine's Day.

JIH and GJBM
Paris
14 February 2012

Jeffrey Herbst is President of Colgate University, a leading liberal arts college in the United States. Holding a PhD from Yale University, previously he was Provost and Executive Vice-President for Academic Affairs at Miami University. As such, he was the chief academic officer for a university with 21 000 students on three American campuses and one in Europe. Dr Herbst started his career as a professor of politics and international affairs at Princeton University, where he taught for 18 years. His primary research interests are in the politics of sub-Saharan Africa, the politics of political and economic reform, and the politics of boundaries. He is the author of *States and Power in Africa: Comparative Lessons in Authority and Control* (Princeton University Press, 2000) and several other books and articles. He has also taught at the University of Zimbabwe, the University of Ghana, the University of Cape Town, and the University of the Western Cape. In 2004 and 2005, he was a Fellow of the John Simon Guggenheim Memorial Foundation. He has served on the Advisory Board of the Brenthurst Foundation since 2005.

Greg Mills directs the Johannesburg-based Brenthurst Foundation. He holds a BA Hons from the University of Cape Town, and an MA and PhD from the University of Lancaster. From 1996 to 2005 he was National Director of the South African Institute of International Affairs. He headed up the Prism strategic analysis group for General Sir David Richards in Kabul in 2006, was seconded as Strategy Adviser to the President of Rwanda in 2008, has served as a member of the Danish Africa Commission from 2008, and during 2010 was deployed twice to regional command (South) in Afghanistan in an advisory capacity, based in Kandahar. He is the author of, inter alia, *The Wired Model: South Africa, Foreign Policy and Globalisation* (Tafelberg, 2000), *The Future of Africa: New Order in Sight?* (Oxford University Press, 2003, with Jeffrey Herbst), *Seven Battles that Shaped South Africa's History* (Tafelberg, 2005, with David Williams), *From Africa to Afghanistan: With Richards and NATO to Kabul* (Wits University Press, 2007), and *Why Africa is Poor: And What Africans Can Do About It* (Penguin, 2010). A columnist for the (South African) *Sunday Times*, he serves on the Advisory Council of the Royal United Services Institute, is a trustee of the SA Military History Museum, and is on the visiting faculty of the NATO Higher Defence College in Rome, the South African Defence Academy, and the Royal College of Defence Studies in the United Kingdom.